JB JOSSEY-BASS

Susan L. Preston

Angel Financing for Entrepreneurs

Early Stage Funding for Long-Term Success

John Wiley & Sons, Inc.

Published by Jossey-Bass
A Wiley Imprint
989 Market Street, San Francisco, CA 94103-1741—www.josseybass.com

Jossey-Bass books and products are available through most bookstores. To contact Jossey-Bass
directly call our Customer Care Department within the U.S. at 800-956-7739, outside the U.S.
at 317-572-3986, or fax 317-572-4002.

Jossey-Bass also publishes its books in a variety of electronic formats. Some content that appears
in print may not be available in electronic books.

Library of Congress Cataloging-in-Publication Data

Preston, Susan L.
    Angel financing for entrepreneurs : early stage funding for long-term success /
Susan L. Preston.
        p. cm.
    "A Wiley Imprint."
    Includes bibliographical references and index.
    ISBN-13: 978-0-7879-8750-3 (cloth)
    1. Angels (Investors)—United States. 2. Investments—United States. 3. New business
enterprises—United States—Finance. I. Title.
    HG4963P74 2007
    658.15'224—dc22   2006101787

Printed in the United States of America
FIRST EDITION
HB Printing 10 9 8 7 6 5 4 3 2 1

⟶ CONTENTS

—~~— Foreword

There are many business books out on the market that give great tips on building your business. Books can be great tools, but they don't match up to the most important tools in your toolbox—people. People are what really help your business move ahead—successful, well-connected people who are willing to share their expertise, their capital, and their connections with you.

Susan Preston is an entrepreneur's most valuable tool. Through her books and her speaking engagements, she willingly shares her expertise and connections with companies seeking capital, with policymakers seeking to attract capital, and with national organizations looking to build an industry.

Angel investors know how to build successful businesses. Susan has firsthand experience as a talented entrepreneur and as a founder and participant in an active Seattle-based angel network. As an attorney with one of the West Coast's leading law firms, she has helped countless companies reach their full potential. In this book, she opens the window to the "inner circle," so we can see into the mysterious world of what investors are thinking—and what we need to do to get access to their capital and their connections.

Honorable Lorrie Keating Heinemann
Cabinet Secretary under Governor Jim Doyle
Wisconsin Department of Financial Institutions
Madison, Wisconsin
September, 2006

To my remarkable children, Michael and Kelsey:

If I have given you one characteristic, it is my passion for life that drives one to seek out life's adventures, big or small.

Always strive to step out of your comfort zone, set high expectations for yourselves, make mistakes, and get messy: some of life's greatest rewards and memories are those experienced on the edge.

I love you.

CHAPTER ONE

Introduction

The greatest challenge for entrepreneurs in starting and growing a company remains simply *money*. Though easy to state, financing your venture is a time-consuming, complicated, inefficient, and frustrating process. Entrepreneurs have often compared it to Winston Churchill's line, "A riddle inside a mystery wrapped in an enigma." This book attempts to provide you with information, guidelines, and resources to take the mystery out of the process. Don't be fooled, however. Raising capital is hard work and you must be well-prepared for every opportunity to pitch your company, either planned or unplanned. Remember the age-old adage: You can only make a good first impression once. It is infinitely true in raising capital.

Traditional funding sources—angels, venture capitalists, commercial banks—have a plethora of investment and funding opportunities. Your ability or inability to clearly and succinctly communicate your market focus and financial projections can make the difference between bringing your dream to life and shelving your brilliant idea. Therefore, preparation is key. This book will help you understand how angel investors think, how to identify their expectations, understand their investment analysis process, and prepare for post-investment requirements.

Just as no two people are alike, no two angels or angel groups will have the same hot buttons or demands. Through this book, you will gain a broad understanding of angels and angel investing. Be mindful that angel investors have varying degrees of sophistication and experience. The book will prepare you to deal with the most knowledgeable angels. Even with experienced angels, preferences on investment terms, depth of due diligence, and post-investment involvement will vary. Therefore, you will learn about multiple scenarios to minimize surprises you may encounter in your dealings with angel investors.

You can use this book as a reference guide for understanding and preparing yourself and your company for the mysteries of angel fundraising. If there is only one message you take away, it must be this: *passion*—every successful entrepreneur has passion. Investors look for passion in entrepreneurs; the willingness to take risks with life savings, to work nights and weekends, to see their idea become reality. It has to be more than excitement. So never lose the passion for your company, and show it each time you speak about your dream.

You also need to understand that professional angel investors are interested in companies with great growth potential; companies with a large market potential and a strong path to profitability. They do not invest in lifestyle companies, small retail operations, or other companies that, while profitable, lack room to expand. In addition, angel investors are interested in companies where the founder has a desire to grow the company. For example, if the entrepreneur only wanted funding for a chain of three boutiques, angel investors would probably yawn and look elsewhere. However, if the entrepreneur wanted funding for a chain that would start with three boutiques and then expand nationally over ten years, angel investors would be likely to take a real interest. Professional angel investors look for entrepreneurs with the drive and capability to build a great company. Angels are looking for strong exit opportunities to realize significant gains on their investment. These are important factors to keep in mind when you think about the possibility of pursuing angel financing for your company.

Over the last several years, private equity financing has created a lot of misunderstandings. During the dot-com bubble (from 1997 through 2000), many companies received massive amounts of financing on little more than an idea (see Figure 1.1).

Webvan.com (1999–2001)
Online grocery store that undersold its products in an effort to gain market share. It expanded too quickly and had no way to get to profitability.
Amount Lost: $1.2 billion

Pets.com (2000)
Quirky commercials could not help the online pet supply business figure out that you cannot make a profit subsidizing the shipping charges on fifty pounds of dog food.
Amount Lost: $282.5 million

Kozmo.com (1998–2001)
An online convenience store that made deliveries to your home, but never figured how to make the costs of the infrastructure work.
Amount Lost: $280 million

Boo.com (1998–2000)
A fashion Web site that attempted to start a global brand in several countries at once, and got hung up on a poor business plan and the technical limitations of the time.
Amount Lost: $160 million

Freeinternet.com (1998–2000)
A combination of excessive spending, poor management, costly lawsuits, and a business model that just didn't make any sense sank this Internet service provider right after its IPO.
Amount Lost: $86 million

Figure 1.1   Examples of Failed Dot-Com Companies

We still have many young entrepreneurs who think venture capitalists are the primary source of financing, even at the very early stages of a business. They also naively believe they need merely slap an executive summary together and the money will beat a path to their door. Well, here's a dose of reality:

- The vast majority of venture capitalists do not invest in seed or start-up financing rounds.
- Most investors require seasoned management, with successful start-up experience, before they will sit down and talk about providing capital.
- To arouse any interest in your proposal, you must have skin in the game; in other words, you have invested your own money.
- Your business plan must be well-written, with detailed financial projections that extend three to five years.

- You are prepared for due diligence and are able to answer any question posed.
- Your corporate structure is clean and uncomplicated, without multiple layers of ownership.
- You own all necessary intellectual property, which has been properly protected.
- Many investors prefer to see completed prototypes, which are already being test marketed or sold.
- Many angels require a board of advisers along with a board of directors.

These are just highlights of what you may encounter as you step into the financing arena. As stated before, angel investors display an almost infinite variety of needs and approaches, so few absolute rules exist. But there's one absolute fact: you can never be too prepared.

CHAPTER TWO

The Basics About Angel Investors

o what is an angel investor? The term has its origin in Broadway plays. Several decades ago, those who funded this form of entertainment were referred to as *angels*. William Wetzel, former director of the Center for Venture Research at the University of New Hampshire, is credited with first applying the term to business, where the financing of early-stage enterprises can feel like "money from heaven" for entrepreneurs. However, like any other financing, angel investments do not just fall from the sky, unencumbered; they are not gifts. These investments come with terms, requirements, and an investor. Much of this book describes the characteristics of an angel investor, as well as ways of finding the right one and assessing the potential value an angel investor can bring to your company—which is far beyond just financial support.

Just as entrepreneurship has many meanings, angel investing has yet to find a definitive definition. For purposes of this book, the term *angel* refers to an individual who typically meets the definition of an *accredited investor* (as defined in the Securities Act of 1933: a natural person whose individual net worth or joint net worth with that person's spouse exceeds $1,000,000 at the time the investment is purchased; or a natural person who had an individual income in excess of $200,000 in each of the two most recent years, or joint income with that person's spouse in excess of $300,000 in each of those years, and who reasonably expects to reach the same income level in the current year). In addition, angels actively participate in their own personal investment decisions.

Statistics from the Center for Venture Research at the University of New Hampshire indicate that in 2005, angel investors poured an esti- mated $23.1 billion into approximately 49,500 deals. Not all these deals involved separate individual companies; they may have been for initial or subsequent rounds of financing. This investment amount and num- ber of deals is fairly constant from 2004, in which $22.5 billion was invested in an estimated 48,000 deals. Most important for young entre- preneurs, 55 percent of angel deals went to seed/start-up ventures, compared to 3.3 percent in 2005 for venture capital funds. In addition, according to a survey by PricewaterhouseCoopers MoneyTree, venture capital firms are averaging around $7 million per deal, while simple mathematics indicates that the average investment amount per deal for angel investors is much lower, around $470,000. Clearly, $500,000 reflects a more appropriate investment amount for the first round of outside or third-party financing when your company's product is still being tested and no proven market exists. Seed/start-up companies garner modest valuations (often $1 million to $3 million). So an ini- tial investment of $500,000 can give you much-needed capital while allowing you to retain majority ownership.

ENTREPRENEURS DEFINE "ANGELS"

Brannon Lambert, founder and COO of VHT, Inc., describes an *angel investor* as "a high-net-worth individual who takes a big risk on one or two people at the beginning stages of a company. They invest locally and provide consultation, direction, and advice." Asked if he would do angel financing again with a new company, he answered quickly, "Absolutely."

Lon McGowan, founder and CEO of iClick, says he prefers "angel investors who have been involved in successful start-up companies of their own." As a result, "They have money to invest in young companies, and enjoy being part of the entrepreneur- ial process without the daily requirements."

How are the various stages of company development defined? One common definition is from the PricewaterhouseCoopers MoneyTree survey, which uses the following definitions for stages of private company development:

- *Seed/Start-Up Stage.* The initial stage. The company has a concept or product under development, but is probably not fully operational. Usually in existence less than eighteen months.

- *Early Stage.* The company has a product or service in testing or pilot production. In some cases, the product may be commercially available. May or may not be generating revenues. Usually in business less than three years.

- *Expansion Stage.* Product or service is in production and commercially available. The company demonstrates significant revenue growth, but may or may not be showing a profit. Usually in business more than three years.

- *Later Stage.* Product or service is widely available. Company is generating ongoing revenue; probably positive cash flow. More likely to be profitable, but not necessarily so. May include spin-offs of operating divisions of existing private companies and established private companies.

THE ESSENCE OF AN ANGEL

What are the attributes of angel investors? Angel investors have one essential and primary goal identical to venture capitalists—they are in the business of making money. Angels invest with anticipation of a healthy return on their investment. They tend to have among the most lucrative returns, which matches the high level of risk they take for providing the earliest professional investment dollars in a company. Angels have an expectation of financial return just like any other investor. But they also have many attributes invaluable to young companies that can set them apart from other types of investors. Angels typically

- Have a sense of social responsibility and enjoy community involvement.
- Take a role in the entrepreneurial process.

- Act as mentors and advisers to the entrepreneur.
- Provide early-stage investment dollars.
- Invest regionally.
- Invest smaller amounts at a time.
- Invest their own money.
- Are able to tolerate the loss of their entire investment.
- Have a diversified portfolio.
- Take a long-term view of their investments—which are often referred to as "patient money."

Participation

Angels typically desire to pass on knowledge. Many entrepreneurs say that once the thrill of building a company is in your blood, you never get rid of the thirst for that emotional roller coaster and thrill of watching an idea grow into a real company, with real customers, providing jobs for others and adding value through innovation. Angel investing becomes an effective means for these "recovering entrepreneurs" to remain engaged but not consumed through the necessary fourteen-hour days and seven-day weeks. These entrepreneurs are the most likely people to seek out new companies and fund them as angel investors. Many angel investors choose to remain involved with their investments out of an active desire to grow companies and act as mentors and advisers to young entrepreneurs.

One of the most important attributes of angel investors is the willingness to bring knowledge to companies during their start-up phase. Many angels are successful entrepreneurs, having prospered in their community often because of local support for their own business. They now have the opportunity to contribute to the wealth of the community through the support of other young, hopeful companies. Angels typically invest in industries they understand, which very often means investing in the same field as their earlier successful endeavors, and they thus bring the benefit of connections to potential customers, vendors, and other resources, as well as possible additional financing sources. Of course, the fit must be right between you and your angel investors. With this match accomplished, angel investors bring experience of having been in your shoes and knowing how to build a successful company, along with industry and professional knowledge and wisdom. Remember, many angels want to be engaged as mentors, advisers, or board members, so take advantage of the opportunity to gain an interested and vested partner.

Consistent with an interest in participating in their community, angel investors typically invest near their home. A sense of connection to the company is important to an angel investor, as well as the ability to keep up on company activities through personal visits, local media, and regional discussions.

Availability

Angels provide early-stage investment. Another feature of angel investors is the focus on early-stage investing. As the statistics bear out, angels are the primary source of outside capital for very young companies. Because other investors such as venture capitalists are not providing investment dollars for seed/start-up companies in any real way, angels provide the first outside professional capital to entrepreneurs at this critical stage of growth when products are being finalized and first customers are being wooed.

Angels cannot invest the large sums of capital that venture capitalists have at their disposal. Some "super angels" do make investments

---

ANGEL OVERVIEW

Angel investments may be small when considered individually, but collectively, they're big business. Here are some overall statistics for the last few years:

- 2005 Angel Investments: $23.1 billion (49,500 deals)
- 2004 Angel Investments: $22.5 billion (48,000 deals)
- 2005 active angels: 227,000
- 2005 Distribution:
    20% health care and medical devices and equipment
    18% software
    55% seed/start-up
    43% post–seed/start-up (10% increase over 2004)

of $250,000 to $2 million a deal, but those are rare. The vast majority of angel investors invest between $25,000 and $100,000 at a time. These smaller sums fit well with the needs of young companies, and may very well have the reciprocal effect of focusing angels on this early stage, where they can play a real role in financing and supporting entrepreneurial growth.

Remember, angel investment does not equal philanthropy. Because of the high risk of investing so early and their interest in helping entrepreneurs, angels can leave the impression of just giving money away. Certainly, even as recently as five years ago, many angels did not understand the finer aspects of intelligent, thoughtful investing, particularly during the Internet bubble, when many people were rushing into the market in fear of being left out of seemingly limitless riches. The bust of 2001 left many angels licking their wounds, in a state of shock or dismay and without the financial wherewithal to continue investing. What seems to be emerging out of these roller coaster years are angels with experience and a cautious approach to investing. So while the bubble-and-bust cycle left an impression of angel financing being "dumb money," active angels who remember those times and the ones joining their ranks now are sophisticated investors, with many of the deal requirements and attributes of the venture capitalist—and first and foremost, they invest to make money.

Investing at the start-up/seed stage carries a very high risk of loss; no prospect has much history or assurance of success. As a result, angel investors must be able to tolerate the complete loss of any or all of their investments. Certainly, this tolerance of loss does not mean that an angel investor goes into a deal expecting to lose the money—quite the contrary. But investing money critical to a comfortable retirement or standard of living is foolhardy at best, and not an indication of a true angel. Angels typically diversify their portfolios so their lifestyle will not be damaged by any problem with their investments.

Conducting intelligent start-up/seed stage investing requires the ability to invest in a number of companies to spread the risk and hedge the investment bets. Venture capital statistics show that the majority of VC investments never show a return despite investors' best efforts in selecting and supporting young companies; the same is true for angel investors. According to professor Robert Wiltbank of Willamette University (2006), the majority of angel investments result in losses. These statistics were collected from 121 angel investors to a detailed survey reporting on 1,038 new venture investments and 414 exit events from those investments:

Angel Exits in Each Internal Rate of Return Category

Total Loss	200
Large Loss	33
Small Loss	27
SUBTOTAL	260
0 to 25% Gain	29
26% to 49% Gain	25
50 to 100% Gain	18
100 to 300% Gain	33
> 300% Gain	49
SUBTOTAL	154

As a result of the broad spread of results and the sheer number of losses, angel investors need a whole portfolio, rather than making only two or three total investments. As the statistics show, the likelihood of failure is so great for any given investment, it's better to take a wide range of relatively small risks than to put a large proportion of available funds into a small number of investments. Angels should also be diversifying through the stage of investments as well as industry.

Because of the early-stage nature of most angel investing, patience is key. The primary exit strategy is a merger or acquisition, providing the investors with cash or liquid stock, or both. Getting a young company to the point of being acquisition-ready takes maturation of products, market, and management; none of these happen overnight. Therefore, most angels anticipate a three-, five-, even seven-year holding period before they can recover their investment, let alone profit from it.

Investment Preferences

Angel investors typically invest in industries similar to the ones venture capitalists choose, which seems logical, since angels and venture capitalists alike are looking for high potential returns (which accompany large potential market caps) in growing, prosperous, and future-oriented fields. Figure 2.1 shows a compilation of survey results conducted by the Angel Capital Education Foundation (currently a

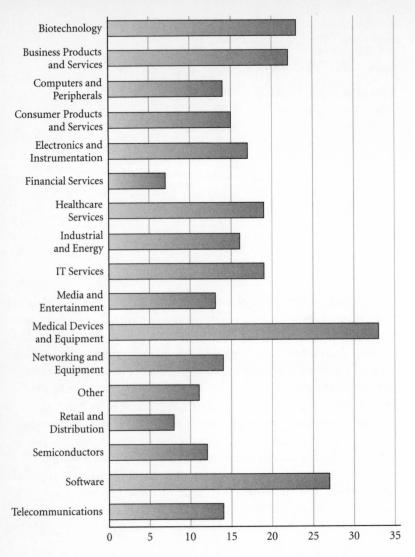

Figure 2.1   Investment Preferences in Percentage for Angel Investors

program of the Ewing Marion Kauffman Foundation) with Angel Capital Association member groups (forty groups reporting).

If one compares these statistics with venture capital investment focus as reported in PricewaterhouseCoopers MoneyTree survey for the period from January 1 to March 31, 2006, shown in Figure 2.2, the similarity of investment preferences is obvious, with the major differ-

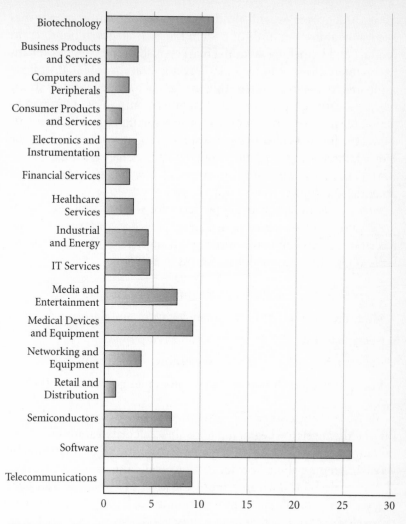

Figure 2.2   Investment Preferences in Percentage for Venture Capitalists

ence being the flip in preference between medical devices and equipment and software, and more diverse investment interests by angels.

ANGEL DEALS

Many companies never need venture capital financing to achieve positive cash flow and eventual liquidity for investors. Software companies are often started in someone's spare bedroom or the proverbial garage and grown organically. In such cases, the entrepreneur may need only minor amounts of cash in the early stages of building the product and launching an initial market push. If the young company has an interesting but limited market capitalization potential, or if the company can create an interesting market niche that generates strong margins, setting up as a limited liability company (LLC) may be preferable to a corporation or sole proprietorship. The LLC structure allows the business to provide investors a return on their investment through the sharing of profits, though they also share any losses. It can work particularly well for companies with low acquisition or merger potential and high cash flow opportunities.

Many deals are simply not appropriate for venture capitalists. Looking at informal statistics compiled and averaged from various sources, it is clear that few companies receive even angel investment dollars and far fewer venture capital dollars for myriad reasons:

- Less than 1 in 100 start-ups obtain angel financing.
- Less than 1 in 1,000 start-ups are venture capital financed.
- Less than 1 in 10,000 new companies go public.
- Less than 1 in 25 angel deals see venture capital money.
- Less than 1 in 100 angel-funded companies go public via IPO.

Because many companies never meet venture capital investment thresholds, angels are beginning to retain a calculated amount of their investment capital for an anticipated second round of financing, by way of "keeping their powder dry." As well, angels often invest in *traunches,* deals in which an investor will agree to a designated amount in a particular financing, contingent on the company's reaching certain milestones or meeting certain preset obligations. For instance, an angel investor may agree to invest $300,000 in a series A preferred stock round, but provides only $100,000 upon completion of the financial documents. The company's receipt of the second $100,000 is dependent upon completion of the first product, and the third $100,000 dependent upon securing the first customer. These investment preconditions typically have other requirements such as timing or size of customer, and are agreed to by the parties as a condition to financing. In addition, these traunch requirements are usually taken from the company's business plan as projected accomplishments with the funding—putting the angel's money where the entrepreneur's mouth is. Staged investment also protects the angel from throwing good money after bad when an entrepreneur cannot deliver on the initial promises, or when conditions arise outside the entrepreneur's control, such as a market shift or a big player entering the market before the small entrepreneurial company gets off the ground, making the prospective investment no longer viable.

Angels' Vital Role in Early-Stage Funding

To appreciate the vital and essential role that angel investors play in early-stage financing, you need only look at the current statistics on venture capital financing and compare those to angel investing.

According to the PricewaterhouseCoopers MoneyTree survey of venture capital investments, venture capitalists invested $21.7 billion on 2,939 deals in 2005. This demonstrates a fairly flat trend line from 2004, when venture capitalists invested $21.6 billion in 2,966 deals. Figure 2.3 shows the recent trend in venture capital investments with the bubble aberration right in the middle (a trend we hope never to witness again, though history suggests we are doomed to repeat it).

While these trends are interesting, a more detailed analysis provides important insight for young entrepreneurs on the source for early-stage financing. The majority of 2005 venture capital dollars went into late-stage investments, 45 percent to be precise, which is the highest proportion in the eleven-year history of the PricewaterhouseCoopers MoneyTree report on venture capital trends. Contrast this percentage in late-stage investments with the venture capitalists' investment in

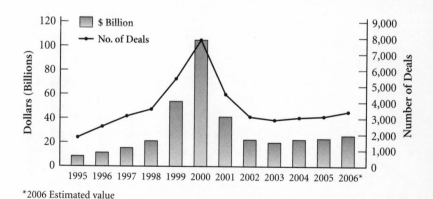

*2006 Estimated value

Figure 2.3   Venture Capital Investments, 1995–2006

VENTURE CAPITAL STATISTICS

Here is a further overview of VC funding and where the money is going:

2005—invested $21.7 billion (2,939 deals)

Average post-money valuation: $81.9 million

2004—invested $21.6 billion (2,966 deals)

2003—invested $19.6 billion (2,865 deals)

Increase due largely to late-stage investments:

$9.7 billion in 2005

$7.2 billion in 2004

$4.9 billion in 2003

In 2005, later stage = 45% of dollars (highest proportion in eleven-year history of MoneyTree)

Only 3.3% in seed/start-up stage

First quarter 2006: $5.6 billion (761 deals)—if this trend continues, 2006 will finish with a higher total investment amount than 2005

First quarter 2006: $187 million in seed/start-up companies (53 deals)—still 3.3% of the dollars and representing 7% of venture capital deals

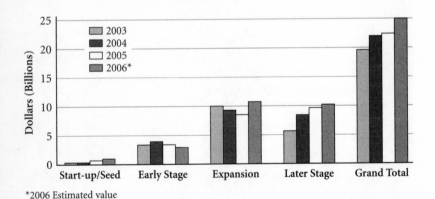

*2006 Estimated value

Figure 2.4   Venture Capital Investments by Stage
of Development ($ Billion)

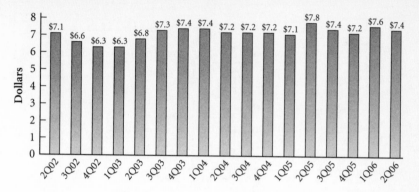

Figure 2.5   Average VC Deal Size per Financing Round ($ Million)

the seed/start-up stage in 2005 (only 3.3 percent), and it becomes clear where the vast majority of venture capitalists focus their investment activities. This reflects a consistent trend by venture capitalists to invest in more mature companies. Figure 2.4 illustrates this point (from PricewaterhouseCoopers MoneyTree).

Further evidence of venture capital migration up the investment and financing chain includes the average venture capital investment amount (see Figure 2.5, from National Venture Capital Association) and the average post-investment valuation for early-stage companies, which was $14.06 million for the twelve months ending with the first quarter of 2006 and $59.16 million for expansion-stage venture capital rounds, according to the National Venture Capital Association. These statistics represent investing patterns well beyond investment needs of early-stage companies. These statistics bear out the need to identify, foster, and expand other sources of early-stage financing—that is, of angel financing.

Even looking at just venture capital seed/start-up round financing investment averages shows numbers above most entrepreneurs' needs, with an average investment amount of $3.9 million in 2005 (in 204 deals), and trending the same in 2006 with $3.8 million in the first quarter (58 deals) and $3.9 million in the second (74 deals). These investment amounts represent the acquisition of a significant percentage ownership on the part of the venture capitalists. Likewise, the relatively small number of deals clearly indicates that traditional venture capitalists are not serving the vast needs of seed/start-up companies.

What investments venture capitalists are doing in seed/start-up companies is at a relatively conservative valuation reflective of the multiple unknowns and uncertainties for success accompanying any

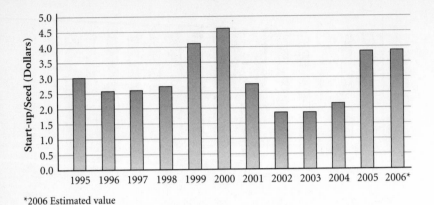

*2006 Estimated value

**Figure 2.6   Valuations of U.S. Venture Capital Seed/
Start-Up Rounds ($ Million)**

seed/start-up company. Figure 2.6 shows a trend between $2 and
$4 million in the last decade for venture capital investments in
seed/start-up companies. These valuations are likely high for the general population of seed/ start-up companies. Because of venture capitalists' adversity to risk, seed/start-up companies they are willing to
invest in are typically by seasoned, successful entrepreneurs whom they
know; thus, this reduces the risk and comparatively slightly increases
the valuation.

The picture for angel investors is very different from that for venture capitalists. For example, the GEM Report (the largest annual measure of entrepreneurial activity worldwide, compiled by more than
150 scholars from 35 countries, under the direction of Babson College
and the London Business School) concludes that angels fund a hundred times as many high-tech seed-stage companies as venture capital
firms do in the United States. This prevalence of angel investors is uniform throughout the countries the GEM Report analyzed. Figure 2.7
provides a global look at venture capital as a percentage of all investments. Clearly, informal investors, which includes angel investors, are
the main source of capital for start-up companies.

In addition, venture capital fund size trends do not speak well for
any reversal of the move toward larger investment amounts per deal.
According to the National Venture Capital Association, far fewer
VC funds exist today, but the average amount of financial resources
per fund is steadily increasing, as illustrated in Table 2.1. With so much
capital to invest, venture capitalists cannot afford to spend time on

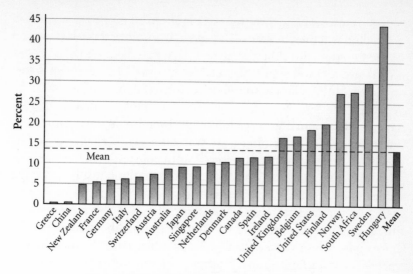

**Figure 2.7   Venture Capital as a Percentage of
All Investments (2005 GEM Report)**

deals as small as $1 million or $2 million (frequent first-round funding needs), when these deals take as much time in due diligence as a $10 million investment; the latter is a more efficient use of human and financial capital for those who have it available.

Why Not Try for VC Financing?

You might look at the statistics demonstrating that venture capitalists need to dispense lots of money at a time and conclude that the best approach is to go for venture financing and obtain all the funding you may need up front and thus avoid the distraction of fundraising in the midst of the serious business of growing a company. Unfortunately, this approach is illogical and often fruitless for many reasons.

Year	Number of Funds	Total $ (Million)	Average $/Fund
2000	637	106,734.4	167,557,928
2001	308	37,718.7	122,436,312
2002	172	3,862.1	22,454,070
2003	141	10,648.6	75,521,986
2004	187	16,986.6	90,837,433
2005 (Q1–3)	130	17,370.2	133,616,923

Table 2.1   Fewer Venture Capital Funds; More Money per Fund

Say your company is valued at $3 million; an investor who puts in $7 million will thereby gain a 70 percent ownership stake, leaving you as the founder with at best 30 percent. (At best, because most professional investors will require the establishment of an option plan before investing, further diluting your founder interest upon their investment.)

When you lose ownership percentage you lose control, and that's far more than a matter of terminology. Even if you don't mind having 30 percent of something great, you stand a good chance of getting forced all the way out if you accept loss of control.

And in any case, you won't often find $7 million just lying on the table these days. The risk of loss is just too high for most venture capitalists at the seed/start-up stage. Remember, venture capitalists are investing someone else's money (not their own like angels), so they have obligations to make the highest possible return on their investments, meaning large return multiples (billion-dollar projected market cap companies) and minimal risk of loss.

Thoughtful growth and creative financing make for better companies and better leaders. The dot-com bubble was a clear lesson that injecting lots of capital into a company at a very early stage does not increase its odds of success—and may, in fact, have the opposite effect.

COMPARISON OF ANGELS TO VENTURE CAPITALISTS

The most usual comparison to angel investors is venture capitalists. Because the two groups are involved in similar businesses and in similar ways, the comparison is natural, but they have some very large differences. It can be helpful for someone starting a new business and seeking funding to have a firm grasp on these similarities and differences.

Similarities

These two investor groups have much in common:

SELECTIVE INVESTMENT. While historically called sources of "dumb money" for investing in ideas with little understanding or up-front analysis, angels are becoming increasingly sophisticated through trial and error, angel organizations, educational programs, and the like. As a result, most angels now go through investment due diligence processes very similar to those of venture capitalists. Therefore, just as venture capitalists are highly selective about investments fitting into their investment profile for maturation stage, industry focus, portfolio compatability, investment terms, and other criteria, angels will often have similarly individualized investment selection requirements. This tells you as the entrepreneur that knowing your audience's interests, preferences, and investment criteria is important if you want to avoid wasting your time and that of the investors by promoting a deal that is ill-suited for your audience. As noted earlier, on average, less than one in a hundred start-ups receive angel investing—and less than one in a thousand receive venture capital financing.

REQUIREMENTS FOR AN INVESTABLE COMPANY. An *investable* company is not just one with a good idea. Investors must see numerous other attributes—a great management team, a realistic exit strategy for themselves, an attractive multiple on the investment, a simple, straightforward ownership structure, innovative technology, and clear intellectual property ownership for starters, and the list goes on.

EXPECTATION OF RETURN ON INVESTMENT. Investing is not a philanthropic activity (though the typical investor will see a strong multiple return on only three out of ten investments, so the effort may seem like charity). Investments by friends and family are often called "love money" because the basis for investment is apt to be affection for the entrepreneur rather than any sort of critical analysis. An angel or venture capitalist is a third-party, professional investor with no established affection for the would-be entrepreneur. Without a reasonable expectation of return on the investment, such an investor simply will not risk putting capital into a company.

SIMILAR INVESTMENT TERMS. Even up to five years ago, angels accepted common stock in return for their investment—then found themselves at a distinct disadvantage when venture capitalists came in and received preferred stock with rights, preferences, and privileges far superior to those of common stock, despite the angel having invested at a time of greater risk of loss. Though some angels still consciously select common stock for investment, most have learned their own lessons or learned at others' peril, and now insist on preferred stock (or debt conversion into preferred stock), placing them on a level similar to that of venture capitalists, who invest after angels and therefore at a less risky time in a company's development.

PROFESSIONAL ATTRIBUTES. Regardless of size, professional investors should bring three attributes to a company, and only the third of which is money. The first is experience and knowledge in their particular field of expertise, which adds value to the company and entrepreneur, and the second consists of connections to potential customers, vendors, resources, and follow-on financing.

Differences

Despite the similarities between venture capitalists and angel investors, significant differences abound. These differences not only involve priorities and deal structure, they involve the preferred stage of investment and the investors' importance to entrepreneurs.

PERSONAL WEALTH INVESTMENT. One of the most significant differences between venture capitalists and angel investors is that the former are investing third-party money and the latter their own personal wealth. As a result, venture capitalists have a fiduciary obligation of maximizing investor returns, and the continued viability of any venture fund depends to a great extent on outperforming other venture funds. Therefore, venture capitalists tend to invest on the home-run theory—that is, they choose high market cap companies at a point in their maturation that minimizes the risk of loss. Because of the size of venture capital investments and the need to create a greater assurance of success, venture capitalists often insist on being more actively involved than angels do, frequently requiring one or more board seats to gain control of corporate decisions.

INVESTMENT FOR REASONABLE RETURN. Many angels do not invest on the home-run theory at all. Instead, they look for more modest returns over their entire portfolio. Because angels are investing their own wealth, they don't face time constraints on showing a handsome profit; the resulting patience allows for the early-stage investing strategy. The social or community involvement aspects of angel investing also provide for involvement in a company at less than a controlling level.

CONTROL UPON INVESTMENT. Unlike venture capitalists, angels are unlikely to take a board position and more likely to play an advisory role for the founder and management team. Many angels refuse board positions because of the potential liability, an unfortunate consequence of the litigious current environment and new laws such as Sarbanes-Oxley. Many angels invest for the enjoyment of being part of a company, being part of the entrepreneurial process.

TIME OF INVESTMENT. As noted, for the most part, angels and venture capitalists invest at different times in a company's maturity. Angels invest at an early stage in a company's growth, taking a very high risk on the entrepreneur, management team, and innovative technology. In contrast, venture capitalists have continuously moved up the investment food chain for the multiplicity of reasons previously articulated, and now invest primarily in later-stage companies with market-proven technology, established sales, and a complete management team.

TIME TO INVESTMENT. While negotiation time varies greatly among investors, on average, angels progress more rapidly to investment than venture capitalists. This does not reflect any less care on the part of angels. Instead, because angels typically invest individually and use their own money, they have the freedom to choose their level of due diligence as well as comfort with sixth-sense feelings about a founder, management team, and company. Venture capitalists have limited partners to whom they owe a fiduciary duty of maximizing investment return and minimizing risk.

A WHOLE WORLD OF ANGEL INVESTORS

If angel investors are high-net-worth individuals (HNWIs) who invest their personal wealth primarily in early-stage companies, are there really enough of them to make a difference? How many individuals are both willing and able to be angel investors? No definitive study has been done on the actual number of angel investors in the United States and elsewhere, but the Center for Venture Research estimates the number of angel investors in the United States at around 126,000 (for the first half of 2005). The number of individuals with sufficient wealth to qualify at an "accredited investor" level under Regulation D of the Securities Act is known, and this forms the pool of potential angel investors. (See Appendix 3 for the full text of Regulation D.) Some estimate the ratio of active to potential angel investors in the United States to be as high as 1:10.

According to the *2006 World Wealth Report* (WWR) by Capgemini and Merrill Lynch, the population of HNWIs has grown steadily in the last ten years, nearly doubling in sheer numbers worldwide from 4.5 million in 1996 to 8.7 million in 2005. HNWIs are defined in the WWR as those having financial assets in excess of $1 million. The aggregate wealth of HNWIs doubled during the same period, from $16.6 trillion in 1996 to $33.3 trillion in 2005. The Ultra-HNWI population—those with individual financial assets in excess of $30 million—continued to grow in 2005 with a 10.2 percent increase to 85,400 individuals, with North America having the highest overall percentage of Ultra-HNWIs, undoubtedly fueled by soaring gas prices and the high profit return of Canadian oil sand fields. What may surprise many is that South Korea, India, Russia, and South Africa witnessed the most growth in HNWIs. The United States still has the greatest overall population of HNWIs and the greatest distribution of wealth, but the aggressive, entrepreneurial nature of foreign markets such as China and India (and Eastern Europe to some extent) are making the distribution of HNWIs a truly global phenomenon. The WWR shows that emerging markets continued to outperform other parts of the world, adding wealth in those countries. Figure 2.8 from the WWR shows comparative HNWI population growth for selected markets from 2004 to 2005.

Savvy entrepreneurs understand the global nature of business today and also understand that an aspiring young business does not compete for investment dollars only with other U.S. companies, it now competes with most of the rest of the world. Part of this broader thinking is

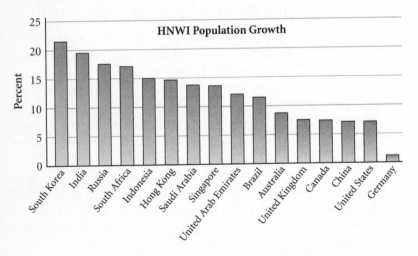

Figure 2.8   Percentage Growth in High Net-Worth
Individuals Globally, Selected Countries

also understanding that wealth generation is driven by growth in GDP and robust public markets; in other words, when the public markets are positive and corporate earnings are up, HNWIs have greater earnings and therefore more disposable income with which to invest in risky ventures such as seed/start-up companies. The inverse also applies. In 2005 and early 2006 the U.S. Federal Reserve kept increasing the overnight lending rate in an attempt to keep inflation in check, ultimately slowing (though not entirely stopping) GDP growth. Interest rate increases, coupled with devastation caused by Hurricanes Katrina and Rita, and with soaring oil prices, all reduced investor and consumer confidence and undercut the willingness and interest of HNWIs, or angel investors, to take greater risk with their investment capital. Therefore, as an entrepreneur, you must understand that even though your company is just taking off, domestic and global factors will influence your access to capital, markets, and talent.

Angel Organizations

Over the last ten years, according to the Center for Venture Research at the University of New Hampshire, the number of angel organizations has grown exponentially. Several factors have been responsible, including the Internet bubble—as evidenced by the large jump in 1999 shown in Figure 2.9. A natural fall-off occurred with the 2001 bust, but the trend for establishing angel groups continued in following years.

Why this proliferation of organizations? One of the key reasons is quality deal flow. Entrepreneurs would much rather present to a room full of accredited investors than make individual presentations to each investor. The best deals want the most efficient course to financing.

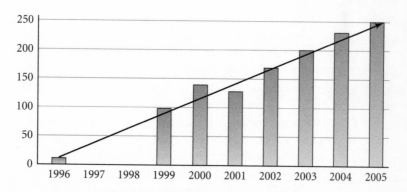

Figure 2.9   Growth of Angel Organizations in the United States

Presenting to fifty potential investors at one time is far more effective than making fifty individual presentations. Additionally, nearly all angel groups have screening committees or other mechanisms for selecting the best candidates for presenting at angel group meetings. Additionally, we know that individual angels have limitations on investment funds, which can restrict an angel's ability to negotiate certain investment terms. With angel groups, several angels may decide to invest, or pooled funds may be invested, increasing the total investment dollars and increasing the angels' collective ability to negotiate terms. Through this collective investment, angel groups help partially meet the ever-increasing funding gap between individual angels and venture capitalists. Equally important, many angel groups can provide a subsequent round of financing, which is necessary for many companies with capital needs under the venture fund radar.

Due diligence (discussed in more detail in Chapter Eight) is not a process to be entered into lightly. Proper and thorough due diligence often requires industry and technical knowledge, as well as comfort with financial documents, legal documents, marketing strategies, and the like. The old saying about two heads being better than one certainly applies to due diligence. Few people have the depth and breadth of knowledge and background to conduct effective and comprehensive due diligence. Therefore, angel groups provide a real solution through collective due diligence, conducted by the group or a subset of group members.

Another great benefit of an angel group is the ability to learn from other angel investors through formal training programs or sessions, as well as through listening to discussions at group meetings, committee meetings, and at other times. Good information and wide experience on the part of the investor make the investment experience richer and more valuable for the entrepreneur as well as safer for the angel investor. Finally, groups provide the social benefits of sharing similar interests. That common interest exists for the potential benefit of the entrepreneur. Most angel investors still invest as lone rangers—by themselves rather than through a group—but the number of investors in angel groups along with the actual number of angel groups is growing because of these obvious benefits.

Because of the real value angel groups present as a source of investors, this book provides an extensive list of angel groups in the United States and Canada, and in Europe, in Appendix 4 and Appendix 5. The source of much of the information on U.S. and Canadian angel groups is the Angel Capital Association (www.angelcapitalassociation.org) and

Angel Capital Education Foundation (www.angelcapitaleducation.org), two leading North American organizations related to angel groups, along with the National Angel Organization (NAO) (www.angelinvestor.ca) in Canada. NAO has traditionally placed a greater focus through its membership and services on individual angel investors, but also certainly promotes the establishment of angel groups. For Europe, information was obtained from the European Business Angel Network (EBAN; www.eban.org).

Angel groups are organized into a number of different legal, organizational, and administrative structures. As a result, angel groups invest in a number of different ways. Most angel groups still leave the investment decision up to each group member. Though the members may conduct due diligence as a group or in subgroups, individual investment decisions are still the typical path. As angel groups are becoming more popular, more angels are forming funds, either as an adjunct to an existing group, called *side-car funds,* or funds from the initial organizational stage. Angel funds are similar to venture capital funds from the standpoint of having members who agree or commit to contribute an agreed amount to the fund for investment. In a venture capital fund, the limited partners (investors) have no say in investment decisions. In contrast, angel fund members participate in the investment decision at some level—deal screening, due diligence, investment decision, post-investment relationships, and so on.

Seed Stage Investing

No statistics exist for Return on Investments for angels. Nonetheless, it is clear that angel investing in start-up/seed stage companies does have the potential for handsome returns. Statistics from early-stage/seed venture capital funds can be used for estimation purposes, as shown in Table 2.2 and Figure 2.10. (All from Thomson Financial/National

Fund Type	1-Year	3-Year	5-Year	10-Year	20-Year
Early/Seed VC	8.3	3.1	-10.9	41.5	20.4
Balanced VC	24.3	11.7	-3.5	18.9	14.6
Later-Stage VC	6.9	8.6	-4.1	11.3	13.5
TOTAL	15.6	7.5	-6.8	23.7	16.5

Table 2.2 **Venture Capital Returns Relative to Investment Stage Focus (Through December 31, 2005)**

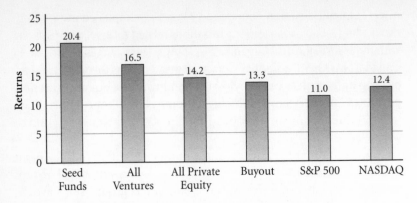

Figure 2.10   Historical Twenty-Year Returns for
Various Investment Alternatives

Venture Capital Association.) Of course, creating these types of returns does require many factors such as diversification of investment portfolio, educated and selective investments, follow-on support for the young companies—and a bit of luck.

SUMMARY

Is it possible to make any generalizations about angel investors? On the macro level, yes. On the personal level, unlikely. Like everyone else, angel investors are all individuals, with unique backgrounds, experiences, and preferences. Therefore, do not expect all angels to react the same, nor to ask the same questions, nor to have the same investment criteria.

Here are the trends angels seem to follow:

- *Angels invest primarily in companies at the seed/start-up stage.* This stage fits well with their average investment amount of around $50,000 to $500,000. Companies should grow thoughtfully, and amounts in this range are generally sufficient for this period of growth, while still allowing entrepreneurs a large amount of control over their companies.

- *Angels invest smaller amounts in a number of deals to create a diversified portfolio.* Because they make more investments for smaller amounts, angels are the investor of preference for seed and early-stage companies. Angels also fill a vital need in supporting entrepreneurs at this early, unknown-future period of development. Angels are more likely to take a bigger risk on you than any other professional investor. Angels are also recently recognizing the possible need to make subsequent investments because a portfolio company is still not ready for venture capital, or simply will never need venture capital.

• *Angels invest for reasons beyond financial return, though profitability is clearly their primary incentive.* Social responsibility and community involvement through local investments also rank high for angels. With domain expertise and entrepreneurial experience, angels also make excellent advisers and mentors.

The population of potential angel investors is growing around the world through the increase in the total number of high-net-worth individuals. Appreciation of angel investing as an alternative source of funds is still a work in progress, but angel organizations are helping make such investing known and accessible. Angel organizations are rapidly growing in number, with sophisticated investment strategies behind this rapid ascent, including quality deal flow, collective due diligence, and greater investment dollar clout.

Angel investors are the primary source of seed/start-up and early-stage funding, placing their belief in the economic process behind young companies. Angel investment dollars plus contribution of expertise and experience amount to an essential and vital part of economic growth for local communities and nations.

CHAPTER THREE

Private Equity Investing

P rivate equity investing is the placement of funds in a nonpublic company in return for a share of ownership. Broadly defined, private equity is any security in a private company that represents ownership or potential ownership in that company. Angels invest in private companies by either financing with debt or using a private equity vehicle. Understanding the complexities of private equity investing is important in dealing intelligently and knowledgeably with angel investors—and, frankly, it is essential if you mean to avoid potentially monumental problems.

This chapter provides general descriptions and discussions of the important topics surrounding equity investment, but it cannot cover specific state and federal requirements for each jurisdiction. Private equity financing has regional and local trends, terms, idiosyncrasies, and regulatory requirements, and you need to work with people who will help your company recognize and work within these parameters. Therefore, before embarking on any private equity financing for your company, you need to secure advisers (including legal counsel) who are experienced and knowledgeable with equity financing on a local and national level. Remember—you only get one chance to make a first impression, and this includes showing you are smart enough to retain advisers who understand the investors' needs and requirements.

Private equity investing certainly comes in many shapes and sizes. Even with the following list of equity investment options, investors continue to come up with creative mechanisms for investing in companies. Table 3.1 summarizes equity investment vehicles, which are explained in greater detail following the table.

Investment Vehicle	Brief Definition
Preferred Stock (voting)	The most common equity investment vehicle used by both sophisticated angel investors and venture capitalists. Preferred stock has rights, preferences, and privileges greater than other types of equity investment. Two important preferences are the entitlement of preferred stock to receive dividends before common stock, and the entitlement of preferred stock to receive a return before common stock.
Preferred Stock (nonvoting)	Gives the same privileges upon liquidation, but does not allow the angel investor to vote shares on important corporate matters, for members of the board of directors, and so on, though certain protective provisions may still allow voting on matters with potential impact on the investor.
Common Stock (voting)	The most basic form of security a corporation can offer. It essentially places the investor on the same financial footing as the founders of the company. This form of investing is generally considered unsophisticated, but still occurs among angel investors. However, some sophisticated angels take common stock because they want to have the same risks as the founders. Also, companies sometimes refuse to offer preferred stock, so common stock is the only type of equity available.
Common Stock (nonvoting)	Same preference as the founders in liquidation, dividends, and so on, but without the ability to vote shares on important corporate matters, for members of the board of directors, and so on.
Warrant	Entitles the holder to buy a proportionate amount of stock at some future time for a predetermined amount, and can be used with an investment for equity or debt. Warrants are generally used as an incentive or sweetener to invest in a company. While warrants are typically for common stock, occasionally a company will use a warrant for preferred stock as part of an investment package.

Table 3.1   Equity Investment Options (Continued)

Option (for common stock)	A right to purchase stock at a predefined value; not a typical investment vehicle for angels. Stock options are typically provided to employees, board members, consultants, and others as a form of reward or alternative form of compensation for past, present, or future services. One circumstance in which options may be granted to an investor would be as an additional benefit or inducement for investing, though warrants are typically the vehicle of choice in these circumstances.
Debenture (promissory note; not convertible—straight debt)	A note carrying interest payable in cash or stock. Investors may insist the note be collateralized (secured), which will make a difference for the investor if the company fails.
Debenture (promissory note; convertible into common or preferred stock)	A debt instrument that automatically converts into equity upon the occurrence of an event or milestone, or at the investor's discretion, or sometimes in either event. Some angels prefer to use a convertible debenture to take advantage of subsequent investment round terms, avoid negotiating valuations, and always have a debt obligation should the conversion fail to occur. This kind of instrument will typically convert to preferred stock.
Stock or Debenture Investment (with associated options or warrants)	Debt instrument with associated options or warrants that provides the investor with an incentive or added benefit for making a risky investment in a start-up company.
Guarantor (on line of credit or other debt instrument)	Assurance that the angel will assume the holder's position should the entrepreneur default on the debt instrument through nonpayment of the outstanding debt balance.

Table 3.1   Equity Investment Options

* *Note:* The table is somewhat simplified and does not include discussion of numerous additional terms and conditions related to various investment forms, such as voting agreements, security agreements, buy-back agreements, co-sale and rights of first refusal, and other rights, preferences, and privileges.

BASIC DIFFERENCES BETWEEN DEBT AND EQUITY INVESTMENTS

Debt carries an obligation of repayment. That is, the fundamental difference between debt and equity is that debts must be repaid at some point, generally described at the maturity date, while equity investments need not be repaid. Of course, assorted nuances and additional terms can modify this simplified definition. For instance, a debt instrument, typically a promissory note, can have terms that automatically convert the debt into equity upon the occurrence of a predefined event or milestone. Appendix 8 is a simple convertible debenture (or note) that contains a clause allowing for the automatic conversion of the debenture into preferred stock upon the company raising $3 million dollars. The debenture also allows the holder (an angel investor in this case) to convert it into equity at any time at a preset price per share; rarely is the right of conversion left to the discretion of the company. As the annotations in Appendix 8 explain, convertible promissory notes can have a variety of structures and terms related to conversion price, rate, timing, and other factors.

Interest is typically due on promissory notes and many investors will agree to accept interest payments in the form of stock (typically common stock) rather than cash. For any entrepreneur, cash is precious; most angel investors would prefer you use 100 percent of your cash to grow your company rather than paying interest on their debt. The issuance of convertible debentures for a short period before a preferred stock offering round of financing is called *bridge financing*. It results only in a minor amount of cumulated interest, so it is generally accepted by most investors.

Convertible debentures such as warrants and convertible promissory notes are the investment vehicle of choice for many angel investors because they are relatively straightforward. The angel investor agrees to automatically convert the debenture into a preferred stock offering for a discount off the price offered to other interested parties. Often the preferred stock financing will be negotiated by a venture capitalist or a group of angel investors, giving the investors a definitive advantage in negotiating investment terms. The original angel investor holding the convertible debenture then receives the investor-favorable terms negotiated in this next round and the entrepreneur has the financing needed to grow the company to a point when a venture capitalist would be interested in investing. The convertible debenture also provides this early-stage, high-risk investor with some security: if the company is unable to raise the next round of financing, the investor still holds a debt instrument that requires repayment upon maturity. This obligation of repayment, while possibly an illusion considering the typical strained coffers of a start-up company, does place the investor in a senior position to the founders and stockholders upon liquidation or dissolution of the company.

One side note: debt-heavy balance sheets, even with convertible debt, can result in difficulties concerning future financing, particularly with venture capitalists. Subsequent investors are not interested in seeing their money go to pay off an investor or shareholder—they want every penny applied to business growth and expansion. Therefore, in subsequent rounds investors will often insist that all debt be converted into equity, even straight debt.

Equity provides higher potential return but carries greater risk of loss. As noted, debt and equity investments differ over the lack of a legal obligation for repayment with the latter. Exceptions or caveats to this statement exist, for instance if the shareholders enter into an agreement obligating the company to repurchase shares at some time in the future. Also, redemption rights or the right to force the company to repurchase shares as a term of a stock offering (almost always preferred stock) would be considered a legal obligation for repayment. Nonetheless, investors approach a stock investment differently from a debt, both psychologically and in terms of benefit expectations. Because of the greater risk of loss, investors often take longer to make an equity investment decision and often require more information in the due diligence process. In addition, because of the higher level of risk, investors expect to receive a greater potential benefit. Preferred stock provides additional rights, preferences, and privileges to create at least a perceived balance for the investor between benefit and loss. Based on this reasoning, equity investments are best for high-growth potential ventures, since debt instruments (unless convertible) have a predefined cap on gain through interest payments (and perhaps some additional stock in the form of a warrant). In contrast, equity investments can achieve major multiples, sometimes returning ten or twenty times the investment—or more, on huge successes. You've surely seen the occasional news clip about angels and other early-stage investors putting in $100,000 that is now worth $10,000,000, which is why many angels get in the business in the first place.

From your perspective as the entrepreneur, equity investing has a lower financial risk since it generally does not carry an obligation of cash payments (except perhaps for mandatory dividend payments), whereas debt servicing will entail interest and principal payments. Also, some debt financing methods, such as lines of credit, have restrictive covenants that could cause you to default. Pure equity investments do not have default conditions unless the investor has a *put option* (right to demand repayment of equity investment after a set time period) or some other future obligation that creates a liability; however, put options and other obligations are not the typical equity investment.

Of course, nothing is perfect. Equity investments do have downsides. Because the risk of loss is higher for investors with an equity investment, investments can take three to six months from introduction to check in the bank. You may not have enough cash to last that long, so while you have a few options, the experienced entrepreneur must keep ahead of funding needs and avoid getting to a zero bank balance. This cash-over-time requirement is often termed "adequate runway," referring to the length of runway a plane will need to land safely—or cash for a company to get to profitability—with different lengths needed for a two-seater and a jumbo jet.

Another downside to equity investing is ownership dilution for the founders, employees, and existing investors. Equity investors reduce your voting control, unless your investors agree to take nonvoting stock, which is quite unlikely. Equity investments can also reduce your management control, though this happens more often with venture capitalists than with angel investors. Venture capitalists will often require one or more seats on the board. This board structure often means greater involvement in management and certainly in strategic direction.

Angel investors often choose to have only information rights (the right to receive information on the company through various communication sources such as quarterly reports, monthly financials, annual report, business plans, and the like), rather than taking a seat on the board. Angels tend to avoid board seats—partly because they normally have a number of investments in their portfolios to provide appropriate diversification, and so do not have the time to serve on all their investments' boards. In addition, angels answer only to themselves, unlike venture capitalists, who have limited partners to whom they owe the fiduciary and financial duties of minimizing risk and maximizing potential returns. Venture capitalists typically invest significantly more than angels and as a result have a greater stake in the company. Meanwhile, Sarbanes-Oxley has caused angels to shy away from serving on boards and thereby raising their perceived liability exposure.

If you must retain 100 percent control indefinitely, it may mean forgoing growth or struggling along with limits on potential financing. If you feel you need control in the short term, then convertible debentures may be a solution to your funding needs. While convertible debenture is considered equity for purposes of your capitalization structure and balance sheet, it does not have voting rights for the underlying shares. Only upon conversion can the holder exercise the voting rights for the stock, which postpones investors' control to a future time.

Another factor to consider in deciding between debt and equity is prioritization upon liquidation—that is, how assets or sale proceeds will be allocated if the company goes out of business and distributes its remaining assets. The general priority of payment works like this:

- First repayment to secured and collateralized debt—senior position
- Second repayment to secured and collateralized debt—junior or subordinated position
- Third repayment to unsecured and noncollateralized debt (any of this debt being straight debt or convertible)
- Fourth repayment to preferred stock—which can be issued in a number of series
- Finally, repayment to common stock—that is, founder stock, employee stock, most friends and family, and some angels

If a company is closing its doors, the likelihood that common stock shareholders will receive payment if all these prior categories exist is slim at best. Note that options and warrants are not listed; until exercised, these represent only the right to purchase stock, not the actual underlying stock itself.

Based on all this information about debt and equity investing, the best advice in deciding your course of financing is to weigh the relative pros and cons of debt verses equity investing, understand your financial needs now and into the future, and know your investor market and their preferences.

PREFERRED STOCK

Preferred stock, quite simply, is stock that has additional rights, preferences, and privileges beyond common stock. Preferred stock is the most popular investment vehicle for sophisticated angel investors because of these rights, which include the preference upon liquidation I just mentioned. Holders of preferred stock also have priority on dividends, rights to control certain corporate actions, and the privilege of choosing to receive a distribution as a preferred stock shareholder or converting the holdings into common stock if financially more advantageous, such as upon an initial public offering. Convertible debentures usually convert into preferred stock with the first preferred stock investment round. Preferred stock is often issued in series, with each series typically having sequential alphabetical identifiers, so the first series or round of preferred stock financing is Series A, the second round is Series B, and so on. In theory, each subsequent round or series should be for a higher valuation.

If your company will need one or more substantial rounds of financing after the angel financing round, simpler early round terms are best. An overly complicated term sheet in an early round can either suppress interest among potential subsequent investors or lead to demands from subsequent investors that early investors accept modified investment terms. Savvy angel investors understand this investment truism: The last gold rules. In other words, the most recent money being invested in a company controls overall terms, even for other rounds. Why? Because subsequent rounds are typically larger than their predecessors, representing a greater potential share of company ownership, and consequently they have greater influence. But most important, without the new round of financing, the company will tank—causing previous investors to lose their investment. So what should the earlier investor do? Stand hard on terms that subsequent investors find unacceptable, or accept compromises and see the company continue to grow? You can hope your investors would see the latter as the obvious choice, but unfortunately not all are that perceptive. This means you, as the entrepreneur, need to have a good understanding of investment options and terms. Several forms of angel investment have been introduced, with convertible debentures and preferred stock structures being two frequently used investment vehicles.

When a subsequent round of financing purchases ownership at a lower value than the prior round, it washes out the ownership percentage of earlier investors, along with the founders, employees, and other holders of common stock. This is called a "down round" and is a common fear among investors who have common stock, and another reason angel investors and venture capitalists favor preferred stock. To better understand the concept of a down round, look at Table 3.2, and also the definition of "Cram Down" in the Glossary, Appendix 1.

Compare Table 3.2 with Table 3.3. The only difference between Table 3.2 (the cram down) and Table 3.3 (normal progression investments) is the price paid per share for the Series B preferred stock. Both

Shareholder Name	Founder's Common Stock ("CS")		Angel Financing Round – Series A Preferred Shares ("A")		Stock Option Pool – Common Stock ("CS")		Venture Capital Round – Series B Preferred Shares ("B")	
	No. of Shares	% of Total	No. of Shares	% of Total	No. of Shares	% of Total	No. of Shares	% of Total
K. Preston	500,000	50%		33.3%		28.6%		6.45%
J. Rubin	500,000	50%		33.3%		28.6%		6.45%
C. Hill-Swartz					50,000	2.86%		0.645%
M. Anderson					50,000	2.86%		0.645%
H. Aldrich					100,000	5.72%		1.29%
S. Ali					50,000	2.86%		0.645%
Subtotal: CS	1,000,000	100%		66.6%	250,000	71.5%		16.13%
C. Mickey			100,000	6.67%		5.71%		1.29%
R. Ayala			200,000	13.3%		11.5%		2.58%
J. Ford			100,000	6.67%		5.71%		1.29%
S. Symonds			100,000	6.67%		5.71%		1.29%
Subtotal: A			500,000	33.3%		28.6%		6.45%
Emerald VC							6,000,000	
Subtotal: B							6,000,000	77.42%
Total Shares	1,000,000		1,500,000	100%	1,750,000	100%	7,750,000	100%
Common:	1,000,000		1,000,000	66.6%	1,250,000	71.2%	1,250,000	22.58%
Preferred:			500,000	33.4%	500,000	28.8%	6,500,000	77.42%
Price/share			$1.00				$0.50	
Pre-money valuation			$1,000,000				$875,000	
Post-money valuation			$1,500,000				$3,875,000	

Table 3.2 Capitalization Table Showing Cram Down (or Down Round)

Shareholder Name	Founder's Common Stock ("CS")		Angel Financing Round – Series A Preferred Shares ("A")		Stock Option Pool – Common Stock ("CS")		Venture Capital Round – Series B Preferred Shares ("B")	
	No. of Shares	% of Total	No. of Shares	% of Total	No. of Shares	% of Total	No. of Shares	% of Total
K. Preston	500,000	50%		33.3%		28.6%		10.5%
J. Rubin	500,000	50%		33.3%		28.6%		10.5%
C. Hill-Swartz					50,000	2.86%		1.05%
M. Anderson					50,000	2.86%		1.05%
H. Aldrich					100,000	5.72%		2.15%
S. Ali					50,000	2.86%		1.05%
Subtotal: CS	1,000,000	100%		66.6%	250,000	71.5%		26.3%
C. Mickey			100,000	6.67%		5.71%		2.1%
R. Ayala			200,000	13.3%		11.5%		4.2%
J. Ford			100,000	6.67%		5.71%		2.1%
S. Symonds			100,000	6.67%		5.71%		2.1%
Subtotal: A			500,000	33.3%		28.6%		10.5%
Emerald VC							3,000,000	63.2%
Subtotal: B							3,000,000	63.2%
Total Shares	1,000,000	100%	1,500,000	100%	1,750,000	100%	4,750,000	100%
Common:	1,000,000	50%	1,000,000	66.6%	1,250,000	71.2%	1,250,000	26.3%
Preferred:	1,000,000	50%	500,000	33.4%	500,000	28.8%	3,500,000	73.7%
Price/share			$0.50				$1.00	
Pre-money valuation			$500,000				$1,750,000	
Post-money valuation			$750,000				$4,750,000	

Table 3.3   Capitalization Table Showing Increasing Valuation Rounds

rounds show a Series B round raise of $3,000,000, but with the cram down round at $0.50 per share for the Series B and previous Series A round raise at $1.00, while the normal progression round is at $1.00 per share for the Series B and the previous A round at $0.50. Note the definitive difference in percentage ownership for the founders, angel investors, and employee option-holders.

Note the significant difference in ownership percentage for all shareholders (and option holders) depending on the valuation, and therefore, the price per share for each round. Protection against this type of negative impact and numerous other reasons, including the need to balance risk with reward, drive the terms of a preferred stock round. Approaches to financing differ in different regions, so you may encounter different preferences for multiples on liquidation and for the extent of protection rights.

Because of the frequent use of preferred stock offerings, the terms of such offerings should be well understood. Exhibit 3.1 provides a comprehensive listing and explanation of terms that may appear in a preferred stock offering. However, angel financing should be a scaled-down version if subsequent rounds of financing must be secured, particularly if those rounds will be venture capital. If a single round of financing will take the company to cash flow positive and to a level of financial confidence for intended growth, the angel round terms can be closer to those in the exhibit. Remember, this is only the term sheet that you should use to familiarize yourself with the construction of preferred stock agreements. Your legal counsel will utilize these or similar terms and conditions to create the final offering documents. The exhibit is set up to first show an example of language for a particular preferred stock term, followed by a discussion of the term. "Great Starts, Inc." is a fictitious company used throughout this book for example purposes only.

Exhibit 3.1   Comprehensive Preferred Stock Term Sheet

SERIES A PREFERRED STOCK FINANCING TERM SHEET
This Term Sheet, dated January 1, 2007, outlines the terms and conditions of a proposed investment by the Investors listed on Exhibit A (collectively, the "Investors") in Great Starts, Inc., a Delaware corporation (the "Company"). This Term Sheet is an expression of intent only, and is not to be construed as a binding agreement, except for the "Exclusivity" and "Confidentiality" provisions contained herein.
Offering Terms
Issuer: Great Starts, Inc., a Delaware corporation

Amount of financing: A minimum of $750,000 and up to a maximum of $1,500,000, including $250,000 received pursuant to outstanding bridge notes (the "Bridge Notes")

Comments: Financing rounds often have a minimum at which the company may start drawing down funds from committed investors. Most investors will insist that the company set up an escrow account that accepts investments but does not release the funds to the company until a minimum amount is in the escrow account. The amount that triggers a release of funds is typically a percentage of the total round raise, but enough to accomplish certain critical milestones. Some investors will not require a minimum raise, but sophisticated ones will insist on it. Also, if you have investors who do not want to be first to invest but are willing to invest later, you can let them all be second or third by setting up an escrow account with a minimum to release the funds.

This term includes Bridge Notes to show how they can be handled in the preferred share term round. In this instance, the Bridge Notes are convertible debentures (or notes) intended to keep the company operational until the full preferred share round is secured. In other words, the convertible debentures "bridge" the funding gap to a round of financing.

Type of Security: Series A Preferred Stock (the "Preferred Stock"), initially convertible on a 1:1 basis into shares of the Company's Common Stock (the "Common Stock").

Price: $1.00 per share (the "Original Purchase Price"). The Original Purchase Price represents a fully diluted pre-money valuation of $3,250,000.

Comments: The price is typically one of the most heavily negotiated terms because it reflects the agreed-to amount investors will pay per share.

Investors: Investors listed in Exhibit A
Bridge Notes listed in Exhibit B

Comments: Some companies will list a lead investor, if they have one, on the first page and then list all other investors on the Exhibit.

At the Closing, the outstanding principal of the Bridge Notes will automatically convert into shares of Preferred Stock at a conversion price equal to the Original Purchase Price. All accrued interest, if any, will be paid at the Closing by the Company.

Comments: Note that only the principal is converted into this Preferred Stock round. Principal is typically a whole number, and therefore, the conversion will not result in fractional shares. Additionally, interest is fairly modest considering the short period of time Bridge Notes are in existence.

Anticipated Closing Date: On or before March 31, 2007 (the "Closing"), with a subsequent closing to occur on or before 15–60 days following the Closing.

(Continued)

Exhibit 3.1   Comprehensive Preferred Stock Term Sheet, Continued

Comments: Because the term sheet provides for a minimum closing amount, you will want the ability to draw funds out of escrow as soon as the total meets that minimum, often referred to as "breaking escrow." Accepting funds into the company's account requires that the participating parties sign all relevant documents, effecting a Closing.

Use of Proceeds: Proceeds from the investment will be used for working capital and general corporate purposes and [_____].

Comments: The description of use of proceeds should fairly summarize the business plan. Few investors will accept merely "working capital and general corporate purposes," and many will require an agreement prohibiting the use of funds to buy out shareholders. Similarly, some investors will even require the conversion of all debt resulting from an investment before Closing.

Dividends: The holders of Preferred Stock shall be entitled to receive noncumulative dividends in preference to any dividend on the Common Stock at the rate of 8 percent of the Original Purchase Price per annum when and as declared by the Board of Directors. The holders of Preferred Stock also shall be entitled to participate pro rata in any dividends paid on the Common Stock on an as converted to Common Stock basis.

Comments: This clause provides preferred shareholders with the right to receive dividends before the common shareholders. This clause offers only noncumulative dividends but investors will prefer to receive cumulative dividends. Also, investors would prefer that dividends are automatically provided rather than based on a Board decision. The preference on first dividends and the added participation with Common Stock are fairly typical.

Liquidation Preference: In the event of any liquidation or winding up of the Company, the holders of Preferred Stock shall be entitled to receive in preference to the holders of the Common Stock a per share amount equal to the Original Purchase Price (as adjusted for any stock splits, dividends, and the like) plus any declared but unpaid dividends (the "Liquidation Preference"). After the payment of the Liquidation Preference to the holders of Preferred Stock, the remaining assets of the Company shall be distributed ratably to the holders of the Common Stock until the holders of Common Stock shall have received a per share amount equal to [$____] per share (as adjusted for any stock splits, dividends, and the like); thereafter, the remaining assets of the Company shall be distributed ratably to the holders of the Common Stock and Preferred Stock on an as converted to Common Stock basis.

A liquidation, for purposes of the application of this Liquidation Preference, is defined as a merger, acquisition, sale of voting control in which the stockholders of the Company immediately prior to the transaction do not own a majority of the outstanding shares of the surviving corporation, or sale or lease of substantially all of the assets of the Company.

Comments: As has been discussed, preferred shares have a number of rights, preferences, and privileges superior to common shares. Liquidation Preference is one of the more important rights. In this clause, preferred shareholders receive an amount equal to the Original Purchase Price before common shareholders receive any distribution. Because this liquidation amount merely makes them whole, investors often require a multiple on the Original Purchase Price—for example, double that price.

Along with asking for multiples on the Original Purchase Price, Preferred Stock investors may ask that they have the right to receive further funds through converting their Preferred Stock into Common Stock and then receiving more funds as a Common Stock holder. This right would have the following language: "After the payment of the Liquidation Preference to the holders of Preferred Stock, the remaining assets of the Company shall be distributed ratably to the holders of the Common Stock and Preferred Stock on an as converted to Common Stock basis."

As the entrepreneur (and therefore the principal holder of common stock), you will want a limit on the amount Preferred Stock investors receive before you receive a distribution. This is how the clause is currently constructed, allowing Preferred Stock shareholders to receive a set amount and then the Common Stock shareholders receive a set amount (the per share price), and then joint receipt of remaining funds.

Conversion: The holders of the Preferred Stock shall have the right to convert Preferred Stock, at the option of the holder, at any time, into shares of Common Stock. The initial conversion rate shall be one share of Preferred Stock into one share of Common Stock, subject to adjustment as provided below.

Comments: Preferred Stock investors will convert when the return on investment is greater on Common Stock than on the Preferred Stock. For example, assume that under the liquidation preference the Preferred Stock investor can receive two times the original purchase price and such potential return equals $2 per share. You are doing an initial public offering (IPO) at $4 per share. Under this basis, the Preferred Stock investors would convert because of the favorable return as a Common Stock holder.

Automatic Conversion: Preferred Stock shall be automatically converted into Common Stock, at the then applicable conversion price, (i) in the event that the holders of at least a majority of the outstanding Preferred Stock consent to such conversion or (ii) upon the closing of a firmly underwritten public offering of shares of Common Stock at a per share price not less than 4 times the Original Purchase Price (as adjusted for stock splits, dividends, and the like) per share and for a total offering of not less than $25 million before deduction of underwriters' commissions and expenses (a "Qualified IPO").

Comments: Investors will agree to automatic conversion of preferred to common shares under circumstances that will provide them this greater return on investment, for instance, an initial public offering (IPO). As the founder, you want your investors to automatically convert upon an agreed event. Investors will not leave a conversion up to you, so the next best alternative is automatic conversion. As with milestone investments in which investors require an entrepreneur to achieve goals and activities the entrepreneur has outlined in the business plan, investors will also agree to automatic conversion that relates to a positive investor event. Therefore,

(Continued)

Exhibit 3.1   Comprehensive Preferred Stock Term Sheet, Continued

an investor may agree to automatic conversion upon achievement of a significant milestone outlined in your business plan that clearly increases investment value and the likelihood of success.

Anti-dilution Provisions: The conversion price of Preferred Stock will be subject to a broad-based weighted average adjustment to reduce dilution in the event that the Company issues additional equity securities at a purchase price less than the applicable conversion price. The conversion price of Preferred Stock will not be adjusted for the following issuances: (i) shares of Common Stock issued upon conversion of or as a dividend or distribution on Preferred Stock, (ii) shares of restricted stock or stock options granted to officers, directors, employees, or consultants as approved by the Company's Board of Directors, (iii) shares of Common Stock subject to outstanding options, warrants, or convertible securities as of the date hereof, (iv) the issuance of Common Stock or rights to purchase Common Stock issued in connection with equipment lease financing arrangements, credit agreements, debt financings, or other commercial transactions approved by the Board of Directors, (v) shares of Common Stock or rights to purchase Common Stock issued for consideration other than cash pursuant to a merger, consolidation, acquisition, or similar business combination approved by the Board of Directors. The conversion price will also be subject to proportional adjustment for stock splits, stock dividends, recapitalizations, and the like.

Comments: As noted earlier, investors are not keen on cram downs or down rounds and would strongly prefer to protect themselves against such actions. These protections are called anti-dilution provisions. Because this book is for entrepreneurs, the example language has company-favorable (or less investor-favorable) terms, but they are still fair and representative terms. The exclusions from the anti-dilution provisions are reasonable for proper operation of your company. For instance, you should be able to issue options to your employees, directors, and consultants without worrying about the implications under a financing round and you should have the ability to issue shares relative to business transactions such as leasing arrangements without making adjustments for your Preferred Stock investors. The terms must be reasonable from the standpoint of not putting a chokehold on the company.

Redemption at Option of Investors: At the election of the holders of at least 66 2/3% of Preferred Stock, the Company shall redeem outstanding Preferred Stock in three annual installments beginning on the fifth anniversary of the Closing. Such redemptions shall be at a purchase price equal to 100 percent of the Original Purchase Price.

Comments: Sophisticated investors know redemption rights really don't have much impact because by the time an investor can typically exercise rights of redemption, the company is probably not in any condition to meet the repayment requirements, that is, it's almost or already out of business. But on occasion, companies do continue on through slow organic growth, riding the ups and downs of the market and slowly making progress. If you wind up with one of those companies, which is the case for many entrepreneurs who dreamed of going public in five years after starting their company (or at least being purchased for a handsome amount), you need to be careful about redemption rights, which can effectively tank a company at a time when you are just turning the corner toward profitability. Therefore, make sure that the time period on redemption is as long as possible, that installment payments are allowed, that the amount is limited to principal, and the investors have no other rights to do things to the company—you don't want them taking over the board of directors at that point.

Voting Rights: Preferred Stock will vote together with the Common Stock and not as a separate class except as specifically provided herein or as otherwise required by law. Each share of Preferred Stock shall have a number of votes equal to the number of shares of Common Stock then issuable upon conversion of such share of Preferred Stock.

Comments: Some investors will ask for special voting rights to increase their influence in certain matters under shareholder control. This language provides equality between the Preferred Stock investors and Common Stock shareholders.

Board of Directors: The size of the Company's Board of Directors shall be set at five. At the Closing, the Board shall initially comprise the following individuals: _____. The Company will indemnify board members to the maximum extent permitted by applicable law. The Company will reimburse directors for their customary and reasonable expenses in attending Board meetings.

Comments: Preferred Stock investors may also ask that one or more board members be designated by the holders of Preferred Stock, thus ensuring the investors a presence on and vote in all board meetings. In addition, with the significant liability issues raised by Sarbanes-Oxley and the general litigious atmosphere in the United States, your investors may insist on the company purchasing director and officer liability insurance. Along the same line of control and observance of laws such as Sarbanes-Oxley, you may also be asked to establish a compensation committee as part of the board to make recommendations, and possibly decisions, on management compensation, benefit plans, and equity incentive plans. Investors may also want to spell out the frequency of board meetings rather than leave it up to management discretion.

Protective Provisions: The Company may not, without the consent of holders of at least a majority of Preferred Stock: (i) declare or pay any dividends or make any distributions upon any of its equity securities; (ii) purchase, redeem, or otherwise acquire any of the Company's equity securities (including warrants, options, and other rights to acquire equity securities) other than the repurchase of equity securities pursuant to existing agreements; (iii) liquidate or dissolve; (iv) merge or consolidate with another corporation in which the holders of the Company's voting equity securities immediately prior to the transactions own 50 percent or less of the voting securities of the surviving corporation; (v) sell, license, or dispose of all or substantially all of the Company's assets, technology, or intellectual property; (vi) change the authorized number of directors; (vii) create any new class or series of shares having rights, preferences, or privileges senior to Preferred Stock; (viii) amend or waive any provision

(Continued)

Exhibit 3.1   Comprehensive Preferred Stock Term Sheet, Continued

of its Certificate of Incorporation or Bylaws in a manner that alters or changes the voting or other powers, preferences, or other special rights or privileges of Preferred Stock so as to affect them adversely; or (ix) increase or decrease the authorized number of shares of Preferred Stock.

Comments: Investors want to know that you cannot take certain actions considered injurious to their investment rights, ownership percentage, or future potential value. As a result, most investors will ask for protective rights. These provisions can be extensive. Again, reasonableness should be the rule. If you are faced with a long list of restrictions of your actions, you may need to ask whether the investor actually trusts your judgment, and therefore, whether or not there is a fit.

Information Rights: The Company shall deliver to each Investor audited annual financial statements and annual report no later than 120 days following the close of the fiscal year, and unaudited quarterly financial statements no later than 45 days following the close of such period. The Company will also furnish each Investor with a copy of the Company's annual operating plan no later than 30 days prior to the beginning of the fiscal year. Each Investor shall also be entitled to standard inspection and visitation rights. These provisions shall terminate upon an IPO or an acquisition, merger, or consolidation of the Company.

Comments: Reasonable information requests should never be an issue. Investors are entitled to know how a company is doing and many investors ask for far more than the rights listed here. Many investors will ask for monthly financials, copies of all business plans, and other information material to the company. You should consistently communicate with your investors, letting them know how the company is progressing and also letting them know about possible setbacks. Better to keep the line of communication open than have your investors find out negative news through the grapevine—or worse yet, in the newspaper.

Registration Rights:
    Demand Rights. If Investors holding more than 50 percent of outstanding Preferred Stock, including Common Stock issued on conversion of Preferred Stock (collectively, "Registrable Securities"), request that the Company file a registration statement having an aggregate offering price to the public of not less than $15,000,000, the Company will use its reasonable best efforts to cause such shares to be registered; provided, however, that the Company shall not be obligated to effect any such registration prior to the fifth anniversary of the Closing. The Company shall have the right to delay such registration under certain circumstances for one period not in excess of 90 days in any 12-month period.
    The Company shall not be obligated to effect more than one registration under these demand right provisions, and shall not be obligated to effect a registration (i) during the 180-day period commencing with the date of the Company's initial public offering, or (ii) if it delivers notice to the holders of the Registrable Securities within 30 days of any registration request of its intent to file a registration statement for such initial public offering within 90 days.

"Piggyback" Rights. The Investors shall be entitled to "piggyback" registration rights on all registrations of the Company or on any demand registrations of any other investor, subject to the right, however, of the Company and its underwriters to reduce the number of shares proposed to be registered pro rata in view of market conditions.

Expenses. The Company shall bear registration expenses (exclusive of underwriting discounts and commissions) of all such demands and piggybacks (including fees and expenses up to $20,000 of one special counsel for the selling stockholders).

Termination of Registration Rights. All registration rights shall terminate upon the earlier to occur of (i) six years following the Company's IPO or (ii) as to any Investor, at such time as such Investor could sell all of its Preferred Stock during any three-month period under Rule 144.

Lock-Up Provision. Each Investor agrees that it will not sell its shares for a specified period (not to exceed 180 days) following the effective date of the Company's IPO; provided that all officers, directors, and other 2% stockholders are similarly bound.

Comments: Registration rights are seldom worth fighting over. Providing registration rights to an investor is significant, but the reality of any investor actually exercising these rights is quite slim. First, if you do have an IPO, the Underwriter will require that all Preferred Stock investors waive registration rights. In addition, if your angel investor requires such language and you anticipate a future venture capital round, the venture capitalists will almost certainly ask for those provisions to be removed. So approach any request for registration rights with all seriousness and take advice from an experienced securities lawyer, but understand the realities of such provisions. If your angel investors are sophisticated, they should understand the realities of registration provisions as well.

Right of First Refusal. Except for gifts to a spouse or children, or transfers to the estate of a deceased shareholder, or transfers of up to 10 percent of all of the Founder's stock (including all preferred and common stock), a Founder may not transfer any shares of the Company's capital stock now owned or hereafter acquired without first offering it to the Company and then to the Investors.

Comments: This particular provision restricts a founder from transferring, in most any manner other than as specifically exempted in the language, his or her ownership to a third party without first offering the shares to the company. Many rights of first refusal provisions also require that after the offer is made to the company for a set period of time, say 30 days, the stock must then be offered to the other shareholders, before the founder can sell to a bone fide third-party purchaser. All of these provisions are intended to keep control of the company in the hands of the current shareholders. Another type of right of first refusal requires the company to offer shares in any offering to the current shareholders before offering them to outside investors. This provision requires that if a company proposes to offer equity securities to any person, the company must first offer these securities to the other shareholders, most typically Preferred Stock shareholders. The latter is true because rights of first of refusal are often rights and privileges related to preferred stock offerings. To restrict these rights, a company can offer these rights to shareholders with a certain percentage ownership. These shareholders would have the right to purchase shares on a pro rata basis. Typically, rights of first refusal terminate upon IPO and should also terminate upon acquisition, merger, or consolidation of the company. Of

(Continued)

Exhibit 3.1   Comprehensive Preferred Stock Term Sheet, Continued

course, just as with other provisions, certain company actions should not fall within a right of first refusal: shares issued upon conversion of preferred stock or warrants, upon the conversion of options, or in connection with equipment leasing, credit agreements, and similar arrangements.

Employee Option Pool. The Company will have reserved [_____] shares of its Common Stock of its fully diluted capital stock prior to the issuance of its Series A Preferred for issuances to directors, officers, employees, and consultants.

Comments: Before they make an investment, most experienced angel investors (and certainly venture capitalists) will require that you set up an option pool for employees, directors, consultants, and the like. Such a requirement protects the investors from being diluted by your establishment of an option pool. In addition, investors want employees and others contributing to a company's success to have a vested interest in the company's future. This future potential for a substantial return from their efforts gives people a greater sense of connection to the company and increases their enthusiasm for seeing the company succeed. Investors typically accept 15 to 30 percent of common stock being committed into an option pool at this early stage. The capitalization table in the Glossary shows angels investing prior to establishment of an option pool.

Founder Vesting. As of the Closing, the Common Stock held by the Founders ("Founder Common Stock") shall vest as follows: 50 percent will vest as of the Closing, with the remaining 50 percent vesting monthly in equal incremental amounts over the next four years. The Company shall have the option to repurchase all unvested Founder Common Stock at cost.

Comments: Just as investors want employees to have a stake in the company to create an incentive for working hard through the long hours of building a company, investors may ask the founders to subject their stock to loss should they leave soon after financing. Angels invest primarily in people. A brilliant, experienced entrepreneur can take an interesting idea and make it a home run, while an inexperienced entrepreneur can tank a brilliant idea. Therefore, investors want management to stick around. One way is to require that a certain percentage of the founders' stock (often 50 percent) be subject to loss. The founder must then earn the stock back over time—so long as they remain with the company; this is referred to as reverse vesting. Of course, exceptions apply, such as full reverse vesting of the stock upon IPO or acquisition or merger. Less frequently, investors will require key employees other than founders to be subject to the same reverse vesting.

Proprietary Information and Inventions Agreement. Prior to the closing, the Company will enter into Proprietary Information and Inventions Agreements with all officers, employees, and consultants, containing standard provisions with respect to confidentiality and corporate ownership of inventions and innovations.

Comments: You should already have agreements in place that essentially state that officers, employees, and consultants must maintain the confidentiality of your company's proprietary information, and that inventions are owned by your company. If these are not in place, investors will almost certainly require their completion before committing resources to your company.

Co-Sale Agreement. The shares of Common Stock held by [_____] (the "Founders") shall be subject to restrictions on transfer and made subject to a co-sale agreement (with the exceptions set forth below) with the Investors such that the Founders may not sell, transfer, or exchange their stock unless each Investor has an opportunity to participate in the sale by a Founder to a third party on a pro rata basis. These co-sale rights shall not apply to and shall terminate upon an acquisition, merger, or consolidation of the Company.

Comments: Investors can require that if founders have the opportunity to sell their shares, they must allow the investors to sell their shares alongside the founders. Obviously, this right reduces the number of shares the founders may sell to accommodate the investors. Just as with other clauses, exceptions should be included, such as transfers to family members and trusts.

Exclusivity and Confidentiality. In consideration of Investor's commitment to devote substantial resources to a due diligence review of the Company and preparation of legal documents relating to this transaction, the Company agrees that during the period between its execution of this Term Sheet and 60 days thereafter (or such earlier date that Investor advises the Company in writing that Investor is electing to discontinue efforts with respect to an investment in the Company), it will not and will not permit any of its officers, directors, or agents acting on its behalf to: (i) take any action to solicit, initiate, encourage, or assist the submission of any proposal, negotiation, or offer from any person or entity other than Investor or the other Investors relating to the acquisition, sale, or transfer of any of the capital stock of the Company or the acquisition, sale, lease, license, or other disposition of the Company or any technology or any material part of the assets of the Company; (ii) offer to sell or transfer any of the capital stock of the Company or to sell, lease, license, or otherwise dispose of the Company or any material part of the technology or assets of the Company to any person or entity other than Investor or the other Investors; or (iii) disclose financial or other information relating to the Company other than in the ordinary course of its business to any person or entity other than Investor, the other Investors, or their agents and representatives.

The Company recognizes that this Term Sheet is confidential and that disclosure of the provisions contained herein could cause irreparable harm to Investor and the other Investors. Accordingly, the Company, and each of the Company's agents, officers, and directors acknowledge and agree that the terms, conditions, and contents of this letter will be kept confidential and will not be published or disclosed except in the following circumstances: (i) disclosure may be made to the Company's directors, officers, employees, or representatives who need to know such information for the purpose of evaluating this proposed investment (it being understood that such persons shall be informed by the Company of the confidential nature of such information and shall be required to treat such information confidentially); or (ii) disclosure may be made with the prior written consent of all Investors.

Investor recognizes that the due diligence materials provided by the Company to Investor are confidential and that disclosure of these terms could cause irreparable harm to the Company. Accordingly, Investor and its agents, officers, and directors acknowledge and agree that the terms, conditions, and contents of this letter will be kept confidential and will not be published or disclosed except in the following circumstances:

(Continued)

Exhibit 3.1   Comprehensive Preferred Stock Term Sheet, Continued

(i) disclosure may be made to the other Investors and their directors, officers, employees, or representatives who need to know such information for the purpose of evaluating this proposed investment (it being understood that such persons shall be informed of the confidential nature of such information and shall be required to treat such information confidentially); or (ii) disclosure may be made with the prior written consent of the Company.

Comments: Some investors will require that you not enter into a term sheet with any other investors for a certain period of time to allow for a thoughtful and thorough due diligence process. In addition, most investors (and you should as well) want the terms of investment kept confidential. In addition, you should always require that materials investors receive in the course of due diligence be kept confidential.

ACCREDITED INVESTORS, PRIVATE PLACEMENT MEMORANDUMS, AND REGULATION D

Don't be misled into thinking you must do a private placement memorandum (PPM) for every private placement of securities. Consultants are constantly telling young, inexperienced entrepreneurs they must put together a full offering document or PPM. The consultant charges $30,000 for the PPM—which is quite an impressive document when completed, but unnecessary if you have only accredited investors. So save your money, restrict yourself to accredited investors, and use your business plan, presentation, and existing documents to wow your prospective investors.

Be aware that in the United States, each state has its own securities regulations. Even though these regulations are fairly uniform and consistent with Federal requirements, never assume anything about state law. Seek counsel within any state in which you have a potential investor to ensure you are complying with that state's securities regulations, along with Federal requirements.

While you were not looking for a legal treatise when you picked up this book, the fact of the matter is that private equity and debt financing, that is, angel financing, has lots of legal hurdles and pitfalls. The better informed you are, the better client you make for your counsel. In theory, this means reducing your legal expenses, but the big advantage is that your knowledge allows you to present yourself to prospective investors as informed and capable of talking their language. So bear with this discussion, as it will serve you well. One caveat—this is a brief review of the securities laws related to private offerings and is by no means complete nor all-inclusive. You should retain legal counsel for interpretation and application of these laws and other requirements related to securities offerings, including state securities laws.

Regulation D is part of the Securities Act of 1933 and governs private equity financings. Under the Securities Act of 1933, any offer to sell securities must either be registered with the SEC or meet an exemption from registration; Regulation D provides three exemptions from these registration requirements. Regulation D allows small companies to offer and sell securities without the burden and expense of registering with the SEC—a significant cost and time savings.

The essence of Regulation D is in Rule 501 through Rule 506. Rule 501 primarily contains definitions, including the definition of an accredited investor (see Glossary for full definition). (Regulation D has been reproduced in this book as Appendix 3 for ease of reference.) The definition of an accredited investor is quite lengthy and contains many categories, with the primary definitions for purposes of angel investing being these:

- Any natural person whose individual net worth, or joint net worth with that person's spouse, at the time of his or her purchase exceeds $1,000,000;

- Any natural person who had an individual income in excess of $200,000 in each of the two most recent years or joint income with that person's spouse in excess of $300,000 in each of those years and has a reasonable expectation of reaching the same income level in the current year; or

- Any entity in which all of the equity owners are accredited investors. (This is most often an angel fund, an arrangement that is becoming more prevalent.)

The first two definitions relate to individual angel investors and the third can relate to an angel fund. The definition of an accredited investor is a bright line test and carries an assumption of financial sophistication. Although not stated, these definitions imply an ability to bear the risk of losing an entire investment. Private equity investments are not for the weak of heart or pocketbook. Therefore, the SEC wrote the definition of an accredited investor to prevent those who cannot afford a loss from making investments without significant information, including explanation of any risk factors related to complete loss of their investment.

These definitions even have requirements. For instance, to qualify as an accredited investor under the $1,000,000 net worth category, investors must purchase at least $150,000 of the securities being offered, by one or a combination of four specific methods: cash, marketable securities, an unconditional obligation to pay cash or marketable securities over not more than five years, and cancellation of indebtedness. The rule also requires that "the total purchase price" may not exceed 20 percent of the purchaser's net worth. The net value of one's residence may be included in calculating net worth.

Section 502 describes the circumstances when information must be provided to investors during the course of the offering and prior to sale, as well as the information that must be provided by the offering company. These information disclosure requirements are extensive, time-consuming, and expensive. Therefore, most sophisticated entrepreneurs will refuse to accept nonaccredited investors, thus avoiding the information disclosure requirements under Section 502.

Regulation D provides for three exempt offerings:

Rule 504 is for offerings up to $1,000,000. Many people refer to this section as the *intrastate exemption* because the company issuing the securities (the "issuer") need not comply with Federal information disclosure requirements if the securities offering is "exclusively in one or more states that provide for the registration of the securities, and require the public filing and delivery to investors of a substantive disclosure document before sale, and are made in accordance with those state provisions." This provision also allows for exclusion from Federal information disclosure requirements for offerings made "exclusively according to state law exemptions from registration that permit general solicitation and general advertising so long as sales are made only to accredited investors."

Rule 505 is for offerings up to $5,000,000.

Rule 506 has no limitation on the size of the offering—large or small.

Rules 505 and 506 are limited to thirty-five nonaccredited investors, but remember, if you accept nonaccredited investors you must comply with all Federal information disclosure requirements—something you want to avoid.

Certain purchasers are excluded from the permitted number of nonaccredited investors:

1. Any relative, spouse, or relative of the spouse of a purchaser who has the same principal residence as the purchaser

2. Any trust or estate in which a purchaser and any of the persons related to him collectively have more than 50 percent of the beneficial interest

3. Any corporation or other organization of which a purchaser and any of the persons related to him collectively are beneficial owners of more than 50 percent of the equity securities or equity interests

4. Any accredited investor

But don't forget, even if you do not count these categories toward the nonaccredited investor limit, you must still comply with Federal information disclosure requirements if any investors are not accredited investors.

In addition, no general solicitation or advertising is allowed by the entrepreneur when looking for accredited investors. This latter prohibition catches many entrepreneurs unaware. The obvious no-no's include advertisements in newspapers or any other general circulation publication and mass mailings offering your securities. But your hands aren't tied; a one-on-one meeting with an accredited investor known to you from a previous business relationship is a great way to get investors without advertising, and you can find a broader audience at angel group meetings, investment forums, business plan competitions, and the like. Whether or not a presentation would be considered a general solicitation or advertising relates to many factors including if the audience is all accredited investors, if they are attending by invitation only, if no detailed offering documents are circulated, and other factors. The best approach is to ask the event sponsors if they have evaluated compliance with Federal and state securities laws. Most programs in which entrepreneurs make presentations on their business have considered these issues in years past because of the obvious importance to presenting companies. Finally, if the program has guidelines on presentation content and limitations on allowable materials for distribution—follow them. Most likely legal counsel has provided guidance on securities law compliance.

What this brief and partial review of Regulation D should tell you is—to make your life easier, either conduct an offering in compliance with Rule 504 (but remember this is for only up to $1,000,000 and you must still comply with state requirements) or sell securities only to accredited investors. Experienced securities lawyers will most often use only Rule 506, which has no offering limit, and strongly advise the acceptance of only accredited investors for the reasons given here and more.

Another attribute of accredited investors is their general understanding and knowledge of the time and energy needed to grow a company. Therefore, outside of avoiding information disclosure requirements, accredited investors are typically less demanding and can actually add value to a company. Nonaccredited investors, on the other hand, can be labor intensive because of their lack of financial and business sophistication and the more significant implications of any investment loss for them. If you question this logic, ask a few entrepreneurs who have accredited and nonaccredited investors which group calls more often and displays more stress about timing of a liquidity event.

To avoid some of the pitfalls associated with these regulations, you can use consultants who make their living raising capital for young companies and take a percentage of the money raised as their fee. Licensed broker-dealers have passed the requisite exams to offer such services and receive this "success fee." Unfortunately, hundreds if not thousands of individuals also raise capital on a success fee basis, *without* having passed the required exams. This is a big no-no from the perspective of securities law compliance. So if you are approached by someone offering to raise your much-needed capital, as tempting as it may be to agree on the spot before they can get away, please confirm their status as an authorized broker-dealer. They should be able to provide you with a copy of their license, and your attorney should be able to verify their standing. The primary way consultants avoid the compliance issue is to charge a set fee, which is due regardless of their success or failure in raising capital, so that any capital raised does not have an associated success fee. These consultants often provide additional services of reviewing and revising your business plan, helping with strategic planning, and so on.

Finally, if you decide to accept nonaccredited investors despite the informed and enlightened advice in this book, provide all investors—even the accredited investors—with all required information. This is particularly true in light of the anti-fraud provisions of the federal securities laws. Also retain experienced securities counsel before talking to anyone about investing in your company. You can commit violations of the securities laws, including the ones that govern general solicitation and advertising, without even realizing it. Violating securities laws in an offering can result in the obligation to offer rescission rights to investors—that is, you have to offer your investors their money back.

CHAPTER FOUR

Understanding Your Funding Needs

O ne of the most difficult aspects of any seed/start-up company is understanding your financial needs. Optimism is a characteristic of many entrepreneurs, along with dogmatic belief in their idea and company. Investors look for these qualities in an entrepreneur, but they also want a dose of reality. So how do you realistically determine your financial needs? How much do you need to get to profitability? What factors impact your finances, anticipated or unpredicted? The scenarios are nearly limitless and no investor expects you to consider every possibility. What an investor does expect is evidence of well-considered, realistic financial projections and a realistic timetable for growing a successful company, a timetable that reflects an understanding of the market in which the company operates.

BUILDING YOUR FINANCIAL STATEMENTS

Entrepreneurs need to ask themselves a few questions when starting to build their financial models:

- What financial documents do you need?
- How many years of projections should you provide?
- How much detail is necessary?
- What are the most important factors or variables for investors?

Just as you need counsel to help with legal aspects of your business, you should retain a qualified financial strategist experienced in early-stage companies to help you answer these questions. The earlier you retain capable professionals, the better prepared you will be for your angel investors. You do have to balance cost with timing. But remember, knowledgeable professional advisers are value-added experts in their fields, as well as resources for investors, partners, and team members.

Building Your Financial Future

Angel investors want to know how you are going to make money, when you will turn profitable, and when they can expect to receive a return on their investment. You need to address these important financial milestones in your executive summary, business plan, and presentation in differing degrees of complexity, and your financial documents need to support your assertions and forecasts. Flowery adjectives are unimpressive and can even turn off an investor, and you will never get funding if your numbers don't back up your assertions. Therefore, building a comprehensive financial model is essential. You need to understand all aspects of your company, including what goes into generating revenues, how much it costs to build your products, overhead, and when you will probably reach profitability. While most investors realize that anything past a couple of years has enormous unknowns, they will want to know you are thinking for the long term, so you need financial projections for three and preferably five years. Because of the inherent uncertainties in future projections, investors often ask entrepreneurs to develop contingency plans in anticipation that milestones take longer to accomplish, market adoption is slow, economic slowdowns occur, and so on. These contingency plans explain how the company can survive (though not necessarily grow) until limiting factors disappear.

Pro-forma (or future projected) financial documents include numerous tables, inputs, calculations, and variables. During due diligence, many angel investors will want to see all backup documentation—staffing schedules including compensation, product distribution schedules, a detailed cost of goods, and the like. You will need to present at least these three "master" or essential documents:

An income statement (also referred to as a profit/loss statement) tracks revenues and expenses. The more comprehensive and complete the expense assumptions and the revenue projections, the more realistic the income statement. Information such as compensation, including fringe benefits, as well as Selling, General, and Administrative Expenses (SG&A), operations, and so on, all go into building an income statement.

A balance sheet that provides information on assets, liabilities, and equity or shareholder ownership, and is computed from estimates based on your current and expected situation. Assets will be anything of value to the company, roughly divided into *current assets* (cash and accounts receivable) and *fixed assets* (equipment, fixtures, furniture, and the like). On the other side, you'll have *current liabilities* (accounts payable and short-term notes) and *long-term liabilities* (typically financial obligations of greater than one year). Shareholder equity is valued on the balance sheet and will show *retained earnings* and net income or loss (with loss being the case for almost all start-up companies). Together liabilities and shareholder equity represent legal claims on the company's assets. Thus, assets must equal the sum of liabilities and shareholder equity.

Cash flow statements track actual cash receipts and cash disbursements, and are often derived from the balance sheet and income statement. These statements will show your cash position at a point in time, commonly on a monthly basis, giving your investors an understanding of when you anticipate to turn cash flow positive, and will also lay out your future financial needs.

Financial documents must have a comprehensive list of assumptions that support and explain your numbers. Assumptions explain how you calculated your financial needs, timing for infusion of money, revenue projections, market growth, and the like. The following box gives a partial list of assumptions used in building financial statements. While not all the listed assumptions may apply to your company, consult with your financial planner before you rule out any factor.

Your documents will have information that depicts your company's current reality in addition to the projected financial values. Actual

FINANCIAL ASSUMPTIONS

- Start-up costs
- Research and development activities and timing
- Capital equipment purchases, including depreciation and amortization expense
- Commercial start date (first sale or shipment) for each product
- Market expansion timing, including increasing unit sales over time along with market expansion costs
- Sales forecasts
- Costs associated with all operations
- Cost of goods
- Financing needs and timing
- Debt issuances and repayment
- Staffing and average salaries by position, along with increases over time
- Necessary license and royalty payments
- Figures in home country currency and exchange rates used if applicable
- Patent prosecution and maintenance expenses, domestic and foreign
- Raw materials costs, inventory, and work in process, including inventory purchase and utilization rate
- Accounts payable and accounts receivable forecasts, including payment periods
- Variable costs such as expected inflation rate and commodities trends
- Analysis period
- Industry- or product-specific factors or variables
- Taxes

numbers and projections based on the numbers behind the assumptions drive the creation of your three primary financial documents.

Building Financial Documents: The Essential Information

Your income statement, balance sheet, and cash flow statement will provide your prospective angel investors with three important types of information that tie back to their primary interest (their eventual exit): revenue, margin, and profitability. First, can you generate impressive, highly scalable revenues in your initial market and eventually additional markets or industry areas? Second, do you have projections for healthy margins that are at least as good as industry average, if not better? Third, when do you become profitable and how do you grow the bottom line to a point of maximum value and ultimate investment liquidity? Fourth, will your business generate more cash from its operations than it will spend?

The best way to understand what information goes into the income statement, balance sheet, and cash flow statement is to look at an example—once again using Great Starts, Inc., a hypothetical software and high-tech scanner start-up company. The documents in Exhibits 4.1 through 4.4 show numbers down to the dollar for the first year, after which no one can anticipate the future that accurately. Therefore, as shown in the following tables, you should round off numbers such as revenue past the first year of projected financials.

Exhibit 4.1 shows all revenue and all operating costs, providing the company's net income or loss. This kind of statement is also referred to as the income or profit-and-loss statement, and it is used to track revenues and expenses so that you can determine the operating performance of your business over a period of time.

Exhibit 4.2 contains information on assets, liabilities, and shareholders' equity. As noted earlier, assets are divided into current and fixed, and liabilities are divided into current (or short-term) and long-term obligations. An asset is anything the business owns that has monetary value. Liabilities are the claims of creditors against the assets of the business, and equity is the shareholders' residual ownership of the assets. In addition, assets must always equal liabilities plus shareholders' equity. Therefore, the balance sheet is a snapshot of a business's financial condition at a specific moment.

Exhibit 4.3 provides information on cash flow in and out for a specific period of time. This information is particularly important for

	2007 First Quarter	2007 Second Quarter	2007 Third Quarter	2007 Fourth Quarter	2007 Annual	2008 Annual	2009 Annual	2010 Annual	2011 Annual
Gross Revenue	$362,268	$540,980	$943,084	$943,084	$2,789,417	$7,900,000	$18,100,000	$25,000,000	$31,400,000
Less discounts & allowances	$0	$0	$0	$0	$0	$800,000	$1,870,000	$2,580,000	$3,218,000
Net Revenue	$362,268	$540,980	$943,084	$943,084	$2,789,417	$7,100,000	$16,230,000	$22,420,000	$28,182,000
Cost of Goods Sold	$319,132	$430,997	$761,322	$761,322	$2,272,772	$5,450,585	$11,092,978	$14,508,505	$17,415,544
Gross Profit	$43,136	$109,983	$181,762	$181,763	$516,645	$1,649,415	$5,137,022	$7,911,495	$10,766,456
Operating Expenses:									
Sales and marketing expenses	$91,115	$103,982	$145,433	$160,433	$500,963	$972,000	$1,290,000	$1,565,000	$1,668,000
General and administrative expenses	$93,303	$95,626	$100,854	$100,854	$390,637	$467,000	$703,000	$792,000	$876,000
Depreciation & amortization (D&A)	$15,870	$16,981	$16,981	$21,981	$71,815	$87,926	$87,926	$87,926	$84,348
Operating Income (Loss) or EBIT*	($157,152)	($106,606)	($81,506)	($101,506)	($446,770)	$122,489	$3,056,096	$5,466,569	$8,138,108
Net Interest Income (Expense)	($16,666)	($22,903)	($26,504)	($29,562)	($95,635)	($137,934)	($103,270)	$6,420	$56,748
Earnings before taxes	($173,818)	($129,508)	($108,010)	($131,068)	($542,405)	($15,445)	$2,952,825	$5,472,989	$8,194,856
Taxes	$0	$0	$0	$0	$0	$4,634	$885,848	$1,641,897	$2,458,457
Net Income (Loss)	($173,818)	($129,508)	($108,010)	($131,068)	($542,405)	($10,812)	$2,066,978	$3,831,093	$5,736,399
EBITDA**	($141,282)	($89,624)	($64,525)	($79,525)	($374,956)	$210,415	$3,144,021	$5,554,495	$8,222,456

* Earnings Before Income Tax

** Earnings Before Income Tax, Depreciation, and Amortization

Exhibit 4.1   Income Statement for Great Starts, Inc.

	2007 First Quarter	2007 Second Quarter	2007 Third Quarter	2007 Fourth Quarter	2007 Annual	2008 Annual	2009 Annual	2010 Annual	2011 Annual
Current Assets:									
Cash	$5,573	$9,016	$15,718	$14,509	$14,509	($1,871)	($28,815)	$3,182,913	$8,625,160
Account Receivables	$107,871	$290,180	$290,180	$280,819	$280,819	$556,525	$1,212,334	$1,669,329	$2,097,975
Inventory	$137,282	$291,010	$326,320	$317,944	$317,944	$581,216	$1,121,637	$1,457,914	$1,741,868
Total Current Assets	$250,726	$590,206	$632,218	$613,272	$613,272	$1,135,870	$2,305,156	$6,310,156	$12,465,003
Fixed Assets:									
Furniture and equipment	$512,546	$512,546	$512,546	$612,546	$612,546	$612,546	$612,546	$612,546	$612,546
Less accumulated D&A	$151,533	$168,515	$185,496	$207,478	$207,478	$295,403	$383,329	$471,255	$555,603
Total furniture and equip.	$361,012	$344,031	$327,049	$405,068	$405,068	$317,142	$229,217	$141,291	$56,943
Total other assets	$149,890	$149,890	$149,890	$149,890	$149,890	$149,890	$149,890	$149,890	$149,890
Total assets	$761,629	$1,084,127	$1,109,157	$1,168,230	$1,168,230	$1,602,902	$2,684,262	$6,601,337	$12,671,836
Current Liabilities:									
Accounts payable	$242,530	$441,197	$487,170	$495,649	$495,649	$801,539	$1,400,659	$1,789,225	$2,122,765
Line of credit	$1,205,607	$1,458,947	$1,546,014	$1,727,677	$1,727,677	$1,896,796	$305,846	$0	$0
Total Current Liabilities	$1,448,137	$1,900,144	$2,033,184	$2,223,326	$2,223,326	$2,698,335	$1,706,505	$1,789,225	$2,122,765
Fixed asset financing	$0	$0	$0	$0	$0	$0	$0	$0	$0
Notes payables1	$518,518	$268,518	$18,518	$18,518	$18,518	$18,518	$18,518	$18,518	$18,518
Total liabilities	$1,966,655	$2,168,662	$2,051,703	$2,241,844	$2,241,844	$2,716,853	$1,725,022	$1,807,743	$2,141,283
Equity:									
Preferred stock	$250,000	$500,000	$750,000	$750,000	$750,000	$750,000	$750,000	$750,000	$750,000
Common stock2	$992,500	$992,500	$992,500	$992,500	$992,500	$992,500	$992,500	$992,500	$992,500
Retained earnings	($2,447,527)	($2,577,035)	($2,685,046)	($2,816,114)	($2,816,114)	($2,859,934)	($787,795)	$3,046,397	$8,783,305
Total shareholder equity	($1,205,027)	($1,084,535)	($942,546)	($1,073,614)	($1,073,614)	($1,117,434)	$954,705	$4,788,897	$10,525,805
Total liabilities and equity	$761,629	$1,084,127	$1,109,157	$1,168,230	$1,168,230	$1,599,419	$2,679,727	$6,596,640	$12,667,088

1. Short-term note of $500,000 provided at no interest by founder's father.
2. Common stock was already issued since the company existed prior to these financials.

Exhibit 4.2 Balance Sheet for Great Starts, Inc.

	2007 First Quarter	2007 Second Quarter	2007 Third Quarter	2007 Fourth Quarter	2007 Annual	2008 Annual	2009 Annual	2010 Annual	2011 Annual
Net Income (Loss)	($173,818)	($129,508)	($108,010)	($131,068)	($542,405)	($10,812)	$2,066,978	$3,831,093	$5,736,399
Add back D&A	$15,870	$16,981	$16,981	$21,981	$71,815	$87,926	$87,926	$87,926	$84,348
Changes in current assets and liabilities:									
Receivables	($68,565)	($182,308)	$0	$9,361	($241,513)	($275,706)	($655,809)	($456,996)	($428,646)
Inventory	$20,197	($153,729)	($35,310)	$8,376	($160,466)	($263,272)	($540,420)	($336,277)	($283,954)
Accounts payable	($15,530)	$198,667	$45,974	$8,478	$237,589	$343,300	$664,890	$409,272	$350,361
Other current liabilities	$0	$0	$0	$0	$0	$0	$0	$0	$0
Cash from Operations	($221,846)	($249,897)	($80,365)	($82,872)	($634,980)	($118,564)	$1,623,564	$3,535,017	$5,458,509
Purchase of furniture and equipment	($77,000)	$0	$0	($100,000)	($177,000)	0	0	0	0
Net change in line of credit	$1,161,107	$253,340	$87,067	$181,663	$1,683,177	$169,119	($1,590,951)	($305,846)	0
Net change in convertible notes1	($638,306)	$0	$0	$0	($638,306)	0	0	0	0
Net change in 5-year term loan2	($223,279)	$0	$0	$0	($223,279)	0	0	0	0
Net change in Invested capital—preferred stock	$0	$0	$0	$0	$0	0	0	0	0
Net change in Invested capital—common stock	$0	$0	$0	$0	$0	0	0	0	0
Cash from Financing	$299,522	$253,340	$87,067	$181,663	$821,593	$169,119	($1,590,951)	($305,846)	$0
Net change in cash	$677	$3,443	$6,702	($1,209)	$9,612	$50,555	$32,613	$3,229,171	$5,458,509
Beginning of period cash	$4,897	$5,573	$9,016	$15,718	$4,897	$$14,509	($1,871)	($28,815)	$3,182,913
End of Period Cash	$5,573	$9,016	$15,718	$14,509	$14,509	$65,064	$30,742	$3,200,356	$8,641,422

1. Convertible note paid off at beginning of year with line of credit in anticipation of angel financing.
2. Term loan paid off at beginning of year with line of credit in anticipation of angel financing.

Exhibit 4.3   Cash Flow Statement for Great Starts, Inc.

young companies with limited resources. This statement serves as an early warning system for impending cash flow problems. The statement shows a beginning cash balance, which includes the starting available cash. Projected cash sources, such as accounts receivable and financings, are calculated for the next period, as well as cash demands for the same period. Therefore, even if you have a positive beginning cash balance, you can end with a negative cash balance if the cash demands exceed the period's cash sources plus the beginning cash balance.

The following list gives you a better understanding of the complexity of information built into just the expense side of the financial documents. Recognizing expenses is important; unexpected revenue is rarely a problem, whereas unexpected expenses can often be disastrous.

Compensation per Employee

- Salary
- Performance Increase
- Medical and Dental
- Social Security, Medicare, and Other Taxes

Balance Sheet Information

- Capital acquisitions:

  Computer and Network Equipment

  Phone Equipment

  Leased Equipment

  Leasehold Improvement

  Office Furniture and Fixtures

  Lab Furniture and Fixtures

  Trade Show Displays

  Lab Equipment

  Manufacturing Equipment
- Accounts Payable Outstanding—for eligible expenses
- Credit Card—Outstanding
- Returns and Allowances
- Inventory

- Debt
- Bad Debt Expense

Employee-Related Costs
- Telecom Service—Data per month
- Office Supplies
- Office Space per person

Fixed Asset Financing—Annual Rate
- Percent Financed

Accounts Receivable Collections, Including Timing

Marketing
- Advertising
- Collateral
- Trade Shows
- Rep Commissions
- Distributor Aids and Supplies
- Market Research
- Sales Training Video

Professional Services
- Accounting, Tax, and Bookkeeping
- Legal
- Consulting

Office Expenses
- Lease and Leasehold Improvements
- Telephone and Internet
- Postage and Shipping
- Office Supplies
- Computer Expense
- Office Operation Equipment
- Rent

Travel and Entertainment
- Trips per Month per Traveler
- Travelers per Month
- Nights per Trip
- Entertainment
- Travel Meals
- Business Meals
- Air Fare
- Lodging
- Car Rental
- Local Mileage, Parking, and Taxi

Employee Related
- Social and Employee Meals
- Dues and Subscriptions
- Seminars, Classes, Presentations, Fees
- Relocation

Federal, State and Local Taxes
- Income Tax
- Business and Occupation Tax
- Sales and Use Tax

Insurance, including general comprehensive, property, professional liability, and health

Bank and Credit Card Charges

Research and Development

Exhibit 4.4 shows the essential information for your business plan financials. It gives an excellent summary of key information your prospective investors want to understand in their initial review of your company. Revenues are shown along with product volume to support the revenue projections. With this single table, an investor can

	2007 First Quarter	2007 Second Quarter	2007 Third Quarter	2007 Fourth Quarter	2007 Annual	2008 Annual	2009 Annual	2010 Annual	2011 Annual
Units sold	41,223	61,559	107,315	107,315	317,412	866,800	1,904,600	2,528,900	3,056,000
Net revenue	$362,268	$540,980	$943,084	$943,084	$2,789,417	$7,100,000	$16,230,000	$22,420,000	$28,182,000
Cost of goods sold	$319,132	$430,997	$761,322	$761,322	$2,272,772	$5,450,585	$11,092,978	$14,508,505	$17,415,544
Gross profit/margin (dollars)	$43,136	$109,983	$181,761	$181,762	$516,645	$1,649,415	$5,137,022	$7,911,495	$10,766,456
Gross profit/margin (percentage)	12%	20%	19%	19%	18%	23%	32%	35%	38%
Operating Expenses:									
Sales and marketing expenses	$91,115	$103,982	$145,433	$160,433	$500,963	$972,000	$1,290,000	$1,565,000	$1,668,000
General and administrative expenses	$93,303	$95,626	$100,854	$100,854	$390,637	$467,000	$703,000	$792,000	$876,000
Depreciation & amortization (D&A)	$15,870	$16,981	$16,981	$21,981	$71,815	$87,926	$87,926	$87,926	$84,348
Total Expenses	$200,288	$216,589	$263,268	$283,268	$963,415	$1,526,926	$2,080,926	$2,444,926	$2,628,348
EBIT*	($157,152)	($106,606)	($81,506)	($101,506)	($446,771)	$122,489	$3,056,096	$5,466,569	$8,138,108
Staffing	18	20	21	23	23	26	28	30	33
Net change in cash	$677	$3,443	$6,702	($1,209)	$9,612	$50,555	$32,613	$3,229,171	$5,458,509
End of Period Cash	$5,573	$9,016	$15,718	$14,509	$14,509	$65,064	$30,742	$3,200,356	$8,641,422

* Earnings Before Income Tax

Exhibit 4.4 Summary Financial Statement for Business Plan

analyze the reasonableness of key assumptions on sales and pricing, as well as staff necessary to support these sales numbers and corresponding services. Expenses against revenues can also be evaluated. Finally, cash flow gives the investor an understanding of your ongoing capitalization needs.

WHAT FINANCIALS TELL AN INVESTOR

If your financial projections show that you will need considerable funds to become cash flow positive, reach profitability, and become a self-sustaining business, you need to map out how you will raise these funds. For example, assume you have an innovative and noninvasive procedure for detecting early-stage lung cancer. You know several phases of clinical studies will be needed to reach a commercial product. After working with your financial strategic adviser, you determine it will take at least $45,000,000 to fully commercialize the procedure. With such a large amount of money needed to fund the start-up, angel financing alone will not come close to meeting your funding needs. As discussed earlier, going out and trying to raise all the funds you need in one round is unrealistic and seldom a good idea. You will need venture capital financing—but because you are so early, venture capital providers may not be willing to take the risk on you. Most important, raising $45,000,000 on a highly promising but untested invention will not yield the kind of valuation you need to keep any realistic percentage of ownership. You will not be able to raise such funds unless you have a long track record of successfully taking inventions to commercialization, so investors have an unusually strong belief in your capability.

The solution to this problem is to raise your capital in phases. You must develop a road map of milestone achievements that will look impressive to potential investors. By having milestones for each funding round, you build value for your company through your accomplishments. Your milestones will lead to further financing, which will fund continued development. Taking this approach also allows you to retain a greater percentage of your company.

The dot-com bubble approach of throwing gobs of money at an idea has greatly diminished or entirely disappeared in many parts of the country, which is a good thing. Being able to live lean and create $50 of value from $5 is the sign of a great entrepreneur. Investors are looking for wise use of funds, so you must be innovative and intelligent in your spending. Do not use invested funds to pay yourself a big salary, no matter what you could make elsewhere—investors want funds to go to growing the company. Do not use invested funds for costly office space and furniture; sophisticated investors will find space in an older commercial building—even one large room and a restroom down a flight of stairs—more impressive. Stretch the first dollar invested; stretch the last. Your brass ring is the value of your stock and the value you continue to build in your company.

As explained in Chapter Two, investments are often made in traunches, meaning that investors require the company to achieve certain milestones to receive a portion of the agreed-to funding. In theory, this approach reduces the chances of an investor throwing good money after bad. If you cannot achieve the goals and milestones set out in your financials and elsewhere in your business plan, investors will decide you have an unrealistic or losing business proposition. Not surprisingly, many of these milestones are tied to financial projections, including commercialization, sales, additional funding, licensing, additional product lines, and the like. Traunching requires the accomplishment of a specific event or events by a certain date.

To illustrate this point, suppose the fictitious company Great Starts, Inc., receives investor commitments of $750,000. The investors were a bit skeptical about sales assumptions Great Starts' founder, Jane Merrill, presented; they asked for an adjustment, but she was emphatic about her numbers. She has confidence in making the numbers because of the advanced stage of discussions with several potential customers; she also knows that adjustment of sales numbers can affect the valuation. The parties agree to traunch investing, with $250,000 at the time of signing financing documents, an additional $250,000 upon two potential customers submitting purchase orders, and the remaining $250,000 upon shipment of goods. No timing is tied to these events in this example, but investors could very well insist on specific dates if the market has potential competitors and being the first to market is one of the founder's stated competitive advantages.

When it comes to providing entrepreneurs with adequate incentive to accomplish milestone events, some investors will require an increase in their ownership if the company fails to accomplish certain milestones, particularly follow-on funding, in a timely fashion. For instance, an angel investor will enter into a convertible debenture or note with you, with automatic conversion upon completion of a subsequent round of financing of $3,000,000. If you accomplish this milestone within three months of signing the convertible debenture, the angel receives only five thousand warrants, exercisable at $0.50. However, if you fail to close on the financing in three months, the angel receives an additional five thousand warrants for each month of delay until the subsequent financing is secured. You can imagine the potential variables, from increasing discounts on conversion to additional shares to even board seats or control of the company. Some requirements can have extreme consequences; these should be critically assessed because investors need to have an inherent level of faith in you. Extreme or severe nonperformance consequences would suggest the opposite. In addition, such terms can have a chilling effect on securing subsequent funding, and you may not want such an investor as part of your company. Be careful when balancing your need of funding against the burdens such funding carries.

REGIONAL INVESTING TRENDS AND HABITS

Not all countries, states, or cities have the same appetite for high-risk investing. Entrepreneurism, investor sophistication, availability of follow-on financing, and acceptance of failure are all cultural variables between nations or regions. In the United States, the two coasts (more specifically, the mid-Atlantic and New England in the East and Silicon Valley, San Diego, and Seattle in the West) have been actively involved in early-stage angel financing for more than a decade. The Midwest has often been referred to as "the fly-over zone," with some pockets of relatively exceptional activity such as Chicago. Recent trends in angel group development show a clear surge of interest in angel investing in the Southeast, Midwest, and Southwest. Outside the United States, Canada is experiencing an increase in angel group formation, but a dearth of early-stage financing remains in different provinces as a result of skyrocketing gas prices (making Albertan oil sands a great investment opportunity), though nothing is ever quite that simple. Parts of Europe struggle with angel financing partly related to cultural and socioeconomic factors in social democracies and the negative perception associated with failure. Other countries are simply not entrepreneurial by nature, again often reflecting social norms.

The question of which comes first, entrepreneurism or early-stage investment interest, seems a bit chicken-and-egg, with complex factors that often defy definition or measurement. What is clear is that most angel investors are prior entrepreneurs interested in building local economic vitality. It's also clear that it takes a few home runs with high public profiles to get investment engines going; and it takes time to build communities like Silicon Valley. If you are in a region with little entrepreneurial activity, you are not likely to find much appetite for early-stage investing in your local market. Therefore, you may need to venture outside your region to find money. Bottom line: being fundable does not have to do solely with the greatness of you, your team, and your idea. Fundability involves complex factors of a greater social and economic nature, so you must understand your financial market as well as your product market.

SOURCES OF FINANCING

To prepare for angel encounters, you must first understand the numerous potential sources of financing that may be available, and the period in your company's maturation when these sources are likely to take an interest. Figure 4.1 gives a rough progression of which financing sources become available in different business phases. You need to understand that product development is seldom linear, and not all funding sources are available to all companies. The oval highlights the development stage at which angels typically invest compared to other financing sources.

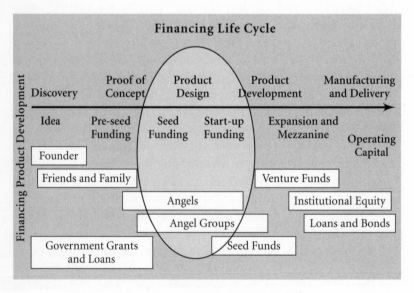

Figure 4.1   Financing Life Cycle

Figure 4.1 puts some of the financing sources into context from the perspective of company maturation and financing stage, with many other sources of financing potentially available to entrepreneurs. These alternative sources of financing may be more appropriate for certain types of businesses, as not all companies are eligible for angel financing. Later, I will discuss what angel investors are typically looking for in companies, but for purposes of the present discussion, it's enough to understand that angels are looking for many of the same attributes as venture capitalists and other third-party investors: a significant return on their investment, leading-edge technology, high growth potential, experienced management, and a clear exit strategy. Therefore, keep your reality hat on when seeking financing and remember that even if your business may not be appropriate for angel financing, you may still be able to develop a solid, profitable venture.

With these thoughts in mind, take a look at the various sources of financing an entrepreneur may want to consider:

Founder: Self-funding—savings, personal loans, credit cards, second mortgage: Most investors today require that the founder have skin in the game. In other words, the entrepreneur has to invest private funds, not just time, to create an attractive company. Some entrepreneurs are fortunate enough to have adequate savings to quit their day jobs and focus full time on making their ideas turn into reality. Most founders must use credit cards, second mortgages, and personal loans to get started. Failure to put yourself and your finances at risk can be interpreted as lack of conviction and unwillingness to make personal sacrifices, which translates for an investor to a lack of passion and determination to succeed.

Bootstrap: Some businesses have a modest amount of cash flow from the very beginning and can be grown through their own activities. Bootstrapping your business usually necessitates at least some initial period of continuing your day job while working on your entrepreneurial venture in the evenings and on weekends. This approach can be effective particularly for entrepreneurs uncomfortable with the idea of taking on debt or giving up equity.

Friends and family: For many entrepreneurs, friends and family members may have the ability to provide some of the initial capital the company needs. The amount that friends and family invest is typically modest and represents the very first funds needed to finish the business plan, create a prototype, or conduct validating research. Friends and family are often referred to as providing "love money" because their investments are made out of affection for you as an individual without the heavy analysis all arm's-length investors insist on. Friends and family typically receive common stock for their investment, or may structure their investment as a debt instrument or promissory note depending on respective comfort levels. Do be cautious as to the number of investors you have in this category. Professional investors can be wary of friends and family because people in those groups are typically unsophisticated and lack understanding of the complexities and often harsh realities of company growth and change. Some professional investors will not invest in companies with more than a few investors in the friends and family round to avoid the hassle they usually entail. Most investors will take a dim view of your Aunt Sally calling every couple of days to ask about her retirement money. They fear you may make possibly inappropriate business decisions based on protecting your friends' and family's investments.

Equipment leasing: You can often leverage your own cash or that of your investors through leasing operational equipment. As an entrepreneur, you must stretch each dollar.

Bartering: Gone are the boom days when entrepreneurs received $10 or $20 million for an idea. Investors now expect entrepreneurs to live lean and make every dollar work like two. One mechanism is to barter or trade services with other entrepreneurs or businesspeople. While certainly not a primary source of funding, trading services or expertise can help stretch those precious dollars. You should be careful in bartering or trading services that ownership of any resulting product is clearly with your company. Therefore, be sure to either secure ownership through a contractual arrangement or avoid bartering for any services related to your products or company assets.

Angels: Obviously—being the focus of this book—angels will not be discussed at length here, but can be summarized as individuals with disposable wealth, almost always "accredited investors" as defined under Regulation D of the Securities Act of 1933, who typically participate at some level in decisions related to investment of their own wealth. Angels themselves put a bit of a twist on this definition—see "Angels Define Angels."

Government grants and loans: The government has a vast array of grant and loan programs for small businesses, research, targeted industries, minority interests, and so on and on. Publications several inches thick are dedicated to information on these programs. There-

---

ANGELS DEFINE ANGELS

David Grahame of LINC in Scotland defines an angel as "A private individual investing their own money into companies in which they can make a difference—an active and direct investment rather than passive. Angels have the ability to make a real contribution to the growth of a company."

Mitch Goldsmith, a serial angel investor, gives a similar definition from a different perspective: "Angels are experienced in the pitfalls of building and growing a company. All businesses have commonalities regardless of industry focus. Angels who have been there and done that can provide unique experiential information to young entrepreneurs."

Knox Massey with Atlanta Technology Angels puts it simply: "Someone who writes a check from their own checkbook. Angel investing is an individual choice; no angel has to make an investment."

---

fore, this discussion is highly abbreviated and provides only nominal information on a few of the larger and more visible programs:

Small Business Innovation Research (SBIR) is a highly competitive program that encourages small businesses to explore their technology potential for commercialization. Since enacted in 1982, the SBIR program has helped thousands of small businesses through federal research and development awards. To qualify for an SBIR grant, you must meet certain criteria including being an American-owned or operated for-profit company with the principal researcher employed in the United States and fewer than five hundred employees. Each year ten different federal departments and agencies award funds. SBIR grants are awarded in phases, with phase I grants providing up to $100,000 for exploration of technical merit or feasibility of an idea or technology. Phase II is for up to $750,000 to evaluate commercial potential.

Another government grant program is the Small Business Technology Transfer program (STTR; the "R" is the second letter of *transfer*). STTR provides fund opportunities in federal innovation and development to expand public-private partnerships through joint ventures, among other means. Grants are awarded to small businesses and nonprofit research institutions. The same eligibility requirements apply to STTR grants as SBIR grants. Five federal departments and agencies issue STTR grants, with a similar phased approach. Many other government grants are available through numerous programs.

With regard to government loans, the Small Business Administration (SBA) offers numerous loan programs. It is important to note, however, that the SBA is primarily a guarantor of loans made by private and other institutions. The SBA's loan program helps qualified small businesses obtain financing when they might not be eligible for business loans through normal lending channels. It is also the agency's most flexible business loan program, since financing under this program can be guaranteed for a variety of general business purposes.

Economic development programs: Loans, tax incentives, tax credits, and other provisions are available for specific industries, certain minority ownerships, or in certain geographic areas. Federal, state, regional, and local government entities have a variety of economic incentive programs that typically focus on economically challenged or underserved aspects of the relevant economy. Such programs number more than 100,000 just in the United States, if you were to total up all programs from all government entities. These programs often also include partnerships with industry associations, foundations, and corporations, as well as multiple government entities. Here's an example of just a few programs, for representative purposes only:

- Federal minority programs
- State economic focus areas
- Regional economically depressed areas
- Local industry focus—like biotech in Seattle

Venture capitalists: Another source of private equity financing, along with angel investors, typically focusing on later-stage companies for a variety of reasons discussed in Chapter Two.

Banks: Most commercial banks do not make loans to young companies because of the lack of assets, operational track record, sales, customer base, and other factors of inherent risk. A small group of banks will extend credit or offer debt financing to a young company after a venture capital round. Some commercial banks do provide a line of credit (LOC) for a small business, but the LOC must be collateralized (secured) with adequate and real business or personal assets, often the business owner's home. Sometimes banks will loan against accounts receivable or inventory, but generally such lending is done for companies with a strong history of sales and a reliable customer base.

Technology licensing: The term is used to describe the process and underlying documents related to a company's acquisition of the rights (most desirably, exclusively) to commercially viable technology. Often technology is licensed from a university or other academic or research institute by an entity interested in commercializing the technology. Technology is also often licensed by larger companies from smaller companies that lack the financial or infrastructure capability to commercialize the technology. An example of the latter would be a pharmaceutical company licensing the right to drug discovery technology from a small biotech company. Appropriately licensing technology and actually having the right to use the technology is one of the major issues for entrepreneurs. Often the entrepreneur has either not licensed the planned technology at all or not licensed the proper breadth of technology, or the license contains restrictions, covenants, or requirements that may cause the loss or reduction of licensed rights.

Corporate partners, strategic partners: The best and most likely investor may be a customer or supplier. Entrepreneurs often overlook these obvious potential investors because they fail to think more broadly about these relationships. Your innovation may be best understood by those in the same field, such as vendors and customers.

Corporate investment arms: Through certainly not present in numbers close to those of the heady bubble years, many large public companies still have strategic investment arms that present a possible alternative source of investment for young companies. Companies like Intel, Dell, and Agilent see their investment arms as providing the company with access to cutting-edge technology and aspiring talent complementary to the company's core platform or future product direction. Investments can be made at various stages of company maturation, but seldom are these investments made at the seed stage. Therefore, strategic partnering is a viable alternative for only a handful of entrepreneurial companies.

Incubator-based financing: Some business incubators have developed a small fund or created a relationship with a small venture fund or other early-stage sources of financing to provide companies graduating from their protection with "launching capital." This type of capital is defined for purposes of this book as a small investment (often in the form of debt financing) to help a company set up operations outside the incubator. The status of companies at graduation is quite varied since incubators set individualized criteria or milestones. Often these milestones include a certain established customer base, an anticipated revenue stream, product maturation, or third-party financing.

From this list of possible funding sources, you should realize that single-source finance thinking is myopic and not entrepreneurial. Many investors insist that entrepreneurs obtain funding from multiple sources to spread the risk around and to create a multiplier on their own investment. Different funding sources will require different financial information. Sophisticated angels have learned to examine financial assumptions closely and to challenge the reality and practicality of an entrepreneur's assumptions. This high level of scrutiny requires a thorough understanding of your own financials and the underlying assumptions, as well as the ability to proffer well-organized and complete documents.

How do you find these elusive angels? What are they looking for in the perfect company? The next chapter will look at these important questions.

CHAPTER FIVE

Looking for Angels and What Angels Are Looking For

A ngel investors are becoming more sophisticated in their investment processes. They take the job of investing seriously and follow procedures established by professional venture capitalists. Angel groups are forming at a rapid rate, reflecting the value of collective due diligence, broad deal access, and the pursuit of mutual interests. Even though most angels still invest on their own, their general level of expectation from the entrepreneur and management team has risen significantly; you must be prepared.

Even with the growth of the angel investor population, they remain elusive beasts. Finding the right angel investor is now easier because of angel organizations and possibly other services such as online matching sites. This book provides extensive lists of angel groups in the United States, Canada, and the European Union in Appendixes 4 and 5 and a list of Internet matching sites in Appendix 9. Lists of this kind are fluid, as groups and sites constantly form and disappear, but the information does give an excellent understanding of the scope of angel organizations in your region, which is an invaluable tool. Most of the Internet matching sites are national in scope, though some have a regional focus, which is reasonable since angel investing is typically on a local basis.

HOW DO YOU FIND ANGEL INVESTORS?

Unfortunately, the process of finding the right angel for your business is not straightforward—there's no Yellow Pages listing under "angel financing"—but it does have a simple answer:

Network, network, network.

So after you put in an eight-hour day at your regular job, attend an evening reception for an investment forum; or before you head off to your day job, attend an entrepreneurial education program, all while putting in several hours a week in the evenings and on the weekend working on your dream. You can never do enough networking. Some will warn entrepreneurs not to over-shop a deal. (Pitching your business plan to dozens and dozens of potential investors creates a perception that your business concept is a losing proposition.) Networking is different; you're not touting your business, you're looking for and seeking out the right connections to the right potential investors. It is simply not true that every angel investor is a good investor for every seed/start-up business, for multiple reasons, including alignment of respective expectations, additional value propositions, and personality fit. Networking has potential collateral value including identifying possible service providers for your company and even possible strategic hires. Networking can also give you a better understanding of your market, while giving you valuable education on investor presentations and pitches, the competition, general resources, and even how to dress.

As you go out the door to a networking event, consider the following points:

- Treat each person as a potential investor, that is be courteous, enthusiastic, and articulate.
- Always have enough business cards with current information.
- Dress up when unsure.
- Have questions to engage others.
- Don't be afraid to request a follow-on meeting.
- Understand "no."
- Be prepared (only one first impression, so get coached).

You will not necessarily know who potential investors are, and many people have dual interests—so be prepared to talk about your company. Rehearse your elevator pitch—a succinct description of your company that gives the listener a clear understanding of your company in a minute or less. It's worth repeating: You only get one chance to make a good first impression. As you are speaking, offer your business card (your up-to-date business card, with no handwritten changes), and be sure to receive one back, or write some quick contact information on another card. Be a good conversationalist, which means not only talking about your company but also finding out about your discussion mates: what they do, what they're interested in, and how there might be a fit. Have some general questions or discussion topics in the back of your mind, to help initiate the conversation and keep it rolling. Remember, people are more willing to help someone who takes a personal interest in them and has something to offer as well as receive. Don't be afraid to ask for the opportunity to meet with them later or at least have a phone conversation, but do understand how to graciously accept a refusal. Often people need more than one encounter to feel comfortable with meeting one-to-one with someone they've just met. Above all, do not take "not interested" (that is, *no*) personally. The reasons for angel investors deciding not to invest are quite varied. You can always ask the uninterested investor the reason for deciding not to go forward, but don't push someone who refuses to answer or seems to have avoided giving the whole answer— accept the response and move on.

Presentations to angel groups are very effective ways to have this first encounter, which opens the door to follow-on meetings. Investor members can get to know you and your company without having a personal conversation. You have the opportunity to wow them with lots of information about your company.

Whatever you do, do not come to an event underdressed. If you are uncertain about the dress code for an event, either find out or dress in business attire. Even though your audience may be wearing chinos and shirts, they are not there to impress the crowd—and you are. So dress as you would run your company, professionally and smartly. If you are uncertain about your wardrobe, your presentation skills, your ability to network, or the like, get a coach or take a course; even Toastmasters International can be valuable. Do not assume you can just learn on the job; remember, you only have one chance to make a first impression.

THE BEST HUNTING GROUNDS

Angel organizations: As discussed in Chapter Two, angel organizations are becoming more common, with the number of groups increasing rapidly in the last decade. Appendixes 4 and 5 provide a comprehensive list of angel groups throughout the United States and Canada, as well as a number of angel organizations in Europe from the European Business Angel Network, EBAN. The lists can't be completely comprehensive because of the constant establishment of new groups and the frequent difficulty of identifying groups. Angel Capital Association (www.angelcapitalassociation.org) and Angel Capital Education Foundation (www.angelcapitaleducation.org) have dynamic Web sites containing links to many angel organizations.

Matching sites on the Web: Multiple matching sites exist and many are listed for you in Appendix 9, but the success of these services is uncertain. The list is provided to give you full and complete information about possible sources for identifying potential investors. Make your own careful assessment before you try any of these online matching and support service sites. The list in Appendix 9 contains information taken directly from these respective sites and therefore does not contain all information on any site, nor is any judgment made as to the accuracy of the information. Additionally, information (including pricing) can change with time.

Professional service providers: Angel investors often put great weight on referrals through their own advisers. Lawyers, accountants, investment advisers, and others who work with high-net-worth individuals and young companies understand the respective interests and needs of both sides. They also have a desire to be seen as providing valued-added services through good referrals of investment opportunities or sources of possible financing. High-net-worth clients also trust the judgment of their advisers because they know these individuals value their own reputations too much to suggest any connection that is less than top-notch.

Investment forums: Most if not all metropolitan areas in the United States, and a growing number abroad, hold investment forums showcasing promising young companies. These investment forums can vary in industry focus, company stage of development, and geographic reach, but most have the common attributes of screening and selecting private companies to make brief presentations to an audience of potential investors, professional advisers, potential customers or strategic partners, economic development partners, and others. They are all designed to showcase a community's top-tier young companies, and are intended to create a favorable impression for these businesses so as to promote investment and establishment of strategic relationships. The bottom-line goal of the sponsoring community is to secure funding and growth of businesses and thus create jobs and a vibrant economy.

From the investors' standpoint, these forums provide a great venue in which to view a number of potential investments in a short time, knowing that the dozen or so presenting companies have been selected from a much larger list of applicants based on predefined selection criteria. Because the screening committee is made up of fellow investors and successful entrepreneurs, angels have confidence that presenting companies will be likely to align with their investment preferences and requirements. Education can also be a component of investment forums, formal as well as informal, and angel investors often seek them out to improve their due diligence techniques and other skills.

Business plan competitions: Cousins to investment forums are business plan competitions. These are typically for very early-stage companies and often associated with a graduate school in business. The formats for business plan competitions are quite varied. Some restrict entry to students and alumni, while others have no limitations. Some have numerous stages in which competitors are successively eliminated or scores are given for different parts of the competition, leading to a final winner. Nearly all have judging on the business plan and an entrant's presentation skills; many have a trade show component. These are great avenues to modest seed financing for first-time entrepreneurs.

Commercial banks: As you know, commercial banks often have relationships with young companies, whether only a checking account or a more complicated debt financing arrangement. Your bank has an obvious interest in your growth and success. Like professional service providers, commercial bankers may have relationships with high-net-worth individuals interested in participating in companies as angel investors.

Venture capitalists: As noted, the vast majority of venture capitalists do not invest in seed/start-up stage companies. They do, however, like to keep their fingers on the pulse of what may mature into a potential investment opportunity at the venture capital level, so many are members of angel investment groups. Venture capitalists also typically know a number of angel investors because of their social and business contacts. Therefore, while you may not be ready for venture capital financing, it's still worth talking with venture capitalists when you get a chance; if they like you and see your company as having good potential, they may help you make contact with angel investors.

Individual angels: Not surprisingly, high-net-worth individuals often know others of the same financial means. In addition, angels who are members of angel groups can recommend your company for presentation—which will boost your chances of getting a place in a program, as greater stock is typically put into recommendations from members for possible presenting companies than applications made at the initiative of the company seeking investors. Recommendations from peers, advisers, and other trusted sources are very important to angels, many of whom have a personal investment rule of investing only in companies referred to them from sources they are sure have their best interests in mind.

Incubators: Business incubators come in various shapes and sizes depending on the source of financial support, criteria for selecting incubated companies and ultimately graduating them from the incubator, presence or absence of a virtual program, industry focus, and the like. Incubators can provide a great deal of value to young companies: reduced rent or rent-free space, able staff, and expert advisers. Some incubators have a small affiliated fund that helps launch graduating companies. Statistics show that companies graduating from an incubator program have a greater chance of long-term success than those that go it alone because of the preselection process and the support provided throughout their incubator residency. Therefore, angel investors sometimes become advisers to incubators—partly to help these young companies but also to get an early view of potential investments. Incubator staff also tend to have contacts with the investment community, if only because one of the key factors for graduating a company is sufficient funding. You may wish to consider applying for incubator residency—or for affiliation if the incubator has a virtual or nonresident program.

Business journals: Just as business journals like to write about successful companies, they also write personal success stories of community leaders, and you might find a mentor or angel investor among their pages. Keep tabs on senior executives of public companies who are retiring, those receiving big promotions, and even other successful entrepreneurs who just cashed out. Do not approach them directly through a cold call, but again, find a trusted referral source. In addition, having a favorable article written on you and your company—profiling your innovative technology—will give you visibility to individual angel investors as well as angel groups. Therefore, creating good relationships with media can be valuable in the short and long term.

Some entrepreneurs need not avail themselves of this diversity of sources. Nonetheless, awareness of all potential opportunities is useful for anyone as a way of staying alert and tuned in to the angel investment community. The bottom line will always be *network, network, network.*

If you haven't already figured it out, finding investors is not a slam-dunk. Even after you have identified potential investors, you have to sell them on you and your company. So do not be discouraged. You will speak and present to dozens and dozens of potential investors to land the handful you need. This is hard work, and it can be incredibly frustrating at times. But keep it up! Great people with great companies get funded because they exhibit passion, project confidence, and understand how to take great ideas and turn them into innovative, profitable businesses.

WHAT ANGELS LOOK FOR

"One man's trash is another man's treasure" may be a bit extreme, but the saying does emphasize the way different companies, markets, and industries appeal to different investors. The statistics in Chapter Two do show a high-tech and biotech focus, but many other categories also receive investments from angel investors. Even with individual investor preferences and personalities, common characteristics do arise. So the best way to start a discussion on what angels are looking for is to describe the perfect investment.

So how do angels determine you match their investment interests and desired personality characteristics? Angel investors look for passion—the excitement with which an entrepreneur speaks of an idea and company. Passion also means absolute commitment to make the dream a reality. Entrepreneurs must also be able to succinctly articulate their company message with that desire to succeed.

Along with passion, the other big message threaded throughout this book is coachability. You must be open to others' opinions; be willing to listen and also hear. No one has all the answers nor all the skills to find all the answers. Respect for others' skills and capabilities is an essential attribute of all successful entrepreneurs. Hiring people smarter than you in their respective disciplines tells the angel investor that you respect others' opinions and understand the necessity of a team to grow a company. Nonetheless, even if you have people who are responsible for sales and marketing, you, as the founder, must sell yourself and your company each day to investors, partners, customers, employees, and even media representatives.

The Winning Company

The ideal company (which, by the way, does not exist) is different for every angel, particularly in priority of importance for the various attributes. But anecdotal evidence suggests the following dream company would appeal to nearly any angel:

Management is *seasoned and capable*. Nearly all angel investors would agree that a great management team is the most important aspect of a winning company. Angels like to see a founder and group of key employees who have already been part of other companies from the idea up, and who have all worked together at some point. That kind of team has strong compatibility, complementary skill sets, and passion.

It's best if the other companies have been successful, but not essential. An interesting phenomenon in parts of the United States—differentiating them from nearly all of the rest of the world—is the acceptance of failure. Failure has been described as experience on someone else's dollar. For the most part, this relative acceptance of failure is confined to the two coasts of the United States, which happen to have the longest history of professional private investors. The United States is also unique in the world, according to the Global Entrepreneurship Monitor, in fear of failure not being an impediment to starting a company, possibly because of the reciprocal lack of stigma associated with failure.

The team, and the founder, must be *coachable*—an absolute necessity for most angels. No single person or group of individuals has all the answers or skills. They must be receptive to input and informed direction. Absence of this characteristic or minimal evidence for its presence, can be a deal killer.

Another absolute for investors is *passion*—that undisputed drive for success and belief in one's ideas. Passion will see entrepreneurs through the lean days of wondering how to meet tomorrow's payroll or purchase raw materials with no money in the bank. Passion creates innovation and fuels creativity.

KNOX MASSEY, DAVID GRAHAME, AND LAURENCE BRIGGS ON MANAGEMENT

Knox Massey of Atlanta Technology Angels states, "Excellent management is a must-have, not a nice-to-have. We are looking for founders who have done it before and will listen to input from . . . advisers and investors. Ethics and honesty are also important criteria."

David Grahame with LINC in Scotland unequivocally agrees— management is the number one factor in evaluating possible investments. David is looking for entrepreneurs who don't take no for an answer, but who understand the difference between determination and obstinacy.

Laurence Briggs adds that entrepreneurs must also be coachable. "Every company will have difficult times, even disasters. Angel investors have to feel comfortable that the CEO will talk to investors—before any possible issue, preferably—and take such advice to heart."

Interestingly, if you asked professional investors to name their top investment priority in 1999, they would have been split between management and technology. Today, management wins hands down. Your experience, knowledge, and capabilities and those of your team are very important because angels and venture capitalists have learned that brilliant entrepreneurs can take an interesting idea and make it a home run, while weak, inexperienced, or ungifted entrepreneurs can take a home run idea and strike out. This is not to say that if you are a young and aspiring entrepreneur you will never get funded; the path to funding may be longer and more difficult, forcing you to prove yourself and your idea through trial and error and grow organically through your own means and those of friends and family, but if your idea is genuinely good and you pursue it firmly enough, you will eventually become fundable.

Because of the importance of management in the determination of investability, looking at individual personality traits is important to understand a star entrepreneur. According to Bob Geras, often referred to as one of the Big Three old-timer angels in Chicago,

The company should have quality management with the ability and experience to make growth happen. The existing team doesn't necessarily need to be presently complete, but should have the qualities to be able to eventually attract a full team needed to build a successful company. These qualities include:

- Integrity
- Experience
- Knowledge
- Perseverance
- Leadership
- Creativity
- Stamina
- Flexibility

In real estate the three most important ingredients for success are location, location, location. In private capital investing it's people, people, people.

A *broad platform technology*, with multiple markets or applications. Investors do not want a single product or market idea, often called a "one-trick pony." Such companies have limited growth potential. If the market doesn't accept that single product, no matter how good it is and even for reasons outside your control, such as timing or an unanticipated competitor, you're out.

The *intellectual property* underlying the technology is protected with broadly written claims in the patents. The company owns all technology necessary, or has appropriate licenses, to develop multiple products and bring them to market. This patent position creates a competitive barrier to entry.

The anticipated products have a *compelling competitive advantage* and resolve a clearly discernable and vocalized market pain. Therefore, immediate market acceptance is highly probable. The company may have already done some beta testing with potential customers, with rave reviews and strong customer need for the final product. Clearly, the ideal is to have low-hanging fruit ready for the picking, and you are the only one in the field with the right harvesting system.

Remember, when you are putting together your list of competitors, consider the consumer's perspective. Even if you see remarkable differentiation between your product and competitors, those unique attributes may not matter to the customer, who may even place your product in a different category—one that in your judgment is inappropriate. In other words, your opinion has little weight when it comes to market interpretation. Perception is reality. If you have to explain to everyone what your product is as well as what market it will move into, you have problems. Consumers simply do not change so dramatically as to think of an entirely new market and the first product in that market.

Ideally, product sales take advantage of an *existing, mature distribution system,* which is recognized and respected within the initial markets. They have a contractual arrangement that is complete or close to complete with no discernable impediments. For the vast majority of young companies, building a distribution system is imprudent and a waste of capital. Few products are so unique that they require their own distribution network. In fact, those that do may face difficulty with market acceptance because of the unfamiliar source of the product. As Mitch Goldsmith, a long-time successful angel investor in Chicago, puts it,

> Consumers, whether in business or retail, are still individuals, because individuals make the buying decisions for companies. Therefore, you have to consider human psychology and drivers for buying, no matter the market. Since you cannot change behavior, you have to somehow make life easier for the consumer to create a compelling need for your product or service. In addition, distribution and credibility are important. Many times companies will not buy from a start-up company because of the uncertainty that the company will still be around in one, three, or five years to provide technology or information support. Therefore, young companies should find a "big brother" or a large, established company to act as their distribution arm.

Professional investors are looking for products or services that have immediate market acceptance. Therefore, *proof of market* through early beta testing with one or more established, recognized potential consumers is very important. Beta testing is often conducted on the young company's dime, because the company is essentially asking potential consumers to spend their time and internal resources on testing the viability and application of an unproven technology or product from an unknown source. You know the product will enhance customers' operations, make their business more profitable, or save them time and money, but they do not. One of the biggest mistakes entrepreneurs make is failing to understand that others simply do not appreciate their fabulous idea and resulting product—and have no need to do so. The same is true with your potential customers or consumers. This idea is true throughout your sales process, including selling your idea to investors. As discussed in Chapter Eight, your investor presentation should not focus on your technology or product. Rather than going on and on about product features, talk about the market, the market need, the way your product provides the ideal market solution, and your competitive edge.

Market acceptance can be a fickle friend. It is worth a bit more discussion with regard to the winning, investable company. It should go without saying that all these attributes of a winning company are reflected in its business plan. Therefore, to demonstrate this investability, the winning company will spell out many market-related attributes:

- *Realistic market size*—relating to your specific product or technology, not a broader general market. (Consider the difference between the security and privacy software market and the software market.)

- *Attractive market size*—a company with a $20 million market size will not attract professional investors, but a $500 million real market will provide investors with the kinds of returns they desire. Where angels start getting interested is individual as well as regional in nature, so you need to understand market size interests for your local investment market.

- *Clear differentiation in the market*—your product must provide a clear advantage. Having to explain its unique value is an impediment to market acceptance.

- *Market readiness and need*—the market is experiencing real pain and knows it. As Lawrence Schwartz, founder and CEO of Stampede Brewing Co., puts it, "Will anyone care? The product or services must be a painkiller, not just a vitamin."

- *Market channel*—the mechanisms by which key markets become aware of your product or services. This is not necessarily the same as a distribution network. Often companies are responsible for making the market into which distributors sell.

- *Market appeal*—most readily understood in the retail market as physical appeal. Market appeal has a broader definition, including product or technology attributes easily identified and understood by prospective customers.

- *Product scalability*—if you cannot build commercial quantities of your product in a profitable manner, you are done before you start.

So far, the hypothetical winning company has seasoned management, broad-platform technology with multiple market opportunities and protected intellectual property, an established distribution network, proof of concept, clear competitive edge, and early proof of market. What more could possibly be needed to win over an angel investor? Well, for one thing, you need a business plan that shows a *path to profitability,* the sooner the better. Angel investors are leery of companies that show a need for substantial capital before reaching a point of self-sustainability. They dislike the uncertainty of future funding for myriad reasons—not just the chance that the company might fail to meet certain milestones before the next funding round (proof of concept, for example) but also the chance of shifts in market preference, market timing, competing investment opportunities, and so on.

Along with early profitability, you must have *realistic financial projections.* Your financial projections must be reasonable and achievable, and balanced against your projected financial needs. Entrepreneurs are notoriously optimistic, and they should be. That optimism, that conviction, is part of the reason you will be successful where others will not, and investors look for that passion and unrelenting drive to succeed. You have to believe in yourself and your company to be successful. So get advice from trusted advisers and knowledgeable friends about realistic financials, and your business plan in general; test your assumptions behind the numbers. Because of entrepreneurs' traditional belief in accomplishing twice as much with half the funding in half the time, professional investors will often internally recalibrate your numbers based on their own experiences. Therefore, in doing their due diligence and financials analysis, investors will often reduce your revenue projections and increase your funding needs. However, you must have defensible, thoughtfully considered financial projections even if investors nearly always recalibrate based on the "founder factor" of optimism and boundless enthusiasm.

Not only do you need to show a clear path to profitability, you must have a strong growth opportunity, with an understanding of what it takes to achieve growth. In addition, you must have *strong margins.* Investors understand that in early growth years, companies invest and reinvest capital, whether brought in from outside or self-generated through early sales, in developing technology, products, and market, hiring key employees, securing space, and the like. But there is a difference between margins and bottom-line profit. If you cannot sell your product for more than a few percentage points above your production cost, you will be unattractive to any eventual acquirer, unless you're in a high-volume, low-margin market. If acquisition is not likely, investors will avoid your company because they can't visualize an exit strategy for liquidity of their investment.

If all the previous "winning company" attributes don't conjure up potential differences of opinion with your angel investors, wait till you get to *valuation.* More deals go south for failure to come to terms on valuation than for nearly any other factor. As discussed in Chapter Eight (on the deal process), getting preliminary agreement on key investment terms, including valuation, is important before entering due diligence. Due diligence is arduous for all parties, and going through hour after hour of discussions, document review, and interviews is distracting and tiresome for you and your employees. Therefore, you want to minimize the number of times you enter the process, so make sure you and your potential investor have certain terms close to agreement, such as basic investment structure, post-investment involvement, and valuation.

Experienced angel investors have much to say on the topic of a winning company; the following excerpts give an understanding of the relative uniform value proposition angels look for:

Henry Vehovec, founder of the National Angel Organization, agrees that the management team is the primary factor and adds, "Experienced angels develop a sixth sense in recognizing a good management team; an innate recognition of a founder with passion and the judgment to select people smarter than themselves to build a company."

David Grahame, with LINC in Scotland, reiterates the importance of the management team, particularly one that is coachable, with "the true gems of the entrepreneurial world being those looking for mentors." He also emphasizes "unfair advantage as an important factor." ("Unfair advantage" is a term of art in this field. It has a positive connotation despite the sound, as it refers to those attributes of a business or technology that give one company a definitive advantage over competition in the market.)

Bob Goff, founder and chairman of Sierra Angels, describes these fundamental requirements for an invest-able company: "validated solution to a valid market requirement that is sufficiently large to offer 10X return on investment; articulated pathway to cash-flow-positive, follow-on funding, and timely liquidity; credible implementation plan with measurable key milestones; relevantly experienced key executives/entrepreneurs who are coachable, and a business plan in which I and fellow Sierra Angel members have relevant domain experience."

Mitch Goldsmith, a partner with Shefsky & Froelich and an extremely experienced angel investor (he has thirty deals in his current portfolio) emphasizes that a "company must be revenue oriented. In other words, a company's business model shows early revenue generation. I will not invest in a company that fails to show a clear path to profitability. You cannot build a product and just expect the market will buy it, no matter how well engineered or the number of bells and whistles. People don't change behavior in the short term."

Steve Robinson, an angel investor for nearly twenty-five years, summarizes his investment criteria in these terms: "First and foremost, people. Second, is this an angel-friendly deal, in other words, the company does not require several rounds of financing or $80 million plus? And third, can the angel investors get a meaningful stake or make a meaningful impact with their investment?"

The Bottom Line—Return on Investment

You now have a clear understanding of how to find angel investors and what angels are looking for as a winning investment. But at the end of the day, if you cannot provide investors with a handsome return on their investment, you are not an angel-fundable business. Table 5.1 gives an idea of the kinds of returns professional investors are looking for at various stages of company development (which roughly equate to time to liquidity):

To provide investors with these types of returns on investments of $25,000 to $500,000, even to $2,000,000, the company must have a large market potential—big returns come from big opportunities,

	Internal Rate of Return (percent)	Return on Investment
Seed	60+/year	10X+
Start-up	50	8X
Early stage	40	5X
Second stage	30	4X
Near exit	25/year	3X

Table 5.1   Rates of Return for Private Equity Investments

which turn into big realities. As a result, most professional angels are not interested in lifestyle companies, restaurants, small retail businesses, and other businesses with limited revenue potential. Friends, family, and angels with a special interest in (or unique experience with) these types of limited-revenue, limited-market businesses, will be the source of funding, along with possible government loans such as small business loans, lines of credit, or personally guaranteed business loans from your neighborhood commercial bank. Professional investors are looking for home runs because the reality is that only a minority of investments provide a real return. As a result, investors look for winning companies of the types previously described in this chapter.

CHAPTER SIX

Preparing for Investors

T he angel investors who back your company are entrusting you with their personal wealth, which they could have invested in stocks, bonds, real estate, venture capital funds, and many, many other opportunities. You are just one of dozens and dozens of entrepreneurs vying for a finite pool of angel dollars. Therefore, you must stand head and shoulders above the crowd just to be noticed, and then you must repeatedly impress your potential investors throughout the investment evaluation process.

Angels are professional investors. They require accurate and complete information from capable, experienced individuals who appreciate the value provided by angels and understand the complexities and uncertainties of growing a company. They are also realists and understand that even the most perfect deal can crash and burn, no matter how good the ideas or how well they are implemented. So they try to pick winners based on the best information they have—including who has impressed them the most.

CORPORATE STRUCTURE

Angels are looking for reasons to rule out possible investments, and one of the big factors for an investor is corporate structure. If it's messy, you will chill a prospective investor's interest. To engage an angel's attention, you need a clean, uncomplicated corporate structure that anticipates an investor's needs. Just consider how your company stands with regard to the potential questions listed in the box—all questions that an angel investor might pose during a discussion of valuation or during the due diligence process. (For a more complete discussion on due diligence, see Chapter Eight.) If you are uncomfortable with these questions, either because you do not understand them or fear you have created a deficient corporate structure, seek legal counsel with experience in start-up companies and early-stage financing. One of the lessons serial entrepreneurs learn from their first venture is to engage a capable attorney early in the process. Cleaning up a mess will take a huge amount of time and cost more money than beginning with a clean corporate structure drafted with the help of your attorney.

Corporate Structure and Governance

Along with these questions and more, the angel investor will probably wish to confirm much of the information you have provided by reviewing your corporate documents. Appendix 6 provides a full due diligence checklist, but here are some of the main documents you may need to provide:

Charter Documents
- Articles or Certificate of Incorporation, as amended to date, including current drafts of pending charter amendments and recapitalization documents.
- Drafts of documents related to proposed reincorporation, if any.
- Bylaws, as amended to date.
- Good standing certificates.
- List of jurisdictions in which the company or any of its subsidiaries or affiliates is qualified to do business, owns or leases real property, or is otherwise operating.

Minutes
- Minutes of stockholders' meetings as well as meetings of the board of directors and permanent board committees.

POTENTIAL INVESTOR QUESTIONS ON CORPORATE STRUCTURE AND GOVERNANCE

What is the company's corporate structure? C corporation, S corporation, limited liability company, or limited partnership? Does this model allow for a liquidity event and return on investment?

Are all corporate minutes in order?

Is the corporate structure overly complicated? If so, why, and can it be simplified?

What are the authorized shares? How many shares are issued? How many existing shareholders? If numerous, then why?

Does the corporate structure fit with the business model?

Does the corporate structure allow for growth? For the short term? For the long term?

What is the founder share allocation? Does the founder have a large enough stake to have the incentive to succeed, but not so large as to be able to ignore the board and other advisers? Is the founder's stock vested over time?

Who is on the board of directors? Do they have the right background for the company? Are there enough outside directors? How are board members compensated?

Does the company have a board of advisers and, if so, who is on the board? Do the advisers actively participate in the company's development? How are advisers compensated?

Does the company have all required permits and licenses?

Has the company already established an option plan for employees and other valued advisers? If not, why? What percentage of stock is reserved for option issuance? How many options have already been issued? What is the typical vesting schedule?

• Authorizing resolutions relating to this offering and related transactions.

Corporate Organization

• List of officers and directors.

• Management structure organization chart.

- Stockholders' lists (including list of optionees and warrant holders), including number of shares and dates of issuance, and consideration paid.
- Information regarding subsidiaries, if any: ownership, date of acquisition of stock or assets, all closing binders relating to acquisitions.
- Information regarding joint ventures or partnership, if any, i.e., partners, date of formation, all closing binders relating to joint ventures or partnerships.
- Agreements relating to mergers, acquisitions or dispositions by the Company of its subsidiaries or affiliates of companies, significant assets or operations involving the Company or any of its subsidiaries or affiliates since inception, including those of any predecessor or subsidiary corporations, if any.

Capital Stock

- Stock records, stock ledgers and other evidence of securities authorized and issued.
- Agreements relating to the purchase, repurchase, sale or issuance of securities, including oral commitments to sell or issue securities.
- Agreements relating to voting of securities and restrictive share transfers, if any.
- Agreements relating to preemptive or other preferential rights to acquire securities and any waivers thereof, if any.
- Agreements relating to registration rights, if any.
- Evidence of qualification or exemption under applicable federal and state blue sky laws for issuance of the company's securities.
- Documents relating to any conversion, recapitalization, reorganization or significant restructuring of the company, if any.

What it boils down to is simple: Be prepared and make sure you have considered your corporate structure from the investor's perspective. The full due diligence process, discussed in Chapter Eight, also includes contracts, intellectual property ownership, licenses, employment agreements, real estate, financials, and so on. The following sections discuss the relative merits of different forms of organization.

C CORPORATIONS. C corporations are the preferred investment structure. Most professional investors are looking for the typical for-profit corporate structure. A C corporation affords the company and investor the greatest flexibility in ownership and liquidity. Publicly traded companies are almost exclusively C corporations. The typical exit strategy for a company involves a merger or acquisition, where the acquiring company wants the acquired company to mimic its corporate structure for ease of integration and transfer of ownership.

C corporations also provide considerable flexibility in stock ownership, allowing for various types of potential investment vehicles that have different structures and rights. For instance, preferred shares may be issued with a variety of differing rights, preferences, and privileges. Options or warrants may be issued as a right to purchase stock in the future for a set amount. A corporation may have one class of voting common stock, another of nonvoting common stock, a third class of stock related to the first angel investment round that consists of preferred shares (often referred to as "Series A," being the first issuance of preferred stock), a fourth class of stock related to a second-round preferred stock offering (the B round), and so on. Individuals, corporations, partnerships, or any other legal entity may own or hold stock or rights to acquire stock in a C corporation.

LIMITED LIABILITY COMPANIES. Limited liability companies (LLCs) offer protection against shareholder liability (if properly structured and operated) like corporations and distribution of profits and losses as in partnerships. This type of direct distribution to LLC members (as opposed to shareholders) avoids double taxation on dividends, which are among the few vehicles for distributing profits to shareholders in a C corporation. Unfortunately, investors do not favor LLCs because of the annual allocation of profits and losses, as well as additional difficulties in selling an LLC in a liquidity event. Further, the LLC is not a recognized legal structure in Canada and other countries outside the United States.

If you cannot provide a legitimate and realistic scenario for providing investors with a return on their investment through merger, acquisition, or IPO, why would they invest? Investors are in the business of making money to increase their net worth, from which to make further investments and further increase their net worth. Having inaccessible wealth halts the investment cycle.

This is not to say LLCs are never a good structure for a young company seeking investors. In a few investment opportunities, an LLC may actually be the preferred structure. A company with limited market potential that makes it an unlikely acquisition target and unrealistic IPO candidate, but with the ability to generate considerable money, may find an LLC structure attractive to investors. If you find your company fits this scenario and you are not attracting investors, consider organizing as an LLC. Taking this alternative does not necessarily solve your funding dilemma—most investors will find it unfamiliar and will need education—but it should be thoughtfully considered and even tested out with interested investors.

So what's unappealing to investors in corporate structures?

1. *Complicated share ownerships held by numerous naive or inexperienced investors.* Professional investors want to deal with other professionals who understand the challenges of growing a company, including its financial needs and length of time to liquidity, and not with the founder's friends and family.

2. *Messy share ownership and pricing through ill-considered financing rounds.* For instance, it can complicate share ownership when you sell shares for a high price per share because a relatively small number of shares are being sold and the resulting valuations are inflated. Also, doing small rounds of financing with complicated and inconsistent terms can create a mess that professional investors may decide is not worth the trouble. The moral of the story is to think ahead, plan for the future, and understand not only what your current investors need but also what future investors will require.

3. *Insufficient authorized shares, which necessitate going back to shareholders to increase the number.* Companies should be capitalized with enough shares to carry them through several rounds of financing. Many people get authorized and issued shares confused or assume they mean the same thing. Authorized shares are the total number of shares a company has or may issue, and do not represent actual ownership. Only issued shares represent ownership. (See the Glossary in Appendix 1 for a more thorough definition of authorized shares.) Sophisticated private equity investors, angels, and venture capitalists would prefer to see a company with 50,000,000 authorized shares rather than 50,000.

This gives it the flexibility to do numerous rounds of financing without continually going back to existing shareholders to authorize more shares. Also, don't forget psychology of numbers. People feel like they are actually getting a real piece of a company when they are issued 10,000 shares instead of 10 shares, even though both may represent 5 percent of the company, since ownership is based on issued shares.

4. *Previous financing rounds that may require offering rescission rights.* As discussed in Chapter Three, private equity offerings must have an exemption from federal and state registration requirements. For instance, if you sold shares of stock in your company to ten people who are not accredited investors (as defined in Regulation D of the Securities Act of 1933) and failed to provide them with all information required under state and federal securities laws, you would be obligated to offer them rescission rights, which means to promise to repay their investment if they want out. By the time that question arises, however, the initial investment is long spent on growing the company— making rescission very difficult to deal with.

5. *Large warrant issuance for a bank loan or line of credit.* Warrants are the right to purchase stock in a company at a future time (or for a period of time) at a certain price. Because of the inherent risk in providing loans or extending lines of credit to young companies, banks will often require not only personal guarantees and security on these instruments but also additional consideration through the issuance of warrants. Investors do not want commercial institutions with impersonal policies to have any real stake in a company. Even 1 or 2 percent potential ownership through warrant exercise (conversion into shares upon payment of price per share) will raise a red flag for investors.

6. *Debt secured with founder's share ownership or the company's intellectual property.* Again, investors do not want debt relationships driving corporate decisions. Nor do they want the company losing key assets through noncompliance.

7. *An inappropriately sized option pool.* Most investors will insist on a stock option plan that provides employees, directors, advisers, and contractors with a non-cash method of payment for services. These options can also provide an incentive for employees to commit themselves to growing the company through earning

ownership. At a very early stage, the pool will be large because you have many hires to make, but you do not want to make the pool too large. While there are no hard-and-fast rules, a start-up company that still needs to place many key hires should allocate somewhere around 25 percent and possibly up to 30 percent of common stock to an option pool.

As an example, Exhibit 6.1 provides a corporate share structure for a start-up/seed stage company with sufficient capitalization for future financings, as well as an option pool.

COMMON VERSUS PREFERRED. As noted, founders generally receive common stock, and employees receive common stock or options to purchase common stock. Friends and family typically receive common stock as well. In most cases the first round of preferred stock issuance is with professional investors such as angels. Unlike "love money" from friends and family, angels and other professional investors require certain superior rights, preferences, and privileges for their investment. This also gives the angel investors a superior position to other investors upon liquidation. Some angel investors use convertible notes (which convert into preferred stock upon the business achieving a certain benchmark or subsequent financing), which still carry these superior rights on liquidation to common stock. In other words, angels get paid first—before friends, family, and founders.

Along with requiring an investment vehicle that has superior rights, angel investors may want rights to purchase additional stock at their discretion. While options may give the right to purchase stock in the future, they are primarily intended for employees, board members, and consultants (and are almost always for common stock). Warrants are the vehicle of choice to give investors the right to purchase stock at some future time at an agreed-upon price. Nothing necessarily prohibits offering an investor stock options, but because of the manner in which option plans are set up and are traditionally used as a form of compensation, options are more appropriate for non–investor-related transactions.

Options provide an incentive for employees and others to put an additional level of effort into their work to build value in the company and consequentially in their options, which represent future ownership in the company. Contrast this with warrants, which are usually considered tradable and are not attached to the party receiving the

Exhibit 6.1   Corporate Structure for Great Starts, Inc.

Initial Capitalization:
50,000,000 total authorized shares in Articles of Incorporation or Charter
35,000,000 designated as common shares in Articles of Incorporation or Charter
15,000,000 designated as preferred shares in Articles of Incorporation or Charter

Founders:
Craig Blond: 4,000,000 issued common shares
Rita Chambers: 4,000,000 issued common shares

Therefore, when the company is first formed, Craig and Rita own 100 percent of Great Starts, Inc., 50 percent each, because they own all of the issued shares. Liken authorized shares to a line of credit. You may have an LOC for $50,000, but if you have drawn down $10,000, you owe only $10,000 rather than $50,000.

Now, Craig and Rita decide to create an option plan for their employees, current and future. They reserve 15 percent or 5,250,000 shares of common stock for the option plan. Now those shares cannot be used for other purposes, as they must remain available as the shares underlying option issuance. They issue 200,000 options for common stock to each of their four employees. At the time of the option issuance, Rita and Craig still own 100 percent of the company because options are a right to purchase stock, not actual stock. Until the options are exercised by paying the per-share price, the employees have no actual ownership or rights incident to stock ownership, such as voting rights. Now suppose one employee, Shay O'Brien, exercises his options and acquires 200,000 shares of Great Starts, Inc. The ownership looks like this:

Craig Blond:	4,000,000	48.78 percent ownership (4,000,000/8,200,000)
Rita Chambers:	4,000,000	48.78 percent ownership (4,000,000/8,200,000)
Shay O'Brien:	200,000	2.44 percent ownership (200,000/8,200,000)
Total:		8,200,000 outstanding or issued shares

Finally, Great Starts does an angel investment round at a valuation of $1,000,000. They issue preferred stock shares at $0.50 per share, or a total of 2,000,000 preferred stock shares. Because preferred stock can convert into common stock, Great Starts must also reserve the number of common shares underlying the preferred shares for possible future conversion. In this example, the conversion is 1:1 (which is quite typical), so Great Starts must set aside 2,000,000 common stock shares. Because the angel investment round is for actual shares, not options or warrants, the preferred shares are considered in calculating ownership.

Now the ownership looks like this:

Craig Blond:	4,000,000	39.22 percent ownership (4,000,000/10,200,000)
Rita Chambers:	4,000,000	39.22 percent ownership (4,000,000/10,200,000)
Shay O'Brien:	200,000	1.95 percent ownership (200,000/10,200,000)
Angel investors:	2,000,000	19.61 percent ownership (2,000,000/10,200,000)
Total:		10,200,000 outstanding or issued shares

warrant. As such, warrants work well to provide additional value for angels, who take the highest risk of professional financing by investing at the earliest stage of a company's development.

Based on this understanding of the need for various stock structures, set up your company with sufficient common and preferred stock. Remember that you must reserve common stock for any issued preferred stock in contemplation of possible conversion (preferred stock is rarely issued without the right of conversion). Therefore, remember to issue enough stock to cover your plans for both preferred and common.

OTHER ESSENTIALS FOR AN INVESTABLE COMPANY

Corporate structure has obvious and significant influence on investment decisions, but it isn't the only critical factor. Contractual relations and intellectual property ownership are among the many other factors which can make a great company or, conversely, limit any potential for investment.

Contracts

While you may not have landed your strategic distribution partner or have multiple customers, you still should have prepared certain essential agreements. As discussed earlier, make sure you have all your employees, including yourself, sign an employee confidentiality and inventions agreement. Your company needs to have clear ownership of everything from ideas to customer lists. Make sure everyone appreciates the importance of these documents and takes them seriously.

Have a standard non-disclosure agreement (NDA) and use it appropriately. Do not disclose confidential information to a third party (anyone outside your company) without an NDA in place. Appendix 2 is a sample NDA. Look at the list of possible confidential information; it is extensive and written to include nearly any conceivable form of confidential information. Also, be sure to mark information as confidential or proprietary to remind employees and third parties of the nature of such information. Remember, once you have disclosed important company information without protection, that information can be provided to anyone outside the company, including your competitors. Also, publicly disclosing information can prevent you from filing for a patent or claiming trade secret protection.

When speaking with potential investors, make sure your investment materials (primarily your presentation and business plan) are carefully tailored not to disclose actual intellectual property, but to reveal enough about your proprietary systems to entice them into further evaluating your company. Make sure all consultants have a consulting agreement that clearly articulates your company's ownership for all works completed on a for-hire basis and for all inventions. Make sure your company owns all intellectual property, including proprietary information.

Even purchase orders should have standard language regarding such topics as guarantees, return policies, shipping costs, and payment methods. Make sure your equipment leases are in order. In general, investors want to see that your company is being run in an orderly fashion, and you are safeguarding important information and protecting the company against liabilities through well-managed procedures and documentation.

Company Policies and Procedures

Along with contracts that help protect your company's assets, have procedures to ensure such protection. If your company relies on trade secrets for its competitive edge and unfair advantage in the marketplace, you must have proper policies and procedures in place to protect this valuable asset. Such policies make employees and others aware of the nature of your assets. In addition, proper confidentiality and trade secret procedures are critical in supporting any claim for damages should a competitor steal your trade secrets. Trade secrets can be quite broad, including formulas, complex code, manufacturing procedures, ingredients, and other critical aspects of your competitive advantage.

If your company's current and future assets include patents, trademarks, copyrights, and other intellectual property, you should have invention recordation policies and procedures. Make sure your employees keep clearly labeled invention and idea diaries that are dated every day to record their observations that may result in intellectual property. Also, to further protect your intellectual property, you may wish to institute a guest sign-in policy to alert third parties to an obligation of confidentiality.

FINANCIALS. In the financial area, policies and procedures abound for compliance with Generally Accepted Accounting Principles (GAAP) and internal controls on spending. For instance, many young companies require two signatures for any check over a certain amount to make sure the funds are being properly and judiciously spent. Lawrence Schwartz, founder and CEO of Stampede Brewing Co., counsels: "Young companies should spend the time and money, early on, to set up appropriate legal and accounting procedures. When your company goes into full gear you will forget about them, or simply not have the time. Then you are spending far more money and much wasted time trying to retrofit your business to operations." Please see Chapter Four for a detailed discussion of the essential financial documents.

INTELLECTUAL PROPERTY. Because intellectual property can be one of the few assets of a young company, you should have a good understanding of the various types of intellectual property and the process for protecting these precious assets. Securing ownership to the exclusion of others is often the primary competitive advantage a company has. Therefore, proper protection will affect your company's valuation and possibly even its suitability for investment. Trade secrets are also considered intellectual property, and in essence, are those aspects of a company that cannot be derived or discovered through examination of the product or technology and are better kept secret to prolong value. In contrast, patents provide protection similar to a monopoly for twenty years from filing, but in exchange you must tell the world all the secrets of your invention. Deciding how to protect your intellectual property can be very difficult, particularly the choice between patenting and keeping something as a trade secret. Hopefully, Table 6.1 will help you better understand the factors and scale for each.

The following questions and answers may help you better understand the complexities of intellectual property:

Patents. What is a patent? A patent is a right to exclude others from making, using, or selling your invention. Contrary to popular belief, a patent does not give the inventor or patent owner the right to practice the invention described in the patent. In fact, doing so may even infringe upon others' patent rights. The patent itself is a printed document that describes the full extent of the invention through the claims made for it.

CONSIDERATION	SHOULD PATENT →				→ SHOULD NOT PATENT
Possible claim scope	Very broad claims covering generic concept in new or pioneering field of technology	Broad claims will cover all reasonable alternative solutions	Specific claims cover your best solutions	Narrow claims limited to one of many solutions	No claims possible (cannot reverse engineer)
Possible use by competitor	Easily detected with no other solution practical for common problem (that is, easy to reverse engineer)	Not difficult to detect; other solutions require more development or are less satisfactory	Other solutions can be detected but are known to have limited uses	Competitive solutions are known and readily available	Detection impossible or better solutions are available
Possible use by your company	Presently in use and considered beneficial	Use in the near future likely	Use in the future possible	No company use planned or likely	Doubtful use by anyone
Possible licensing income	License presently in effect and licensee wants patent	Active licensing prospect requires patent filing	Good potential for licensing	Little royalty likely to result from patent	No real expectation of royalty income or trading value
Possible effect if similar patent claims obtained by third party	Patent would be easily enforced with great expense to your company and settlement unlikely	Royalties to other patent holder would adversely affect your profits	Reasonable royalty would be possible with moderate effect on your profits	Nominal royalties will have little effect on your profits	No chance that patent would be enforced

Table 6.1 Criteria for Determining Patent Action

Are there different kinds of patents? Yes, patents come in three types:

Utility patents relate to new and useful processes, machines, articles of manufacture, or compositions of matter. This is the most common type of patent and what most people think of when referring to a patent. *Design patents* relate to new, original, visible, and ornamental (nonutilitarian) designs for an article of manufacture. *Plant patents* may be granted on asexually reproduced, distinct, and new varieties of plants.

How long does patent protection last? Generally, the patent term is twenty years from the date on which the application is filed with the U.S. Patent and Trademark Office. U.S. patents are effective only within the United States, U.S. territories, and U.S. possessions. This means that obtaining a U.S. patent entitles you to prevent others from making, using, or selling your patented invention only in the United States. You must file for separate patents in each country where you would like to maintain patent protection.

Can an inventor lose the right to file for a patent? Unfortunately, yes. Several actions can cause the loss of the ability to file for patent protection (or bar patentability) if they occur prior to filing a patent application, including commercial use of the invention, publication, or public disclosure of the invention. Because matters that can lead to bars on patentability can be very complicated, err on the side of caution and consult with competent patent counsel early in the process.

Trademarks. What is a trademark or service mark? A trademark is a word, symbol, or device used in trade to indicate the source of the goods and to distinguish them from the goods of others. As a result, trademarks create a marketing advantage through consumer awareness and association. A service mark is the same as a trademark except that it identifies and distinguishes the source of a service rather than a product.

What are trademark rights? Trademark rights may be used to prevent others from using a confusingly similar mark, but not to prevent others from making the same goods or from selling the same goods or services under a clearly different mark.

Is registration of my mark required? No. Actual use of a trademark in commerce can establish rights in the mark, without registration. However, the rights are not as strong and could be limited by someone registering the same or a confusingly similar mark in good faith. The rights outside of federal registration are called common law rights.

What rights are associated with a federally registered trademark? Federal trademark registration on the Principal Register (the primary federal registration) provides three main advantages:

- National ownership of the mark and the corresponding exclusive right to use the mark nationwide in connection with the goods or services listed in the registration
- The ability to use ® next to the trademark as indication of federal registration
- Rights related to bringing an action against infringers

When can I use the trademark symbols TM, SM and ®? If you want to claim rights on a mark (and the mark is not registered to another party), you may use the "TM" (trademark) or "SM" (service mark) designation to alert the public to your claim. You may do so regardless of whether you have filed an application with the U.S. Patent and Trademark Office. However, you may only use the federal registration symbol (®) after the Trademark Office actually registers a mark, and not while an application is pending. Also, you may use the registration symbol with the mark only on or in connection with the goods or services listed in the federal trademark registration.

Copyright. What is a copyright? Copyright gives protection to authors of "original works of authorship" that are in a tangible form, published or unpublished. Therefore, because of the tangible form requirement, a speech (orally spoken) is not copyrightable, but the electronic record or written copy is copyrightable. Works of authorship can be in numerous forms, including writings, computer software, architectural works, musical works, pantomimes, dramatic works, and motion pictures. The Copyright Act generally gives the owner of a copyright the exclusive right to reproduce the work, prepare derivative works, distribute copies, and publicly perform or display the work. The copyright protects the form of expression rather than the subject matter of the writing. For example, a description of a machine could be copyrighted, but this would only prevent others from copying the description; it would not prevent others from writing a description of their own or from making and using the machine. Copyrights are registered by the Copyright Office of the Library of Congress.

Why should I register my work if copyright protection is automatic? Registration is recommended for a number of reasons. Many choose to register their works because they wish to have their copyright a matter of public record and have a certificate of registration. Registered works may be eligible for statutory damages and attorneys' fees in successful litigation.

Who is an author? Under the copyright law, the creator of the original work is its author. The author is also the owner of copyright unless there is a written agreement by which the author assigns the copyright to another person or entity.

What is a "work made for hire"? Although the general rule is that the person who creates the work is its author, there is an exception to that principle for a *work made for hire,* which is a work prepared by an employee within the scope of employment, or a work specially ordered or commissioned in certain specified circumstances. When a work qualifies as a work made for hire, the employer or commissioning party is considered to be the author.

How long does copyright last? For works created after January 1, 1978, copyright protection will endure for the life of the author plus an additional 70 years. For anonymous and pseudonymous works and works made for hire, the term will be 95 years from the year of first publication or 120 years from the year of creation, whichever expires first. The Sonny Bono Copyright Term Extension Act, signed into law on October 27, 1998, amends the provisions concerning duration of copyright protection. Under this Act, terms of copyright are generally extended for an additional twenty years.

Do trademarks, copyrights, and patents protect the same things? No. Trademarks, copyrights, and patents all differ. Table 6.2 compares the relative attributes of these different forms of intellectual property protection.

Employee Compensation

Start-ups are expected to attract the best and the brightest, but not pay them anywhere close to their value. Just like the founders, the early employees should be willing to take a minimal salary in exchange for stock and stock options. Investors want all employees to focus on building value. As a result, investors consider stock options an important—and often essential—part of employee compensation. The opportunity to own a piece of the company provides an incentive that, in theory, will be worth far more than ordinary compensation. Keep employee salaries at a level competitive with other start-up companies, not with

Forms of Protection	Subject Matter Protected	Sample Items Protected	Scope of Protection
Utility patent	Machines, processes, articles of manufacture, compositions of matter, and improvements thereof	Products, chemicals, software, manufacturing processes	Right to exclude others from manufacturing, using or selling
Design patent	Ornamental design or appearance—refers to nonutilitarian exterior features	Appearance of medical instruments, lamps, and any other object	Right to exclude others from manufacturing, using or selling
Copyright	Literary, musical, dramatic, pictorial, graphic, sculptural works, motion pictures, sound recordings, and so on	Books, artwork, photographs, software, databases, graphics, advertising copy, text	Exclusive right to reproduce the work, prepare derivative works, distribute copies, perform the work publicly, and display the work publicly
Trademark	Words, names, symbols, and devices used to identify products and services	Words, logos, shapes, nonfunctional container and product shapes, distinctive color schemes	Right to prevent use by others likely to cause confusion, and to prevent dilution

Table 6.2   Comparison of Intellectual Property

publicly traded companies. Talented people who are willing to take a risk on you in building value in your young company have the right kind of entrepreneurial spirit.

As mentioned earlier, unlike straight stock, stock options are a right to purchase stock in the future at a set price. Options can be either incentive, that is, *qualified* stock options, which can only be granted to employees, or nonqualified stock options, which can be granted to directors, advisers, and consultants, as well as employees. There are accounting and tax differences between the two types, and you should consult your tax attorney or accountant to better understand the details. In addition, you should consult an attorney experienced in stock options to set up all relevant documents and handle all necessary corporate activities to put a stock option plan in place.

The timing for setting up your option pool is also important. Recall from earlier discussions that the founder of a seed/start-up company should aside around 20 to 30 percent of the authorized common stock for an option pool for later granting to employees, directors, and others. Many investors will insist that you establish your option pool prior to their investment in order to avoid the dilution of their ownership. You need to set aside shares for options because the shares must be reserved for possible exercise of the options, upon maturity, into the underlying shares, by paying the option exercise price.

As the founder and majority owner of your start-up, you should follow another truism of employee compensation: always pay your employees even if you don't get paid. Unless you have an up-front agreement with your employees, do not damage their good will by failing to meet your payroll. Despite their willingness to bet on the long-term success of the company partially through their hard work, it is still your company and your dream. Just as you are up-front with investors, be up-front with employees as well. Let them know the status of the company; keep them informed of setbacks and mutually celebrate accomplishments. You are building a culture as much as a company.

Board of Directors and Board of Advisers

Many angel investors require companies to have a board of directors or a board of advisers, or both. The board of directors has a fiduciary responsibility to the shareholders and is elected by the shareholders. The members help decide the strategic direction of the company. In start-up/seed companies, directors provide critical expertise in many areas not adequately staffed—finance, operations, manufacturing, design, marketing, and so on. As indicated earlier, investors want to see nonemployee directors. Individuals considered leaders in their field or with known expertise who are willing to roll up their sleeves and help you think through growing your company could provide you with invaluable third-party validation.

You can organize advisers in a board structure or have a single relationship with each. Regardless, advisers, just like directors, can provide significant value. Do not simply add your advisers' names to your company's business plan, use them. Many investors will ask what each director and adviser is contributing to your business. You simply cannot get enough outside support, comments, and direction. So talk to people, use your advisers, ask friends to read over your business plan, and practice your presentation. Do not try to do this on your own. Soloing just does not work in creating a company; it takes a team.

Compensate your directors and advisers with stock options. People experienced with start-up companies do not expect to be compensated in cash for these board roles. Some advisers will require cash if they are acting as consultants, providing more than general advice. Just as there is no hard-and-fast rule about the percentage of stock to set aside for option plans, so too there are no exact numbers for option issuance to directors and advisers. Some companies consider 0.5 percent to 1 percent as more than adequate long-term compensation for directors and half that amount for advisers, though the percentages vary greatly. The percentage depends on many factors, including the importance of the respective roles in the company, the industry (often advisers are more valuable than directors for biotech companies), the market value, and trends in the industry.

Preparing for investors can be a lengthy process, but if you execute it properly, you have a much greater chance of securing your professional angel investor. Taking care of these matters does not happen in a vacuum, but in an orderly sequence with all other activities associated with securing investors. Most entrepreneurs put their company in order while networking, polishing their presentation, mapping out the marketing plan, securing a first customer, and answering the phone. Juggling all of these tasks and more while still looking calm and controlled is the mark of a true entrepreneur.

Now that you are well on the road to being prepared for your investor, how do you make the match?

CHAPTER SEVEN

Making the Match

Y ou now have an appreciation of the significant role angels play in early-stage financing, as well as of the basic types of private equity financing and the usual terms for it. You've made a start at understanding your funding requirements into the future and how to prepare your company for professional investors. But you haven't spoken to anyone yet. The next phase in preparing to engage prospective angel investors is communicating everything about your company. How do you tell your company's complete story in twenty-five pages? Or in one minute when you run into a potential investor in an elevator? You need to communicate to investors through a variety of methods depending on the investor interaction opportunity.

These are the four most important investor communication tools you need to have well developed:

- Elevator pitch
- Investor presentation
- Executive summary
- Business plan, including detailed pro-forma financials

From these four, you can create almost any communication an investor needs to hear. Other documents are also valuable, but they are developed for reasons other than investor communication: Product fact sheets and flyers, advertisements, articles, awards and recognitions, testimonials, and the like. But the four essential communication tools must be polished and complete before any meeting with potential investors. You may be asked at any time for a quick summary of your business (elevator pitch and executive summary), or to give a visual and discussion overview of your company (investor presentation) or deliver a detailed discussion of your company (business plan).

Once you're ready, never miss an opportunity to make a connection with a potential investor or referral source. Take advantage of these situations whether spontaneous or staged. Make sure you get contact information from your audience and give them your business card. Never step out of your house without business cards, even to coach a Pee-Wee Football game. Opportunities occur when you least expect them.

ELEVATOR PITCH: YOUR TAG LINE IN A PARAGRAPH

You really can explain your company in sixty seconds. Your elevator pitch is an articulate, concise statement of your idea, business model, company solution, marketing strategy, and competition, designed to be delivered to potential investors during an elevator ride. While it may seem difficult, you can do it. Creating a great tag line is a place to start: a one-sentence statement of the essence of your company, which should be based on your mission statement. Once you have your tag line, a way to create your elevator pitch is to use a whiteboard and write down your tag line, vision, and four to six bullet points about your company. Now take this information and see what you can combine; underline the essential words and key phrases. From this condensed information, draft your paragraph. Capturing a prospective investor's interest is key, so you need to communicate what makes your company the one to invest in: the size of your market and the strategy you'll use to approach it, along with your competitive advantage.

Test your new statement out on friendly audiences and individuals familiar with your company to make sure you have covered all essential components. Next, test it on those unfamiliar with your company to find out if your brief description is simple, straightforward, immediately understandable, and exciting. Modify the statement as necessary. It needs to explain why you are a perfect match for potential angel investors, and how you will meet their goals for a robust return on their investment.

INVESTOR PRESENTATIONS

Your first impression is your investor's most important memory.

Guy Kawasaki, founder of Garage Technology Ventures and an inspiring author and speaker, has a rule for investor presentations: 10/20/30. Your visuals should be limited to ten slides that you can present in no more than twenty minutes, and the font size should be at least thirty points. Great rules to live by. As hard as it may be to imagine, you can describe your company in ten slides and twenty minutes. Going through the process of condensing your presentation makes you review and revise, again and again, both your assumptions and your messages. You will discover two or three essential attributes of your company. Approach content development from the investor's perspective.

Bob Goff, founder and president of Sierra Angels, emphasizes the need to pitch the plan, not the product. In the first couple of minutes of a presentation, he wants to know six specific things, in this order:

1. What business the company is in

2. What important need it fills

3. Why the solution is superior to the competition

4. Why the plan and management team are credible

5. How the management team's relevant experience will influence the execution of the plan

6. Why the plan is a superior opportunity for the investors, compared to the other deals under consideration

Remember, investors want to know, first and foremost, how you will make them money—what exit strategy they can look forward to. What is their realistic return on investment (ROI)? And what is the timetable for their exit?

Content of Investor Presentations

Getting your slide presentation right is very difficult, and everyone will have an opinion on how to make it better. You should practice your presentation several times before friendly audiences, experienced and inexperienced. How you present yourself and handle the fundraising process is a key indicator to potential investors of how you will handle customers, strategic partners, new hires, and the other challenges of running a business. You must have a complete presentation that covers all essential components and is also readily understandable by potential investors without any industry expertise. Never assume anyone understands your market, technology, or industry, and always assume your audience is intelligent and savvy with investment experience. Remember, you get one chance to make a good first impression.

Many angels and angel groups have set information they require in all presentations; make sure you understand these information needs. You can often obtain this information from angel organization Web sites and from individual angels simply by asking. Nothing is absolute with investor presentations, but following the structure outlined in the following paragraphs should give you a strong first presentation for beta testing on your safe audiences.

SLIDE #1: COMPANY INTRODUCTION
Content:

  a. Company name—with your slogan if you have one

  b. Your name and position

  c. One-sentence "essence of your company"—what you do, the market, and your solution

Objective:

  Set the stage for your presentation so your audience understands who you are, what your company does, and in general who your customers will be and the problem or pain you are solving for them. Most important, this slide should capture their attention and pique their interest, so they're ready to hear more.

SLIDE #2: MARKET
Content:

  a. Who are your customers?

  b. What need creates the market demand? Why your solution? What is your value proposition?

c. What is the size of the market?

d. Quantify your opportunity.

e. Explain how the market is growing and why.

Objective:

You want to define your customers so that your audience can relate to them and appreciate their needs. Investor audiences want to understand the customers' specific problem or need, and why the problem is important—a hindrance to maximizing a customer's business. In sizing the market, reference third-party, independent evidence. If you have broad-platform technology, with multiple market opportunities, mention the others, but focus on the first market you plan to pursue and why.

SLIDE #3: TECHNOLOGY OR PRODUCT
Content:

a. How is your product a solution to market needs?

b. Explain your technology or product from the customer's perspective.

c. Will the customer see your product as either an entire solution or the main, critical component in a multi-sourced solution? Identify your product's value-add.

Objective:

Rather than focusing your presentation on the novel and innovative characteristics of your technology or your product, focus on the solution you provide. Through this approach, you will answer questions on what your product does, why customers would buy your product, and what makes your product unique. If you have proprietary technology, say so. If you have patents or patent applications—list them and then speak to their value.

You are highlighting product or technology benefits and superiority from a customer solution perspective. If there are customer system, behavior, or procedure conversions required, make sure to mention these and how and why they will occur.

SLIDE #4: WHAT MAKES YOU SUPERIOR TO THE COMPETITION; BARRIERS
Content:

Who are your competition? Again, approach from the customer's perspective. If you have defined the market as X, don't do comparisons to companies in market Y.

One method of communicating competitive positioning is a competitive analysis matrix or four-square diagram, comparing your company with the competition on two leading factors. The lower left box typically represents lowest rankings for both factors, and the upper right box the highest rankings for both factors. Place each company measured in the appropriate location within the boxes based on X and Y axis factor scaling.

Objective:

When considering competition, think like your customers. How would they categorize you? What are their needs? What problems are you solving for them? The fundamental objectives for this slide are to show why you have the superior solution for solving critical customer needs, to identify the big players in your field and show your persuasive differentiators, and to explain how you will keep your competitive edge over time. If customers will have to make behavioral or system conversions to use your product, how will you get them to change? Also, if you are successful, how will you prevent a bigger, better-known, or better-funded company from creating a competitive product and grabbing your market?

SLIDE #5: MARKET APPROACH
Content:
   a. Sales: Explain how you propose to reach your market. What channels of distribution will you use? If you are using third-party distributors, what sales incentives will you use? Is your sales cycle seasonal? How long is your sales cycle?

   b. Support: How do you plan to provide customer support before, during, and after the sale? Access to information and rapid response are crucial at all steps.

Objective:

At the end of the day, sales are the true evidence of success. Your financials will show your revenue projections (which directly relate to sales), so how will you drive those sales? Make your market approach and sales program simple for prospective investors and customers to understand. Investors need to readily grasp your customer awareness and buying stimulus programs and systems—from the salesperson's and customer's perspective. How are you conditioning the market to receive the product?

SLIDE #6: OPERATIONS; BUSINESS GROWTH STRATEGY
Content:
   a. How is your product or technology scalable?

  b. How is your business scalable?

  c. How will you manufacture products at a competitive price?

  d. Where are you in the product development and commercial launch time line?

  e. What is left to accomplish and when?

  f. Are there any risks or challenges to commercialization?

Objective:

    Technology can be very exciting and products can clearly meet a significant market need, but if you cannot make commercially useful quantities at attractive prices, you have only an interesting idea. Recognize any necessary strategic partnerships, licenses, or contracts (such as manufacturing or distribution) needed to achieve success.

SLIDE #7: MANAGEMENT

Content:

  a. Previous companies, positions, and relevant accomplishments for key management.

  b. Key positions that still need to be filled, and timing of filling positions.

  c. Background and qualifications (in general terms) of prospective hires whose identity can not yet be revealed.

  d. Members of the board of directors and the board of advisers. Describe their general level of involvement and highlight any strategic contributions.

Objective:

    Investors want to know that key management has relevant experience, knowledge, or background. Therefore, leadership and entrepreneurial experience should be emphasized for the CEO, while technical expertise and impressive credentials should be noted for the chief technology officer.

    Investors put considerable weight on the caliber of board members. An industry leader's willingness to participate on a board speaks volumes as third-party validation of you and your company.

SLIDE #8: FINANCIAL PROJECTIONS

Content:

  a. What is your road to profitability?

  b. How big are the potholes?

  c. What is your time line?

Give broad five-year financial projections in a table format with annual total product units sold, revenues, cost of goods, gross margin, SG&A, pretax profit, and cash flow. Show when and how you will be cash-flow positive and ultimately profitable.

Objective:

You are showing well-considered financial projections. Investors want to know you have realistic projections for market adoption, timing, and product pricing. Investors also want to understand, from a financial perspective, if and when you will need follow-on financing and the milestones that will be accomplished with each funding round. Different angels may want other numbers in the initial presentation— so ask.

SLIDE #9: MILESTONES

Content:

You may wish to use a Gantt chart to highlight key steps and milestones, including key hires, product development and funding needs, and timing. Show a stepwise, methodical process to success. Start with earlier activities, even showing the date of company formation. Include key financial milestones such as prior and subsequent funding rounds and revenue targets.

Objective:

The primary objective for this slide is to communicate your understanding of the steps to profitability, and to show how you plan to reach it.

SLIDE #10: FUNDING SOUGHT AND EXIT STRATEGY

Content:

a. Funding sought: How much are you raising in this round? Any previous rounds? What is the timing? Have you already raised part of this round? If so, how much did you raise, and by what investment vehicle (debt or equity—common or preferred)? If not already shown, your future funding needs and timing. Is this a debt or equity offering? What was the valuation on any prior financing rounds? What is the pre-money valuation for this round?

b. Exit Strategy: Give your best estimate of timing to exit and liquidity for investors. Recognize that a merger or acquisition is the most probable exit strategy, unless your revenues and market sector strongly suggest an IPO opportunity. Give suggestions of appropriate potential acquirers.

Objective:

Now that you have the audience excited about your business and future opportunities, let them know how they can participate. Investors want to know your timing for due diligence. They also want to know the percentage of ownership resulting from this financing round.

At the end of the day, investors want to know how and when they will realize a return on their investment. They also want to know the exit strategy is well considered and the long-term target.

Once you've covered the basics, leave the participation info on the screen. Say thank you, then restate your name and contact information. If you have a follow-up meeting date set, give that information. Restate your slogan. Ask for questions.

TEN-MINUTE PRESENTATIONS. The Alliance of Angels, the first angel organization in Seattle, which has an impressive investment record and member list, has a great diagram on the ten-minute pitch, shown in Figure 7.1. The diagram gives a nice perspective on relative time spent on each subject and an alternative approach to the order of your slides.

The slides outlined in this chapter and the diagram in Figure 7.1 work well for nearly any size audience. How you present—from sitting at a table with one other person beside you to standing at the front of a packed room—is mechanical.

The Presentation

Once you know what to present, how do you present it? Remember, potential investors are going to judge your whole approach to business by your presentation. Find out the amount of time you have, the meeting and presentation format, the possible room setup, the equipment you may need to bring and if you can bring other materials, products, or anything else. In other words, find out all audience expectations. If you're thinking of video or multimedia presentations, coordinate with the forum employees. Find out beforehand if you can bring another member of your team along, if you wish to do so. Consider developing a set of questions and answers for your own use, to help you prepare for what the audience may ask.

Finally, show your passion. Angels invest in you. They enjoy being part of a company and its growth. Your passion, excitement, and energy are infectious and will remind your prospective angel investors of their own heady days of building a company.

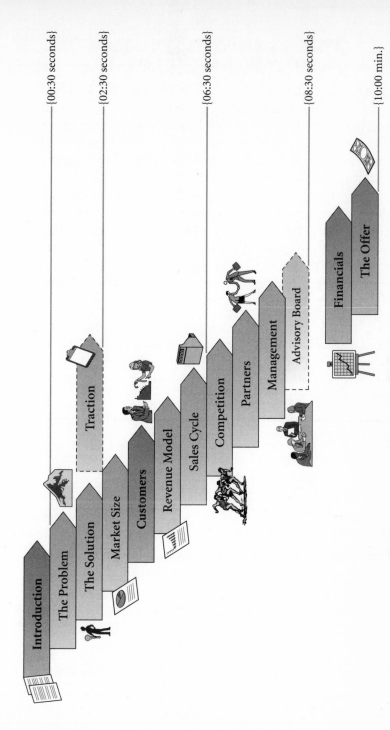

{00:30 seconds}
{02:30 seconds}
{06:30 seconds}
{08:30 seconds}
{10:00 min.}

Introduction
The Problem
The Solution
Market Size
Customers
Revenue Model
Sales Cycle
Competition
Partners
Management
Advisory Board
Financials
The Offer
Traction

Figure 7.1   Ten-Minute Pitch Time Line

COLLEEN STONE ON SPEAKING WITH POTENTIAL ANGEL INVESTORS

Colleen Stone, founder and CEO of InSpa, offers the following advice: "If you are going to have angel investors, do not approach them until you have refined your ideas and business proposal into a simple, straightforward, easy-to-grasp presentation. This is not to say angels are dumb; quite the contrary, angels make exceptional advisers and mentors because of their experience and background. Rather, angels are not going to take raw data and turn it into analysis. Angels will take you at face value on the size of the market, potential, et cetera, so make sure those are verifiable. Simply put, if you don't have your elevator pitch and presentation down cold, you are not ready for prime time."

Presentation Dos and Don'ts

Proofread everything and have a second set of eyes look over the documents, too. Don't let a single typo slip past; investors are likely to take it as a sign of slipshod work in your whole company plan.

Make sure your format, font size, and slide layout is consistent throughout your presentation.

Don't read your slides—have bullet points only and add content and context through your presentation.

Include your company name and logo on each slide. Use a unique background developed for your company, one that you plan to use for building brand.

Bring copies of your slides and executive summary. If product samples are practical and permitted, bring them along.

Don't use multiple flowery adjectives or statements like "world's leading," "the first and only solution," "massive market share potential," and the like—investors will be skeptical unless you can prove such claims through third-party evidence.

During the presentation, if you are asked a question, briefly answer it and then indicate you will expand on that point in a minute. Do not just say you will get to it later.

Don't spend time explaining your technology in great detail. Investors want to understand how you plan to make them money—which means sales—which means meeting customer needs in a competitively advantageous manner.

Always have enough business cards, hand them out shamelessly, and collect as many business cards as possible in return.

The bottom line? Be prepared.

BUSINESS PLAN AND EXECUTIVE SUMMARY

A business plan tells your company's story; it is your most comprehensive and dynamic communication tool. It gives investors a road map for your company, from incorporation to exit. It states your value proposition for the investor, customer, partner, and employee. An okay business plan takes a week to pull together; a great business plan takes several weeks, is reviewed by many people, is rewritten numerous times, and is always considered a work in progress. This is not to say you submit a partial document to investors. Rather it means you are open to suggestions and comments about fine-tuning and advancing your company, and the changes you adopt are reflected in your business plan. So you don't just write a business plan in June and expect it to be current in November. You must continually update the plan to reflect the actuality of your business.

As Bob Geras, a successful businessman as well as an active participant in the Chicago venture capital and angel communities for more than forty years, puts it, "Any entrepreneur with an ounce of common sense will be sure that this document puts his best foot forward and tells his story in a well-organized, concise, and believable fashion. It often will indicate whether the promoter [meaning the entrepreneur] has thought through his proposed course of action thoroughly, analyzed the potential pitfalls, and detailed a credible plan to cope with them." Never underestimate the power and value of your executive summary and business plan. These documents are your face, words, and window to the public. If you do not spend the time creating the best business plan you can afford, investors will read it as an indication that you lack the intense commitment to your idea that would give them a chance of making money on it.

What's in a Business Plan?

Libraries, bookstores, and the Internet are replete with books and information on how to build a business plan. You can also hire professionals to help you draft your plan, though be sure to do background research on them so they fit into your larger group of advisers and provide further value down the road. Here is a condensed overview of business plan essentials:

1. **EXECUTIVE SUMMARY.** Your business plan in two pages. Your executive summary must be a synopsis of your business because it needs to work as a separate, stand-alone document. Quite often, investors will read your executive summary as an initial introduction to your company. Many angel organizations will take only executive summaries when considering companies for presentation. In writing your executive summary, focus on the points you include in your full slide presentations, whether it runs ten or twenty minutes. Some entrepreneurs find it easier to write the entire business plan first and then go back to the executive summary, which makes sense since writing the entire business plans helps sharpen your perception of the essential, key strengths of your business and plan.

Focus on market and customer definitions (market description and market need for your product or technology), competitive analysis, your distinct advantages (how your company is uniquely qualified to fulfill market needs), brief financials, management overview, and exit strategy. Don't worry about operations, unless your technology would suggest large commercialization issues such as scalability or potential patent infringement. Don't worry about company history unless you have accomplishments such as landing a first major customer, entering a foreign market, resolving technology difficulties, or getting patents issued; then by all means, highlight the milestones accomplished prior to this funding round. Early accomplishments give prospective investors comfort about your abilities and sixth sense about the market, as well as your ability to make progress on little funding.

Remember, many investors will read only your executive summary to see if their interest is piqued. You want to whet their appetite and interest in these two pages. As Laurence Briggs of InvestINForum in Dallas so eloquently puts it: "We are not looking for an opportunity— we are looking at opportunities." Angels see dozens and dozens of business plans, so yours needs to stand out starting with the first sentence.

2. COMPANY HISTORY. The date you started your business has relevance, but what you want to emphasize are any accomplishments to date. Your company's past track record is the best indicator of a bright future. You can state your formation date, office locations, and legal structure in one sentence. Spend time discussing accomplishments that give a nice introduction to the company.

3. INDUSTRY DISCUSSION. Make sure you understand and define your relevant market. Avoid large, generic market size numbers. Do not overestimate market size or make projections overly aggressive. As noted earlier, a software company focused on privacy and security applications, for example, should not talk about the entire software industry; it should stick to the part the company could capture if it owned 100 percent of its relevant market. Also provide information on market trends showing the increased demand for your product or technology, along with increased market pain such as the billions of dollars lost each year to fraud your technology could uncover. Trend discussions should focus on prospective numbers, but historical data can be important to set the stage by describing a definitive increase in market need, particularly if the market growth has been recent, say in the last one to five years.

Industry discussion is an excellent section in which to provide third-party validation through references to studies by professional market research firms. Then explain how your company will provide the preferred market solution. If you have broad-platform technology with cross-industry applications—perhaps your security and privacy software may have applications for wireless technology as well as Internet—spell them out. Identify all markets, then explain which industry vertical you plan to address first and why. If your product is so new that you will be the first mover, say so—but you need not be the first mover in a particular market. In fact, being second can be advantageous, especially if the technology requires creating the market or changing customer habits, and your plan should make this point clear to potential investors.

4. CUSTOMER DEFINITION. You must show a crisp and clear understanding of your customers' needs. You are appealing to well-defined customer wants and needs, and the first market you choose must exemplify these characteristics. Describe customer decision-making processes and explain how your offering fits a customer's approach to

the market. Explain customer demographics and how you plan to appeal to those characteristics. Make sure you cite third-party independent sources for customer definitions and habits.

5. PRODUCT AND TECHNOLOGY. You need to provide a description of your product to give your prospective investor an appreciation of key attributes. Do not give a technical white paper. Instead, continue to focus on those aspects of your product or technology that meet customer wants and needs. If you have filed for patents, or better yet received issued patents, highlight these potential barriers to entry and unfair advantages over competition. Exclusive licenses can provide a significant competitive edge. Again, investors do not necessarily want to know how your product or technology works; they want to know why it will matter to the customer.

6. COMPETITIVE ANALYSIS. Your analysis of competition is a particularly tricky section because your definition of competition may differ from that of prospective investors and even from what your customers perceive. You must look at your company through these other lenses. It does not matter how slick your technology is if the customers don't want it. Make sure your list of competitors is complete and reflects your specific market. If you have only a few companies listed, investors may be concerned that the market is not big enough; if you list too many, then the market will look too saturated to support another entrant.

More important than identifying competitors is recognizing their strengths and weaknesses and the key factors for your competitive differentiation in the market. Again, use third-party information to portray an objective analysis—particularly when discussing competitors' weaknesses. In addition, you need to show barriers to entry and advantages your company has over the competition. Examples of useful advantages can include a world-class management team, proprietary or patented technology, key exclusive partnerships, being first to market with impediments or barriers to entry by competition, long-term contracts with major customers, and successes to date.

7. MARKETING PLAN. Very simply, the marketing plan explains how you will penetrate the market. How will the company promote its products? Will you need a strategic partnership for distribution? And what are the chances of securing the right agreement if you don't already have one in place? How will the products be priced? How will the products be delivered to the market? Internet (Web site), direct sales, distribution chain, retail outlet? The cost varies significantly depending on the distribution mechanism.

Just as important as promoting, selling, and distributing products is retaining customers. The easiest sale is a repeat sale. In the dot-com era, terms like *sticky* and *gooey* became popular because they were actually fairly descriptive of a desired attribute, getting and keeping customers. This retention will depend on after-sale performance and follow-on, so customer service, maintenance, and regular contact with customers are quite important.

8. OPERATIONS. This portion of your business plan focuses on execution. Operations relate to short-term goals such as completion of product development and scaling to commercial manufacturing levels, as well as long-term goals such as multinational expansion and effective outsourcing. The operations plan spells out how you are going to accomplish milestones, with execution squarely on the shoulders of management. It is useful to include a time-line chart showing each step to product launch and customer shipment, along with target due dates. Some entrepreneurs find it best to start with the end result and then work backward to define each step—each milestone needed to achieve the end result. Since accomplishing various end results involves actions such as acquisition of equipment, hiring employees, and further financing, make sure your financial plans are consistent with your operations plan.

9. MANAGEMENT TEAM. As noted elsewhere, the credibility of the founder and the initial management team is the number one factor for most angel investors. Keep the description of each member of key management to a brief paragraph—you can provide extensive résumés during due diligence. Emphasize industry experience, relevant background, prior relationships among team members, and start-up experience. At an early stage, you may have key functional areas missing from the team. This is acceptable so long as you recognize the need and describe key characteristics of the position and timing for hire. This section should also include a discussion of your board of directors and board of advisers. Many angel investors will not invest in companies lacking outside strategic advice and oversight. Having well-known or well-credentialed advisers adds credibility to your company,

gives third-party validation, and suggests you understand the value of outside advice and direction. Make sure you explain the respective roles of your advisers.

10. FINANCIAL PLAN. After the executive summary, many angels turn to the financials to see how you plan to make money and how you plan to grow the company. They want to know how you will use the proceeds, what funding you need to get to profitability, and whether you are thinking too pie-in-the-sky with aggressive, unrealistic financials. Angels can even be concerned if you seem too conservative in your numbers, suggesting you have tempered passion or you are pessimistic. Modest but realistic financials are fine, but it may mean your company is not appropriate for angel investors unless you have a creative mechanism for return on their investment.

All revenue streams should be included, along with their relative importance and timing. Make sure your financials are consistent with all other parts of your business plan. Discuss all key assumptions including operating margins, headcount, compensation and benefits, SG&A costs, market penetration rates, and cost of goods. All sources and timing of funding should be defined.

11. EXIT STRATEGY. Also known as "And they all lived happily ever after." All potential investors want to know how you plan to make them money. Describe your anticipated timing and likely method of providing liquidity. Do not just say "IPO or acquisition." Investors want to know you have thought about and will continue to plan for the most viable exit strategy. You may even wish to describe comparable companies and their eventual exit strategy to support your choice.

Your business plan should be concise and succinct. Anything more than twenty to twenty-five pages is unnecessary and probably won't be read. Reread, revise, review, get outside input—and do this all over again a number of times until anyone could pick up your business plan, understand your business proposition, and get excited about it. Investors will first read the executive summary to see if their interest is piqued, will then look at the financials to see if they seem reasonable, comprehensive, and likely to provide handsome profits, which would set the company up for an appropriate exit strategy. If they are still interested, then investors will read the rest of your business plan.

Side Note

As discussed elsewhere, do not ask prospective investors to sign a non-disclosure or confidentiality agreement (NDA) to see your business plan. Most angel investors will not sign an agreement at this stage. Only upon entering due diligence should you need an NDA.

Remember that you can choose among multiple business plan models, so if the outline presented here does not suit your needs or interests, find another one, or better yet, take what you consider the best of many sources. Just make sure that your business plan reflects your thoughts and plans for your company—your fingerprint. Sophisticated investors can tell if you have had a business plan written for you. Even if you use a consultant, make sure the business plan uses your voice.

One big overriding *don't* is the inclusion of numerous adjectives and meaningless statements. Use realistic terms. Sophisticated angel investors are not impressed with claims like *enormous, infinite, paradigm shift,* and *revolutionary,* because they know that 99 percent of all ideas are not, and the other 1 percent are likely to have difficulty with market acceptance. If you insist on using such terms and phrases, back them up with facts. Whether supporting an adjective or otherwise, use third-party statistics and references often to validate market and products. In fact, without third-party sources, your business plan will be weak and possibly unpersuasive. It isn't that investors don't trust you, but they expect you to be dogmatically enthusiastic about your company and will read anything you give them in that light. Let independent information support your statements.

Along with these must-have sections of a business plan, consider including some appendixes:

- A full set of financials (income statement, balance sheet, and cash flow statement)
- Some partnership or customer letters of commitment or endorsement
- Some product or technology drawings

HOW INVESTORS MAKE INVESTMENT CHOICES

Through your various interactions—from the brief encounters of elevator pitches to the full slide show on your business plan—you are portraying your personal interests and preferences as well as giving prospective investors a good understanding of your personality. Angel investing is personal. Angels are looking for a connection with you and your company on more than a financial level. This personal fit is more than simple compatibility, it is also alignment of goals. For instance, are you happy to have a company with ten employees? Do you feel unsure about growing your company because of control issues, either from an ownership standpoint or from that of making sure that operations reflect what you would choose to do? If so, your personality will probably not fit with angel investors. Big ideas, big markets, and big dreams match better because these represent traits essential for providing angels with a handsome return on their investment.

A strong dose of reality is also a telling factor for angel investors. Do you have a realistic understanding of your overall market and what portion you can capture in what time period? Do you clearly understand your competition? Are your financials realistic? Have you considered all potential costs, seasonal issues, timing of customer uptake, and further financial requirements? Do you have a contingency plan? And do you have a realistic valuation? Asking for a valuation higher than what angels consider reasonable for your stage of development can be an early deal killer. Prospective investors will ask themselves, If you are out of touch with reality on your valuation, how else are you unrealistic? Your revenue projections, product pricing, or product uptake? Today, few seed/start-up companies will support a valuation above $3 million, possibly $4 million at best. At this stage, you have no proof of market or technology. Angels are investing on your previous track record, their comfort with your capabilities, and their belief in your anticipated products or technology.

Making a match is not just from the angel investor's perspective. Are you ready for professional investors? Do you have the personality for receiving input from others, for sharing ownership in your company? Obviously, these are critical questions to ask yourself. Do not assume that you can just make it work. If you know that professional investors are right for you and that angel investors are preferable because of their characteristics, your funding desires, or your stage of development, you still need to make sure any given deal is a fit.

One fundamental point of compatibility is alignment of interests. Do you want passive investors? If your potential angel investor is interested in and will likely insist on a board position, or will be calling on you each week to find out status and provide input, you don't need the headache and the angel investor does not want the frustration of

NELSON GRAY ON MONEY

As Nelson Gray, a highly experienced angel investor in Scotland, puts it: "The first priority is how the company will make money. In other words, does the business plan work? Likewise, the management team's interests must be aligned with yours in driving the company toward a liquidity event. Entrepreneurs must keep their eye on the exit strategy not just creating a company to provide large salaries. Equally important is simply: Do you [the angel] like the management team? Compatibility is key as you will be working closely with the team over an extended period. Remember, angels don't have to invest—so make it work in all respects."

dealing with someone whose basic interests differ that much. Having a conversation about control with investors can be difficult if you have not picked up on their interests during the initial meetings. Nonetheless, you must make sure you have such a conversation prior to entering due diligence. In Chapter Eight, on the investment process, I point out that one of the steps prior to due diligence is agreement on basic investment terms. Such discussions help bring matters like investor involvement to the surface. You then have agreement on general investment terms, including the post-investment relationship.

Before entering due diligence, ask your investor some of the following questions:

- What is your expectation for your relationship with the company? Board seat, adviser, information only, executive position, periodic visits?
- Do you understand the risk of early-stage investing?
- What is your expectation on ROI (return on investment) and timing for liquidity?
- What is your background, expertise, experience?
- What connections can you share?
- What other skills can you provide the company?
- What additional capital could you attract?

- Are you anticipating and planning to invest more than once in the company? If so, do you expect a right of first refusal entitling you to invest before new investors?
- Why are you interested in investing in the company?

And if you have unique expectations or desires for your investor's involvement, that your prospect doesn't ask about, describe them up front.

Desirable angel characteristics include tolerance for risk, patience on liquidity event, industry experience, and subject matter expertise. Funding is important, but money is not the most valuable angel investor attribute. Angels can be remarkable mentors and advisers to young companies. Their experiences help you avoid pitfalls and see hidden opportunities. In addition, angels often have key industry connections and gladly make introductions on your behalf to prospective customers, suppliers, and strategic partners.

Once your essential documents and presentations have gone through several rounds of drafting, reviewing, revising, and testing, and you understand your basis for wanting angel financing as well as what angels are looking for, you are ready to move on to the next phase of angel investing: the actual investment process.

CHAPTER EIGHT

The Investment Process

From the time you first meet a prospective angel investor to the time you put that big check in your bank account, it seems like an endless series of interviews, requirements, hoops to jump through, discussions, and document reviews. The entire process can seem like a complete disruption to your business, dragging you away from the things you need to do to earn money. But remember, you are asking someone to trust and invest in you rather than in dozens, possibly hundreds of other opportunities.

It can't be said too often: angel investing is not a philanthropic venture. Angels are in the business to make money. So consider how you would approach investing in a company if you had no prior relationship with the founder. Put yourself in the shoes of the investor. In fact, that kind of approach will bode well for you in all steps of the investment process. Understanding how your prospective investors think, including what motivates them, will make it much likelier that you will be able to engage and hold their interest. Part of the value provided by this book is understanding the mind and motivation of the typical angel investor.

The investment process includes numerous steps and varies from investor to investor. Although each potential investment takes its own course, if you are prepared for any possible request, you will make the process move smoothly and generally impress your prospective investor.

These are the steps the investment process generally follows:

- Get a referral to investor
- Make initial contact with prospective investor
- Send executive summary
- Make the follow-up call and set a first meeting date
- Do your presentation for potential investor
- Allow investor to review your business plan
- Draft term sheet
- Go through due diligence process
- Validate business and technology
- Agree on final term sheet—parallel with due diligence
- Prepare or approve final documents reflecting term sheet
- Close the deal
- Accept investment—often in traunches based on milestones

As discussed in Chapter Five, finding angel investors is not straightforward, but many avenues do exist. Persistence is important, as well as patience.

OPENING NEGOTIATIONS

For purposes of this discussion on the investment process, the referral process will occur through a professional adviser, but any of the other resources previously discussed can be substituted for the initial step.

Referral to Investor

Referrals through a resource trusted by an angel carry far greater weight than many other introductions. Angels rely on their lawyers, accountants, close friends, and business partners—people they are sure are looking out for their best interests. Making a good impression on a trusted referral source is also important because these professionals are not about to compromise their clients' or friends' trust by referring an unprepared, unworthy investment candidate. So consider even meetings with referral sources as networking events and put your best foot forward.

So you are fully prepared for the introduction (having followed all of the prior steps in the book), and have gained the confidence of your accountant—Ms. Archer, CPA—who just happens to have several clients who are angel investors. Please note that you did not pick Ms. Archer at random; you used networking and contacts to find an accountant who specifically works with angel investors. You should ask Ms. Archer for a referral and to provide you with an introduction to any angel she regards as an appropriate match for your business. These introductions often happen over e-mail, and are known specifically as "warm introductions" to prospective investors. Mr. Collins—one of the angel investors receiving these warm introductions from Ms. Archer—decides he is willing to speak with you. (Note: If Ms. Archer is very busy, then instead of asking her to give you a direct introduction, ask instead if you could use her name as a reference when you contact Mr. Collins and other potential investors. Also, ask for some background on each referral, including any communication preferences such as whether the investor prefers written rather than electronic mail and any other quirks.) The more you know about a prospective investor, the better communication you will craft, increasing your chances of making a good impression.

Initial Contact

Consider the first contact carefully, based on the information you received from Ms. Archer as well as any information you can obtain through your network contacts and the Internet about Mr. Collins. Do not use a standard introduction for all angels; customize each communication. Think about your audience and their background and possible interests. Also make sure you include some pithy comments about your company, including any recent accomplishments such as landing your first customer. Do not go on for pages about your product or services. Make the cover communication short and sweet. Attach your executive summary. End with a statement that you will follow up by calling in the next week, never less time.

Some thoughts at this step:

Ms. Archer does not want to waste her time or that of Mr. Collins. Time is always among the most precious commodities for a busy person. If Ms. Archer is reluctant to provide you with referrals, your company may not be ready for prime time with sophisticated angel investors. Alternatively, you may need help preparing your executive summary.

Many angel investors will rule out entrepreneurs on typographical errors or bad grammar. Proofread every communication. As trivial as this may seem, many investors believe typos and poorly written documents reflect a lack of attention to detail, lack of commitment to spend the time to do things right.

Follow-Up

As promised, make the follow-up call and set a first meeting date. Even if Mr. Collins does not respond to your e-mail, call to set up your first in-person meeting. While not receiving a response may seem like a bad sign, people do get busy, and you should go ahead and call. Also, some investors want to see if you will be persistent. To continue the example, say you contact Mr. Collins, who seems somewhat interested, and you set up an in-person meeting.

Some thoughts at this step:

Know the difference between being persistent and being annoying. Don't obnoxiously pester or pursue Mr. Collins. If you do not get a call back after leaving two messages, leave him alone. You may want to follow up with Ms. Archer to find out if unrelated circumstances are causing Mr. Collins's nonresponse.

Know a "no." Say you contact Mr. Collins and have a phone conference with him. If Mr. Collins indicates that he is not investing at this time, that you are outside his area of investments, or you simply do not fit his investment profile, take those as a polite no. It's OK to send an occasional update after this refusal, as most investors will accept occasional news of your company's progress, and this gives you some continued connection with an investor who may be interested at a later stage. Mr. Collins may simply not have appreciated or understood your company the first time. Third-party validation, especially news of customers, patents, strategic partners, and the like, is far more effective than any statement you can make since you are supposed to be passionate about your company. Finally, turn a "no" into a networking opportunity. While you may not be a match for Mr. Collins, you may be a match for one of his contacts or associates.

Go to the investor. Make the meeting convenient for him. Work around Mr. Collins's schedule. Bring your own equipment if you want to do a presentation (this does not include a screen since most offices have a white wall, and carrying a screen is a bit over the top.) If you meet in a restaurant or coffee shop, you can bring your laptop, but try to present off a paper copy of your presentation. If you have video clips or other technical aspects of your presentation that should be displayed on a computer, such as a Web page or calculation process, you should choose a private location to avoid making viewing difficult and ineffective. Bring a copy of your presentation, any product fact sheet, and a professional attitude. Also bring a copy of your business plan, which you can provide if the conversation seems to go well or if the investor asks for a copy.

Ask for a reasonable period of time, such as forty-five minutes. Let Mr. Collins decide if he wants a shorter or longer period at the time of scheduling the meeting or during the meeting.

Do not stack meetings. You never know if your prior meeting will start or end on time. Traffic can be a problem. Parking may be difficult to find. Even if you have a legitimate excuse, you run the risk of putting a blemish on your relationship before you start.

Presentation

For your first meeting with Mr. Collins, choose a quiet location that gives some privacy, preferably Mr. Collins's office. Make sure the location is convenient for Mr. Collins. Arrive a few minutes early, especially if you need to set up equipment.

Now comes the hard part. How do you start your conversation? Some people prefer to get to know you better while others prefer that you launch directly into the presentation. You need to be attuned to Mr. Collins's preference. To find out, have a couple of preset questions to ask Mr. Collins about his background or company. Note your surroundings if you're in his office. These ice-breaking questions are quite important in discovering possible mutual interests and Mr. Collins's personality. They also fill the time while you are setting up your equipment if unable to do so before the meeting. Remember, angel investing is always personal, so try to connect with your investor.

Make sure your formal presentation is no more than fifteen to twenty minutes. You may be in the meeting far longer because of questions, side conversations, and so on, but your presentation itself must not be overly long. Know the difference between enough information and too much information. An investor who is interested will make time to know more. Refer to Chapter Seven for more on presentation and pitch content.

Some thoughts at this step:

Practice your presentation on safe audiences repeatedly. That's an absolute and uncompromising rule. Your idea or company is your baby, and parents always see their baby as the most beautiful, perfect bundle ever created. You need objective opinions from many sources about content, order of presentation, image, and other details.

Customize your presentation if possible. If you know Mr. Collins will be particularly interested in patent protection, spend an extra minute emphasizing your intellectual property protection. Also, you can have additional, more detailed slides at the ready for various subjects to drill down to if it turns out to be beneficial.

Don't directly ask for money, but open the door for the money. Confusing? The following conversation illustrates the point:

"As you know, Mr. Collins, we are in the process of raising capital, and we are looking for $500,000 in this round. Your participation as one of our angel investors would be outstanding."

"Well, initially, I am impressed by what you have shown me. Of course, I have many questions."

"Absolutely. I'd like to answer all your questions through further discussions, and you're welcome to a copy of the business plan now. May we schedule a follow-up meeting after you have a chance to review the business plan? I can also give you some preliminary contacts and references if you like."

"That sounds like a good plan. Give me a couple of weeks. And a couple of references would be nice, even though you were recommended by Ms. Archer."

This first meeting is far too early to make a formal request for an investment, but do not leave the meeting without having a concrete next step.

Promptly after the meeting, follow up with a thank-you note, preferably handwritten. Add two to three salient points—your prime messages—to your note, along with any information the investor requested during the meeting.

Opening Moves

For purposes of this example, assume everything progresses nicely with Mr. Collins. Expect this to be the exception, not the rule. As the old joke goes, you have to kiss a lot of frogs before you meet your prince, and the same is true of angel investors (or any other source of financing, for that matter). Not to say that most angel investors are frogs, but most angels are former entrepreneurs and it makes them hold you to a higher standard. If they feel they are not a good fit with your company, they are probably right. However, because of their experience, most angels are compassionate and knowledgeable businesspeople who have been in your shoes at one time, and any opportunity to meet with one is valuable as an opportunity to network.

So suppose Mr. Collins has had two weeks to review your business plan, and you call to set up the next meeting. Now you should invite him to visit your office. He most likely wants to see what your operations look like and get a feel for your company's environment and culture. Make sure your employees are aware of Mr. Collins's visit; you may even want to give them some information about Mr. Collins. The people you hire speak volumes about your business acumen and judgment. The caliber of senior management makes a statement about others' views of your business. So hire capable, experienced people—people who are smarter than you in their respective fields.

Now is the time to request that Mr. Collins sign a non-disclosure (confidentiality) agreement. Many entrepreneurs ask for an NDA far too early in the process. Your initial presentation and business plan should not contain any proprietary or confidential information. Prospective investors see dozens and dozens of presentations each year and review numerous business plans. Remembering which information is confidential and which is public knowledge is almost impossible and investors are not going to take the risk of inadvertent disclosure. Some angels, who look at only a few deals a year, may be willing to sign an NDA earlier in the process, but you should not plan on this being the case. Venture capitalists routinely refuse to sign NDAs until they are into due diligence, and most angel investors will take the same position.

Some thoughts at this step:

In your correspondence with Mr. Collins setting up the office visit, make sure you mention the need to sign a non-disclosure agreement. Mr. Collins should know by now that your business has proprietary technology. Even so, take the time to explain that you would like to discuss the details of your technology, share specifics about your customer list, and really give Mr. Collins a chance to see and understand every aspect of your company. Having this discussion with Mr. Collins will let him know what information you consider confidential, and will also establish that you take your intellectual property rights seriously.

Find out what Mr. Collins is particularly interested in discussing. Ask him what questions he has so you can address these right away. Have technology or product demonstrations ready.

Clean up the offices. Have copies made of materials you plan to go over with Mr. Collins. Offer him something to drink or to eat depending on the timing of the meeting. If you have any product posters or trade booth materials, put them up in the office. Mr. Collins should not care if your offices are in an older building. In fact, he will probably prefer to see that you are frugal, using every penny for business growth rather than expensive office space. (One exception to the charms of frugality: if you're expanding a service-based business that caters to upscale clients, you need to appeal to that audience.) But inexpensive is not the same as chaotic; Mr. Collins will observe and note if things seem disorganized or dysfunctional.

So Mr. Collins spends a couple hours in your offices. You conduct the product or technology demonstrations, allow Mr. Collins to talk with key management, and answer questions he may have about your business. Again, anywhere along this investment process, he may indicate he is not interested. Investors do not have to have a reason, so be careful how you ask what the basis is for not proceeding. It may be confusion about your technology, which you can correct, but it may also be personality incompatibility. As discussed before, know a "no." If this happens, ask if you can send follow-up communications to keep him informed of your progress, and if he can be used as a reference.

Assume Mr. Collins is quite intrigued and wants to start due diligence. If you thought the prior process took time, wait until you get to the *real* details. So don't rush in. To avoid headaches (and wasting Mr. Collins's time), get a few essentials taken care of before you start due diligence.

Draft Term Sheet

First, if you have not already touched on it, talk about your desired investment vehicle. Talk about general terms. Do not go through the hours of due diligence just to find out you cannot agree on the basics.

Is this a debt or equity investment?

If debt, what time length? Convertible debt, with automatic conversion upon certain milestones or benchmarks, is generally the preferred debt investment vehicle. Also, unsecured debt is preferred to keep assets available for commercial bank debt financing through a line of credit. If he insists on security, Mr. Collins should be willing to subordinate his investment to such debt financing.

If this is an equity investment, does Mr. Collins want common or preferred stock? As discussed, most sophisticated angels require preferred stock. Make sure you have a general idea of Mr. Collins's essential terms.

Mr. Collins should already know what amount you are looking to raise. Understand his possible investment range limits.

Understand Mr. Collins's post-investment expectations. Do not accept an angel's money if you know you just want a passive investor, but the angel wants to be directly involved. Mr. Collins may require active involvement in the company such as a board position, a primary advisory role, or actual position in the company. Know these requirements up front. Fundamental incompatibilities and differences in expectations spell trouble, headache, and possible disaster.

Have a preliminary discussion of valuation. If respective valuations are logarithmically different, there is slim likelihood of finding a satisfactory middle ground. Before you have even these preliminary discussions, seek out a third-party, unbiased opinion on valuing your company. Be ready for numbers lower than you expect. Investors will not pay more than what they independently determine a company is worth. While valuation discussions are often emotional, and while the company is your passion, which is a trait investors look for, investors also expect you to be realistic. So do not take statements about your company's weaknesses and lack of progress personally.

Have your due diligence materials ready. Pulling together all your corporate documents, contracts, marketing materials, lead sheets, customer lists, references, and so on can take weeks, so have them prepared beforehand. Again, Mr. Collins will be evaluating you on responsiveness. You want to keep his enthusiasm and interest on the front burner, so try to stay two steps ahead of him.

After these discussions, create a rough term sheet to memorialize these very broad, general terms. Don't expect Mr. Collins to sign anything, but rather send him an e-mail message or paper note addressing other matters related to due diligence, such as timing of meetings, document production, and the like, and mention in the correspondence your understanding of the general terms under which he may invest. No more than a paragraph or a half dozen bullets should be necessary at this point.

Work with your advisers to assist you with this process. This is an area where advisers can play a key role in making the process less of a headache, mediating between you and the investor to make sure both sides have the same understanding of the terms and requirements.

You should have already completed the steps outlined in Chapter Five on preparing for your angel investor. While some investors will not care if you have all corporate matters covered, why take the chance? You will eventually need corporate documents such as option plans and disclosure agreements, so do not risk losing an investment opportunity for lack of preparation.

Valuation

Negotiating valuation can be quite emotional for some entrepreneurs. Ego, greed, arrogance, and ignorance have probably killed more deals than any other factor. This is one of the reasons for early valuation discussions. Price per share is not everything, and receiving a high valuation is not always the best deal. Consider the entire value proposition of each angel investor. Do they bring value-adds such as market contacts, high visibility, and access to follow-on funding? These attributes can increase your valuation immediately after the investment, offsetting a small compromise in valuation on your part.

Chapter Two provides information on typical seed/start-up valuations for venture capital deals. Since at this time no one has published data on angel round valuations, you can only extrapolate from VC values to angel investing at a similar stage. There are many industry-recognized methods of valuing a company, particularly ongoing companies with existing revenue. These methods include book value (a liquidation-oriented valuation), market value (doing comparables), income value (using discounted cash flow), and, more often, a weighted average of the various methods.

For a pre-revenue company—meaning most seed/start-up companies—a multiple on expected return on investment in a certain time period is probably the most common. What pre-revenue valuation often comes down to is what the currently accepted market value is—in other words, what will the market bear?

A number of factors can impact valuation, all of which are covered in due diligence and carry various weights of importance, differing by the angel investor, region, market, and industry. These factors can include, among many others, the quality of the management team, the size of the market, the industry focus, the company's stage of development, its competitive advantages and their strength, and its current and long-term funding needs.

Finally, angel investors all have a number of biases that go into their valuation calculations, either consciously or not. Be aware of concerns like these, and be prepared with answers:

- Is management capable and focused?
- What are the chances product development will go as planned?
- How much can you anticipate competitive behavior?
- Has pricing been accurately forecast?

THE DUE DILIGENCE PROCESS

Nelson Gray, experienced angel investor, catches the essence of the time-consuming, detail-oriented due diligence process in three simple questions:

- So what?
- Who cares?
- Why you?

Of course, the devil is in the details, and details are the core of due diligence. But these three questions do provide the big picture on what your angel investor is trying to bring out in due diligence.

By the time you get to due diligence, investors have already decided they are more likely than not to invest. They are looking for potentially serious problems with your business—deal killers. Be completely transparent and willing to answer questions honestly. Provide any information or documentation a prospective investor requests. Angel investors realize your company is not complete; you're not expected to have all key hires, an established market, and a long list of customers. They understand you have steps and milestones ahead of you with numerous potential pitfalls and setbacks. Angel investors want you to recognize your current limitations and needs, and your potential future obstacles. Don't make your prospective investor ask questions or dig for answers. Be forthright because experienced investors have a sixth sense about matters, and when they find inconsistencies and loose ends, their radar goes off and tells them that you are not giving them the full story. As in most cases, the cover-up is a far greater sin than the actual problem itself.

No two angels will conduct exactly the same level or intensity of due diligence, so prepare for the most diligent angel investor. You will probably receive many document requests and questions specific to your industry, market, and company. Have your documents in order and preferably in notebooks with tabs and tables of contents. Appendix 6 is a lengthy document checklist that you can use as you create your due diligence notebooks, and Appendix 7 is a list of possible due diligence questions. Having all your documents in order will impress your prospective investor and further solidify the relationship.

Making your investors wait while you compile documents, making them have to ask repeatedly for documents, or providing them with incomplete or disorganized documents will either kill the deal outright or raise serious concerns in your prospective investor's mind. These are matters you should have taken care of without investor demand; if you cannot adequately prepare for someone as important as an investor, what will you do with customers, suppliers, or strategic partners? So get your act together and present yourself as a capable, experienced, prepared entrepreneur.

Reviewing documents and asking endless questions is just part of due diligence. Many angel investors will conduct a number of other activities to assess your company. Most angels will want to visit your company office. As noted, potential investors are interested in experiencing team interaction. They also like to talk to your other employees to get a sense of their commitment to the company and develop a firm grasp of the company's goals and strategies.

Be open about interactions between your angel investor and your employees. In the example used in this chapter, you should have other members of your management team participate in presentations to Mr. Collins. Show Mr. Collins around the office, no matter how small it is, because you are proud of what you have already created. Give your team some background on Mr. Collins and ask them to spend time with Mr. Collins if he so desires.

Investors will often conduct due diligence on your team as well as on you, to see what attributes you all have as a group. You are the inspiration, the fearless leader, the inventor, but a company is not one person. One deal killer for angels is a founder who feels able to do it all; no one is that talented nor has forty hours a day to handle every task necessary to grow a successful company. These are the main characteristics Mr. Collins will be looking for in your team:

- High-quality, experienced people covering key functional areas with complementary skills.
- A full-time commitment to the company either now or at the time of funding.
- Team compatibility and fit, often resulting from team members' past experience in working together.
- Agreed-to and respected systems, controls, and reporting structure.
- A stake in the outcome through ownership.
- Interests aligned with those of investors to build a great company that is highly profitable with a strong potential exit strategy.
- Coachable, willing to listen and hear input, and then integrate that information into their work.
- Passion.

Mr. Collins will ask for references, possibly from a number of different sources including other investors, customers, suppliers, bankers, previous employers, and even competitors. Do not be obstructive about references. Unwillingness to allow a potential investor to speak freely with references is a big red flag, indicating that you are trying to hide something or being less than honest. You should also know that most angel investors take what your direct references say with a grain of salt, because they expect you to give the names of people you trust who will sing your praises. So angels typically ask your references for further references and they often make their own calls to others they know who will have information about you. If you believe Mr. Collins could compromise a particular relationship by calling someone, talk with him about it. He may be willing to limit questions or let you participate in the call. You may even be able to satisfy his needs with another reference or source of information.

Remember that angels invest locally for the most part and so live in the city where you're starting your business, or a neighboring city. Because many are successful entrepreneurs, they are connected with the same service providers, suppliers, and so on that you expect to use. For them, the "six degrees of separation" that allegedly connect everyone on earth to everyone else are in practice about two degrees—they'll know how to find out whatever they need to know about you and your team. Many angels consider references one of the most important aspects of due diligence. Investors look for third-party validation of you and your company. They know you will wax eloquent about your company, so don't be offended by their need to independently validate everything you say.

Some angels will run a background check on you and your team, so don't be surprised if they ask for your driver's license number. Investors are looking for criminal records, particularly related to business-related felonies. They may also check Federal databases and consult the SEC and NASDAQ for possible securities violations.

Market and Technology Validation

Just as with other steps to independently validate your assertions, Mr. Collins will likely conduct his own market and technology analysis and validation. Discussions with references can provide some of this information. Be willing to provide market analyst reports on your product and your market—both must be validated. If you have patents or patent applications, provide copies and also a list of any prior art you may have cited in the application. The same is true for trademarks and copyrights. If you have not filed for intellectual property protection and plan to keep your inventions and ideas as trade secrets, make sure you can explain how you will keep this information confidential and unavailable to competitors. Also, practice what you preach; if you plan on keeping trade secrets or filing patents, make sure all third parties sign NDAs. Few things will make an investor lose confidence in a company faster than failure to protect valuable intellectual property.

In conducting his market and technology analysis to validate your claims, Mr. Collins will look at several sources, particularly third-party market analyst reports, recent IPOs in related industries, and the reports filed by public companies in the industry, as well as public and private databases, reports, and publications. Mr. Collins will run comparable financial models. He will also talk with friends and business acquaintances who are well-versed in your field, along with the extensive reference checking already being conducted with vendors, suppliers, customers, previous investors, employees, and anyone else he believes likely to provide useful insight.

The market and technology analysis and validation will also include Mr. Collins's independent assessment of your competition. He will make his own decision on what constitutes a competitor and will probably talk to some of them. Be sure to have a complete and accurate section on competition in your business plan. Missing a key element of a competitor's product will be seen as sloppy research or a lack of understanding of your market—or, worse still, as an attempt to hide something. You must have well-considered reasons for your position against each competitor.

Intellectual Property—Ownership and Protection

If intellectual property is key to your company's success and you plan to file for patent, trademark, or copyright protection upon securing your funding, make sure you have taken all appropriate steps to prevent the loss of intellectual property rights prior to filing. Chapter Six contains a primer on intellectual property and protection. Make sure you take all necessary steps—maintaining confidentiality, filing provisional applications, proper recordation, limiting commercialization, and so on—outlined in Chapter Six to ensure protection.

Employee proprietary information and inventions agreements are a must even if you plan to patent, trademark, or copyright all protectable intellectual property. These agreements are essential no matter what intellectual property strategy you plan to follow. Confidential and proprietary information goes far beyond inventions and trademarks: to customer lists, business strategies, contractual arrangements, and the like. Employees must observe and respect these valuable assets. These agreements should have all of the following characteristics:

- They must be signed upon employment to show adequate consideration, that is, employment.
- Their wording must sensitize employees to the importance of maintaining the confidentiality of company information.
- They must provide employees with a clear understanding of the breadth and depth of your company's proprietary and confidential information.
- They should describe the full extent of activities considered to be work done on behalf of the company or during work hours,

that is, activities whose results are owned by the company. The agreement also recognizes independent activities outside the scope of employment and company.

- They should clearly articulate company ownership of inventions, ideas, and proprietary or confidential information.
- They should state the continued obligation to the company for maintaining confidentiality.
- They should recognize possible reciprocal care of third-party confidential information.

Clear and unfettered ownership of intellectual property is essential to your business. The earlier discussion has assumed that key (and even collateral) intellectual property was developed by the founder and within the company, giving clear ownership to your company. Often, internal development is not the case; instead, technology has been licensed from a university, corporation, research institute, or individual. These license agreements must be clear, clean, complete, and uncompromising.

Note: Even development made within your company can be challenged in the absence of prior agreements regarding ownership. Therefore, an employee proprietary information and inventions agreement must be signed upon employment. Additionally, as founder, you should assign all your intellectual property rights to your company. The value of such an asset can often operate as the consideration for your founder's stock issuance. A red flag for investors is an arrangement in which the founder only licenses technology to the company rather than assigning ownership. Investors want the entire bundle of rights for any intellectual property owned by the company.

Financial Analysis

Chapter Four provides a comprehensive discussion of what financial documents you need and what goes into building these documents. These documents need to be completed before you begin due diligence, as your angel may ask to review your financial documents before anything else. Mr. Collins does not want to waste his time looking at your legal structure, contracts, and business procedures if you have not thought through the financial aspects of building your company. Therefore, have all documents and backup information well organized and ready for review. Know the contents backwards and forwards so you can answer any question about any number or assumption. Be ready to explain why you decided on certain assumptions and not others. Prepare to have your financials compared and contrasted with those of other start-ups in your field.

Investors want to see things like these:

- Financial projections that include a diversified customer base with multiple products off a broad-platform technology
- Markets being entered in a thoughtful, calculated manner, with strong support for your choice of the first market
- A well-mapped-out process for introduction of products
- Enough flexibility in your numbers and your mind to adjust your projections should an unanticipated market show strong interest

In other words, you need a well-developed view of the future, and you need to demonstrate the ability to recognize the signs for needing to rethink your projections if necessary.

Board of Directors and Board of Advisers

Mr. Collins wants to see that you are thinking outside your insular team. He also wants to know that you recognize the contributions experts can make in forming and growing your company. Equally important are outside board members to provide validation. If one or more noted leaders in your industry are willing to attach their names to your business and give of their time to help you grow the company (generally in return for stock or stock options), you have elevated your status in the eyes of an investor. Just as important as having outside directors and advisers is having them add value rather than just contribute names and résumés to your documentation.

Due Diligence Red Flags

Every angel has a mental list of factors that raise serious questions about the merits of a potential deal. These factors differ with each angel investor since they are all unique individuals, but the following list does give an idea of potential red flags that can turn into deal killers:

- *No investment by founders:* Investors read this as, "I do not really believe in my idea."

- *Numerous small investors, especially friends and family:* Professional investors recognize the need for pre-seed funding and know that friends and family are among the few potential sources. However, having dozens of very small investors, particularly ones who are unsophisticated, spells a potential headache and distraction for the entrepreneur.

- *One-trick ponies:* If your company has only one product or a single-application technology, the available markets are very limited and the investor is essentially betting on acceptance in a single market.

- *Claims of "no competition":* Every company has competition. Saying you have no competition will cause angels to run, not just walk away.

- *Any portion of funds being used to cash out earlier investors or pay liabilities:* Angels want every penny of their investment used to grow the company.

- *Lack of participation by earlier investors (if relevant):* If none of your prior investors step up to reinvest, it shows a possible lack of confidence in your company.

- *Prior financings have greater protection and more favorable terms:* "The last gold rules." In other words, the most recent money in the door will expect the most favorable terms—and will not enter without them.

- *A history of failure by the management team:* Though experience often comes in the form of a failure, investors are not interested in supporting someone who does not learn from past mistakes.

- *Family business:* Most angels refuse to invest in family businesses because nepotism and family drama can create unfavorable dynamics and cause the retention of marginal performers, which prevents real growth.

- *Multiple licenses required for practicing technology:* Licensing involves many different possible scenarios, from a concern that the field is already flooded to the chances of being sued for patent infringement, making the value of your technology or product questionable. It can also result in low realizable margins due to the license fees' impact on the cost of goods.

- *Heavy debt:* If a young company is already carrying a disproportionate amount of debt, investors will interpret this as poor financial management skills, overspending, poor business judgment, or some other unfavorable sign about the company's worth.

• *Hockey-stick growth projections:* It is just not realistic to project a sudden, explosive rise in value. That kind of success would require every assumption to be 110 percent true, the market to react perfectly, no technical glitches to occur, and almost limitless funding to be at hand. You need exceptional proof for exceptional projections.

• *Key assumptions missing in financials:* Not having considered many of the basics in developing financial documents can mean many things—starting with inexperience, poor business judgment, and a failure to retain skilled advisers. In general, incomplete financials will cause angels to seriously question your abilities and their interest in your company.

• *No board of advisers or board of directors, or only internal parties on either board:* If you don't have boards with external participation, it suggests that you do not seek advice beyond your team, creating a question of your coachability. Remember, external board members and advisers validate your ideas.

• *An entrepreneur who wants total control:* In a start-up, the entrepreneur typically does everything from five-year strategy to answering customer support calls. One of the reasons for raising investment funds is to hire smart people to take over various responsibilities; people who have years of experience in their area of expertise. An entrepreneur who wants to be the ultimate Renaissance businessperson will ultimately fail to meet investors' expectations, either keeping a small and interesting (but exit-proof) company or burning out and leaving the company and investors high and dry.

• *Unrealistic valuation:* If you are asking for a $20 million valuation on a seed/start-up and your prospective angel is coming in thinking around $2 million, you are unlikely to have a meeting of the minds. No matter how much you love your idea, it is still only worth what the market will pay for it.

FINAL TERM SHEET AND RESULTING DOCUMENTS

As mentioned earlier, you should already have discussed high-level terms with your angel investor before entering due diligence to avoid wasting their time or yours. To continue with Mr. Collins, assume that he is quite impressed, has not found any red flags, and is ready to move to finalizing the terms of his investment. Chapter Three provides a thorough discussion of alternative forms of investment and term sheet content. The final terms should be a win-win. If either party feels resentful about the compromises made in the terms of the investment, it can sour the whole future relationship. Be up-front about your desires and especially about wanting a mutually positive outcome. Also think about these questions:

Who is driving the investment terms? Angels generally expect you to draft the term sheet and have your legal counsel create the underlying documents. Therefore, you will bear most legal costs. Venture capitalists almost exclusively require that the company cover their legal costs as well, but angels typically foot their own legal bills.

How many angel investors do you want? Mr. Collins may be quite interested in providing all the funding you need for this round, but are you really interested in just one angel investor? One of the many advantages of angel groups is the access to many angels and the likelihood of multiple investors from the same groups or a couple of different groups.

What are your long-term funding needs and how does this affect decisions on early investors? As discussed elsewhere, if your pro-formas call for subsequent funding rounds, particularly venture-capital-level funding, keep the terms relatively simple and straightforward with your early angel rounds. Sophisticated angels will understand your need for creating incentives rather than disincentives for follow-on funding. At the same time, you need to understand that angels are entitled to protect themselves—they are taking a great risk on you.

In negotiating the deal, know your strengths and weaknesses. Understand long-term ownership dilution for you and your angel investor. Understand your investors' needs. You may even wish to conduct an "angel investor interview" with each of them to make sure you understand their needs and desires. Ask questions like these:

- What is the single most important factor in your determination of investment? Why?
- What are your expectations for return?
- What level of dilution are you willing to tolerate?

Understand each of your angel investors as an individual and let them get to know you, because angel investing is a personal decision.

After all the negotiations, you finally have your term sheet. Your lawyer will then generate the multiple documents related to these terms. If you are doing a convertible debenture (note) the documents may be relatively simple. If you are doing a preferred stock round, the number of documents will depend on the complexity of terms. Make sure your lawyer is experienced in early-stage funding and able to guide you through the document creation process.

Shareholder and Buy-Out Agreements

Some investors will ask for a shareholder agreement that governs the disposition of shares by the founders and other major shareholders. Most often, angels do not want shares to go to the spouse or significant other. Rather they want the company to have the obligation to repurchase the shares, and then (or simultaneously) they want the right to purchase the shares on a pro rata (equal) basis with other investors. Control of ownership is important in any company, and this is particularly true for professional private equity investors.

Buy-out agreements create an obligation by the company to purchase back investor shares at a designated time or upon demand after a certain period. If some uncertainty surrounds your ability to execute on an exit strategy, contractually mandating a return on investment may induce your prospective angel to invest. Buy-out agreements are particularly useful for companies that forecast high margins and strong cash flow but have limited ability to realize the traditional exit strategies, an acquisition or IPO. The parties agree to the multiple on investment or the formula to be used for calculating the investor's payout. As previously discussed, limited liability companies (LLCs) can work well to attract angel investors if your business model does not project large market share but does show a handsome profit potential. One aspect of an LLC that you may not desire is that investors become members (like shareholders) in the LLC, and unless you have a buyout agreement or provision, they are members forever. Therefore, a buyout agreement can work well as a stand-alone agreement or in conjunction with an LLC structure.

Deal Closing

At last! Finally receiving your investor's check can seem almost anticlimactic after making it through this entire process. Make sure not to rush the close. After having gone through this entire process, one key lesson should be to plan ahead so you do not run out of money before investors are ready to invest. You do not want to be desperate, so estimate the amount of money you need to get through six months. Finally, go ahead and celebrate.

SUMMARY THOUGHTS

If you have learned anything from all this discussion, it should at least include these maxims:

- Be prepared; stay two steps ahead of your prospective investors.
- Act professional; be professional.
- Recognize that investors enter due diligence with the thought of doing a deal and are looking for deal killers.
- Make sure you have a rough term sheet done before entering due diligence to avoid wasting your time and that of the investors.
- Discuss mutual expectations sooner rather than later. Don't think you can make an ill-fitted relationship work.
- Be open and honest at all times. Do not hide bad news; better you say something than the angel find out through other means.
- Angels don't expect a fully staffed company, but you should know what else you need to cover.
- Have the best advisory board you can assemble. Remember, angels put more stock in third-party opinions of your company than in your own self-praise. You are supposed to be enthusiastic and totally committed—that's passion, and essential, but it means angels will take what you say with a substantial grain of salt.

CHAPTER NINE

After the Investment

───〜〜〜─── So all your hard work has paid off and you've closed
the deal. You are happy, the investor is pleased, and everyone is enthusiastic about expanding the company. So how do you interact with
your angel investors effectively so you maintain the current positive
relationship? Regardless of whether any given angel remains passive
or becomes actively involved as an adviser, director, or confidant, you
should stay in touch with all your investors and shareholders.

COMMUNICATE REGULARLY—
ALL THE NEWS

If you send out quarterly updates on the status of the company,
including financials, that is often enough for investors. Communicate honestly and in a timely manner. Most angel investors will take a
relatively passive role, so proactive communication is essential to keep
them satisfied. You want them to feel comfortable, knowing that you
are working hard to grow their investment. Remember to express
your appreciation for the trust your angels have placed in you.
Colleen Stone, founder and CEO of InSpa, puts it well: "Say thank

you—frequently. Let your angels know that you appreciate them and the trust they have placed in you to grow their investment."

These days, with more and more angels and professional private equity investors in general making their investments in traunches against clearly defined milestones or benchmarks, communication is even more important than with one-time financing. Keep your angels informed of all progress toward accomplishment of the agreed-upon milestones. If you're going to miss a date, regardless of the reason, inform your investors as soon as you suspect it will happen. Do not wait until a couple of days or even a week before the date. Most investors are quite understanding so long as you are honest and up-front with them about the status of the milestone. Your investors might even be able to help you resolve the issue or remove an impediment. They will also probably give you more time to meet the milestone without losing this traunch of funding. As with all relationships, the secret to success is communication.

The same approach should be taken when events take a turn for the worse. Communicate early about challenges you are facing. At the same time, explain how you plan to resolve these issues. Investors, and people in general, are impressed when you point out a problem and a solution at the same time. Consider how you would react to an employee who failed to inform you of a major issue, trying instead to resolve it quietly and ultimately creating a bigger problem. Then consider an employee who presents you with an issue before it goes out of control, and who has also outlined several possible solutions for your consideration. Employees of the latter type endear themselves to you, while the former type creates larger messes for you to clean up. The same is true of your relationship with investors. Be up-front about problems and also tell them how you plan to handle these matters. Again, relationships evolve around effective communication.

Keep your investors comfortable with your progress. Your openness will likely bode well when it is time for your next funding round. You want some of your prior investors to reinvest as a showing of confidence in you. As mentioned earlier, repeat investments are a form of third-party endorsement. Angels often have connections to other angel investors, and can work these contacts for investment in subsequent rounds. They also often have connections with venture capitalists. Ask for these introductions early on, even before you are ready to go out for your next round of funding. Preparing the capital market is important. You can show prospective investors where you are today—and then, when you come back a few months later, you will have lots of progress to show. Notes that begin, "Look what we have done since you last spoke to us" or "We would like to let you know the progress we have made since last speaking" are great mechanisms to impress current and prospective investors and get them excited about talking to you.

LEVEL OF INVOLVEMENT

Robert Wiltbank, an assistant professor of strategic management at Willamette University, conducts research on angel investors and has provided some interesting empirical data in a January 2006 white paper titled, "At the Individual Level: Outlining Angel Investing in the United States." Dr. Wiltbank's data is based on responses from 121 angel investors to a detailed survey reporting 1,038 new venture investments and 414 exit events from those investments. The responding angels had invested approximately $100 million in 624 ongoing new ventures. A series of questions related to participation after investment. From his analysis, Dr. Wiltbank concluded, "Overall, these investors spend about 12 hours per week on new venture investing; over 30% of that time is spent with ventures in which they have already invested." Therefore, this study indicates that active angels are spending about four hours a week on existing investments. Spread this time over a portfolio of companies and you can surmise that most angels are passive investors, reading periodic communications and making occasional phone calls. The primary role angels take is monitoring their investments' performance, but they also act as an informal sounding board for the management team. Dr. Wiltbank also points out an obvious caveat to this average time spent on existing ventures; investors, he says, generally "take a greater interest/role when larger amounts of money are riding on the success of the venture."

Most angels remain passive investors because they feel comfortable with the capabilities of any team they choose to invest in. Again, Colleen Stone of InSpa eloquently states this point: "If you pick the right angel investors, they can relate to your company and you. They will understand your business model and market. They have an emotional connection with your company, rather than taking a hands-off approach. You are not just one more company in a portfolio; it's personal."

You should have a good understanding of your investors' expectations regarding the post-investment relationship. Many angels can bring important experiences and background to your company. For those angels, you should have discussed their post-investment role in general terms prior to the investment, to ensure alignment of interests. Now, sit down and outline the specifics of each investor's contributions and interactions with you and your team. Angel investors typically have a very good idea where they can add value, and ultimately their level of involvement is their choice. You should have already read your investors' résumés and understand where they can provide contributions to your business. Your investors will be impressed and appreciative if you take the lead on suggesting possible areas where they can provide value. These topics will probably have arisen during the investment process, so make sure you have kept track of those conversations.

In defining your angels' roles, some mechanical questions should be addressed:

How often will they be in the office? You do not want your investor just dropping in and engaging team members in conversations without pre-planning. An energetic angel willing to help out can be invaluable, or a disruption to the flow of work. Make sure each angel appreciates the difference. Your team will look to you to manage the investor relationship.

Who will they be working with? Make sure those key members of your team are involved in the discussions of setting expectations and developing mutually agreed-to processes for the investors' activities and contributions.

What goal should be set for the angels' involvement? Advisers are not typically responsible for accomplishing goals for your company, but rather for sharing their knowledge and their connections. Make sure your team is involved in developing the goals and strategies for your investors' activities. Just as the investment process involved your team, so should the post-investment relationship.

Because angel investors are often successful entrepreneurs themselves, they have the wealth of knowledge of the right and wrong strategies. Learn from their experiences. Many aspects of business are not intuitive. In addition, your angel investors did not invest in you because you had all the answers but because they believe in you, your team, your idea, your path to profitability, and your ability to execute on your business plan. Angels also invest because of the personal connection they make with your company and you. They will relate to your struggles, frustrations, and triumphs.

ANGEL VALUE

As discussed much earlier, angels invest for reasons beyond making money. It is worth looking at the list from Chapter Two again to review the reasons angels invest outside the desire to receive a financial return. Angels typically:

- Have a sense of social responsibility and enjoy community involvement.
- Take a role in the entrepreneurial process.
- Act as mentors and advisers to the entrepreneur.
- Provide early-stage investment dollars.
- Invest regionally.
- Have a diversified portfolio.
- Take a long-term view of their investments—which are often referred to as "patient money."

One of the overriding themes of these attributes is that investing for angels is personal. Remember, angels do not have to make an investment. Investing is not just business for angels. Their personal passion shows in their investment choices and style, just as their passion made them successful as entrepreneurs. So angels will take their involvement and desire to help you grow the company personally. They will give you insights on employee management, finding key hires, market realities, and how to get those purchase orders. Individual businesses are not unique; every company faces similar issues. Listen to your angel investors. They have your best interests in mind since they also have their money in your company.

Just as important, angels will help you understand what not to do. Do not kid yourself that setbacks will not happen to you. Angels can help you by pointing out possible future problems based on your market, operational structure, and other factors both within and outside your control. You cannot necessarily avoid problems such as a downturn in the market, but you can be prepared with a contingency plan. No one has a crystal ball to tell the future, but experienced angels can give you the benefit of their insights based on the past. As you have heard before, history repeats itself.

Angel investors can also be great confidants. Sometimes you may need someone to talk to about the challenges of growing a company, the stress of being responsible for your team's livelihood, and the endless demands on your time. Many angels are glad to lend support, but keep it professional. Do not let an angel become concerned about your ability to cope. Everyone has meltdowns—just avoid them in the office.

Angels facilitate company growth, but they do not make it happen. Often, investors can open doors for you through their contacts and prior professional relationships. They have built one or more successful companies, giving them a positive reputation in the market. This local, regional, or national visibility can be part of your company's growth strategy. Remember, angels bring much more than money to your company—they also bring experience and connections.

Your investors will be glad to introduce you to prospective customers, vendors, or strategic partners. But they will not make the presentation or close the deal. On a rare occasion, an investor may accompany you to the first meeting, possibly to reinforce the message of enthusiasm about your company. Typically, your investor will give you a very warm introduction and some background information on the individual you will meet, including key interests to highlight and any individual quirks to address or avoid. You are expected to take the introduction from there, follow it through, and create value. Angels are advisers and mentors; they are not employees. It is still your responsibility to run and grow the company.

As with other communications issues, it is very important to keep the angel informed in a timely manner of your interactions and progress with the introduction. Many times the party you're scheduled to meet will call your angel, so you want that angel fully and accurately informed of all activities. You may even suggest emphasizing certain points you want to drive home or clarify. Again, your angel should gladly support your efforts.

PATIENCE TO EXIT

One of the other attributes of angel investors is patient investment. They understand that building a company takes time. Whether that is two years or eight years, maintain a connection with your angel investors. Be disciplined about your regular communications. Keep a copy of your angel investors' skills and contacts and occasionally review the list. Even two or three years after an investment, you may want to ask for an introduction, or for help in thinking through a particularly complex matter. Even if you do not hear from them, your angel investors have not forgotten about you.

Exit Strategy

Angels are patient, but they do want an exit event to reap the benefits of their investment. As discussed before, the two primary exit strategies are acquisition (or merger) and initial public offering (IPO). While IPOs may draw much attention from the press, they are relatively infrequent in the United States, and almost nonexistent in the rest of the world. Figure 9.1 provides information from Dow Jones/Venture One on IPO activity in the United States from 1994 through 2005. Comparatively, the rest of the world showed a fraction of this level of activity.

This information should reinforce the hard truth that IPO is not the typical exit strategy for private companies. Instead, acquisitions (being bought) or less frequently mergers (being combined with another company) are the most likely route to liquidity and a return on investment. Figure 9.2, from VentureSource, shows a definitive trend toward mergers and acquisitions (M&A).

What this tells you is the need to operate your company to maximize value for your likely exit—an acquisition or merger. Clean corporate structure, financial controls, comprehensive policies and procedures, and strong intellectual property protection all influence valuation. In addition, private companies must now think about Sarbanes-Oxley Act compliance. While Sarbanes-Oxley applies only to publicly traded companies, the enormous expense of compliance can

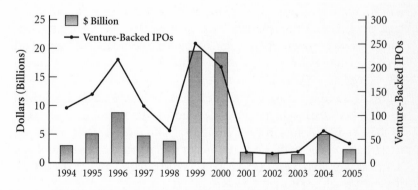

Figure 9.1   U.S. IPOs: 1994 Through 2005

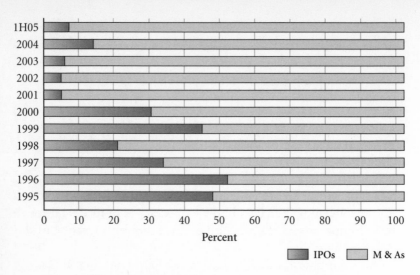

Figure 9.2   IPO and M&A Trends in the United States

have a serious impact when a public company acquires a private company. The logic behind the effect on valuation is that if the publicly traded company has to put considerable time and money into making an acquired private company compliant with Sarbanes-Oxley after incorporation into the public company, the private company will feel the effect of this cost rather than the public company. In other words, the cost of getting the acquired private company compliant is passed down through the private company, ultimately to the shareholders, in the form of reduced valuation.

Sarbanes-Oxley is a complex set of laws and regulations with significant requirements pertaining to a public company's accounting and legal practices. Entire treatises have been written on this legislation, which resulted from corporate and accounting scandals like Enron and Tyco International. Provisions place controls on the accounting industry, as well as requirements for internal company financial controls, reporting, and accountability. Therefore, seek experienced financial and legal counsel to help you understand when to implement many of these requirements in your company. Taking a proactive approach to Sarbanes-Oxley will save significant dollars in the long run. Even better, if you do have an IPO as your exit strategy, you are already on the right track for post-offering public status.

Remember

Just as landing your angel investor involves much preparation, so does managing the post-investment relationship in concert with growing your company. Themes run through this book that describe characteristics of successful entrepreneurs:

- Passion
- Coachability
- Preparedness
- Open, consistent, and timely communication
- Honesty and forthrightness
- Team approach—within the company and with outside professional advisers
- Strong advisers
- Focus on the end game: developing profitability and setting up an exit event

Live by these edicts and you have a great chance to become an angel investor yourself one day, providing much-needed capital, experience, and a sympathetic ear to young entrepreneurs eager to learn and grow their own companies.

Best of luck—because it never hurts to have a bit of luck.

Glossary of Terms Related to Private Equity and Debt Financing

Accredited Investor: According to Regulation D of the Securities Act of 1933, specifically §§ 230.501–230.508, which provides rules for private equity offerings, "accredited investor" shall mean any person who comes within any of the following categories, or who the issuer reasonably believes comes within any of the following categories, at the time of the sale of the securities to that person:

(1) Any bank as defined in section 3(a)(2) of the Act, or any savings and loan association or other institution as defined in section 3(a)(5)(A) of the Act whether acting in its individual or fiduciary capacity; any broker or dealer registered pursuant to section 15 of the Securities Exchange Act of 1934; any insurance company as defined in section 2(13) of the Act; any investment company registered under the Investment Company Act of 1940 or a business development company as defined in section 2(a)(48) of that Act; any Small Business Investment Company licensed by the U.S. Small Business Administration under section 301(c) or (d) of the Small Business Investment Act of 1958; any plan established and maintained by a state, its political subdivisions, or any agency or instrumentality of a state or its political subdivisions, for the benefit of its employees, if such plan has total assets in excess of $5,000,000; any employee benefit plan within the meaning of the

Employee Retirement Income Security Act of 1974 if the investment decision is made by a plan fiduciary, as defined in section 3(21) of such Act, which is either a bank, savings and loan association, insurance company, or registered adviser, or if the employee benefit plan has total assets in excess of $5,000,000 or, if a self-directed plan, with investment decisions made solely by persons that are accredited investors;

(2) Any private business development company as defined in section 202(a)(22) of the Investment Advisers Act of 1940;

(3) Any organization described in section 501(c)(3) of the Internal Revenue Code, corporation, Massachusetts or similar business trust, or partnership, not formed for the specific purpose of acquiring the securities offered, with total assets in excess of $5,000,000;

(4) Any director, executive officer, or general partner of the issuer of the securities being offered or sold, or any director, executive officer, or general partner of a general partner of that issuer;

(5) Any natural person whose individual net worth, or joint net worth with that person's spouse, at the time of his purchase exceeds $1,000,000;

(6) Any natural person who had an individual income in excess of $200,000 in each of the two most recent years or joint income with that person's spouse in excess of $300,000 in each of those years and has a reasonable expectation of reaching the same income level in the current year;

(7) Any trust, with total assets in excess of $5,000,000, not formed for the specific purpose of acquiring the securities offered, whose purchase is directed by a sophisticated person as described in § 230.506(b)(2)(ii); and

(8) Any entity in which all of the equity owners are accredited investors.

(The bolding emphasizes those parts of the definition most applicable to angel investors, as individuals—subsections 5 or 6—or as part of an angel fund or group of angel investors—subsection 7.)

Accrued Interest: The interest due on preferred stock or a bond since the last interest payment was made.

ACRS: Accelerated Cost Recovery System. The IRS-approved method of calculating depreciation expense for tax purposes. Also known as Accelerated Depreciation.

ADR: American Depositary Receipt. A security issued by a U.S. bank in place of the foreign shares held in trust by that bank, thereby facilitating the trading of foreign shares in U.S. markets.

Advisory Board: A group of external advisers to a company that is less formal than the fiduciary board, that is, the Board of Directors. Advisory boards typically do not have authority to determine company direction but can be vital in providing subject-matter-specific guidance and expertise. Many technology companies have advisory boards made up of industry-related experts for guidance as well as validation of technology.

Allocation: The amount of securities assigned to an investor, broker, or underwriter in an offering. Allocation often occurs when a share offering or distribution is less than the total of all investors', brokers', or underwriters' entitled percentage of total shares. For instance, if investors have rights of first refusal (defined later in this appendix), but the number of shares available for allocation is less than previously agreed, an allocation would be made among the entitled parties according to a preestablished or agreed-to formula.

Amortization: An accounting procedure that gradually reduces the book value of an intangible asset through periodic charges to income.

AMT: Alternative Minimum Tax. A tax designed to prevent wealthy investors from using tax shelters to avoid income tax. The calculation of the AMT takes into account tax preference items.

Angel Financing: Capital raised from independently wealthy investors who are not family or friends of the business's founders. This capital is generally seed financing.

Angel Investor: An individual who typically meets the definition of an accredited investor (defined earlier in this appendix) and who actively participates in, or independently determines, decisions of investment of personal wealth. These wealthy individuals often provide the first professional funding available to a young company. People who are relatives or friends of the business's founders are typically not considered angel investors. Angel investors typically follow the initial funding provided by the founders and their friends and family.

Anti-dilution: A provision in private equity financing that protects the early-round investors from being washed out or their ownership from being diluted (that is, proportionally reduced) through later rounds of financing. There are many different forms of anti-dilution including: 1) broad-based weighted average, which is most favorable to the company; 2) narrow-based weighted average, which looks only at the outstanding stock (as opposed to all stock on a fully diluted basis); and 3) a "ratchet" provision, which is quite onerous from the company's perspective as it provides that upon a down round, the conversion price of preferred stock is adjusted downward to the issuance price of the dilutive financing. Another provision, the so-called pay-to-play provision, is burdensome to the investors because it requires that investors must participate in dilutive rounds to retain anti-dilution protection for their shares.

Balance Sheet: A condensed financial statement showing the nature and amount of a company's assets, liabilities, and equity on a given date.

Bankruptcy: An inability to pay debts. Chapter 13 of the bankruptcy code deals with individuals in reorganization of personal debt. Chapter 11 of the bankruptcy code deals with companies in reorganization, which allows the debtor to remain in business and negotiate for a restructuring of debt. Chapter 7 deals with liquidation proceedings for either an individual or a company.

Best Efforts: As opposed to an underwritten offering (see definition later in this appendix), "best efforts" indicates an offering in which the investment banker or broker-dealer agrees to distribute as much of an offering as possible, and return any unsold shares to the issuer, without further obligation.

Blue Sky Laws: A common term that refers to state securities laws as opposed to Federal securities laws. Each state has its own set of securities laws pertaining to public and private offerings made within that state. The term originated when a judge ruled that a stock had as much value as a patch of blue sky.

Bond: Specific type of debt instrument most commonly sold by government entities.

Book Value: Book value of a stock is determined from a company's balance sheet by adding all current and fixed assets and then deducting all debts, other liabilities, and the liquidation price of any preferred issues. The sum arrived at is divided by the number of common shares outstanding, and the result is book value per common share. Book value is not commonly used for early-stage company valuation determinations because of the typical absence of actual fixed or other booked assets. Instead, early-stage companies often have their value determined on the basis of future earnings or projected value of intellectual property.

Bridge Financing: Short-term (usually one to six months) debt or equity funding (typically a convertible debenture—see definition later in this appendix) of a limited amount, provided to private companies immediately prior to a round of financing and meant to "bridge" a company to the next round of financing.

Burn Rate: The rate at which a company expends net cash over a certain period, usually a month.

Business Judgment Rule: The legal principle that assumes the board of directors is acting in the best interests of the shareholders. If the board is found to violate the business judgment rule, it would be in violation of its fiduciary duty to the shareholders.

Business Plan: A document that describes a business idea or existing business in detail and sets out the company's plan for the future through the discussion of a number of different aspects of the business. Typical structure: 1. Executive Summary, 2. Company History, 3. Industry Discussion, 4. Customer Definition, 5. Product and Technology, 6. Competitive Analysis, 7. Marketing Plan, 8. Operations, 9. Management Team, 10. Financial Plan, and 11. Exit Strategy for the Coming Years. The brief executive summary that opens the typical business plan is probably the most important element of the document, because the time constraints of venture capital fund representatives and angel investors mean they start there and may not read anything else.

CAGR: Compound Annual Growth Rate. The year-over-year growth rate applied to an investment or other aspect of a firm using a base amount.

Capital Gains: The difference between an asset's purchase price and selling price, when the selling price is greater. Long-term capital gains (on assets held for a year or longer) are taxed at a lower rate than ordinary income.

Capital (or Assets) Under Management: The amount of capital available to a fund management team for venture investments.

Capitalization Table: Also called a "Cap Table," this is a table showing the total amount of the various securities issued by a firm. This typically includes the amount of investment obtained from each source and the securities distributed—for example, common and preferred shares, options, warrants, convertible debentures, and so on—and respective capitalization ratios. An investor will typically ask for a fully diluted Cap Table to understand any and all securities (anything that represents or could convert into ownership interests; see definition later in this appendix).

Carried Interest: Typically referred to as just "the carry," it represents that portion of any gains realized by a venture capital fund to which the fund managers are entitled, generally without having to contribute capital to the fund. Carried interest payments are customary in the venture capital industry, in order to create a significant economic incentive for venture capital fund managers to achieve capital gains. A typical carried interest for venture capital general partners is 20 percent.

Cash Position: The amount of cash available to a company at a given point in time.

Chapter 7: The part of the Bankruptcy Code that provides for liquidation of a company's or individual's assets.

Chapter 11: The part of the Bankruptcy Code that provides for reorganization of a bankrupt company's assets.

Clawback: A clawback obligation represents the general partner's promise that, over the life of a venture capital fund, the managers will not receive a greater share of the fund's distributions than they bargained for. Generally, this means that the general partner may not keep distributions representing more than a specified percentage (for example, 20 percent) of the venture capital fund's cumulative profits, if any. When triggered, the clawback will require that the general partner return to the fund's limited partners an amount equal to what is determined to be "excess" distributions.

Closing: An investment event occurring after the required legal documents are implemented between the investors and a company and after the capital is transferred in exchange for company ownership or debt obligation.

Co-investment: The syndication of a private equity financing round or an investment by an individual (usually a general partner) alongside a private equity fund in a financing round.

Collar Agreement: Agreed-upon adjustments in the number of shares offered in a stock-for-stock exchange to account for price fluctuations before the completion of the deal.

Committed Capital: The total dollar amount of capital an investor pledges to a private equity fund.

Common Stock: A unit of ownership of a corporation. In the case of a public company, the stock is traded between investors on various exchanges. Owners of common stock are typically entitled to vote on the selection of directors and other important events and in some cases receive dividends on their holdings. Investors who purchase common stock hope that the stock price will increase so the value of their investment will appreciate. In the event that a corporation is liquidated, the claims of secured and unsecured creditors and owners of bonds and preferred stock take precedence over the claims of those who own common stock, and as such the former will receive distribution of cash or other value before the holders of common stock.

Conversion Price: The price at which an interest in a convertible debenture or note (defined later in this appendix) is converted, or can be converted into, stock. For example, if an investor enters into a convertible debenture with a company at a conversion price of $0.10 per share, and exchanges $50,000 for a convertible debenture, the investor could convert (or possibly will be required to convert upon a predefined event) into 500,000 shares based on the investment amount of $50,000 and the conversion price of $0.10 per share.

Conversion Ratio: The number of shares of stock into which a convertible security may be converted. The conversion ratio equals the value of the convertible security divided by the conversion price. Preferred stock is typically convertible into common stock.

Convertible Note or Debenture: Debt instruments that automatically or voluntarily convert to some other security. By way of example, a company may issue a convertible note to investors and have the note automatically convert into preferred stock of the same nature and kind as issued in the first round of financing. Appendix 8 of this book is an example of this type of debt instrument.

Convertible Preferred Stock: Preferred stock that may be converted into common stock or another class of preferred stock, either voluntarily or automatically.

Convertible Security: A bond, warrant, debenture, or preferred stock that is exchangeable for another type of security (usually common stock) at a stated price. Convertibles are appropriate for investors who want higher income or greater liquidation preference protection than is available from common stock, together with greater appreciation potential than common stock offerings. (See Common Stock, Dilution, and Preferred Stock.)

Corporate Charter: The document prepared when a corporation is formed, also referred to as the Articles of Incorporation, depending on the state of incorporation. The charter sets forth basic information about the corporation, such as principal place of business, authorized shares, classes of stock, and rights related to the stock.

Corporate Resolution: A document signifying an action by a corporation's board of directors.

Corporate Venturing: Investment capital distributed by in-house investment managers for large corporations to further the company's strategic interests.

Corporation: A legal, taxable entity chartered by a state or the federal government. Ownership of a for-profit corporation is held by the shareholders. A for-profit corporation typically has a board of directors. Nonprofit corporations do not have shareholders, since no individual may receive a personal benefit through an ownership interest in a nonprofit company. A nonprofit or not-for-profit corporation typically has a board of trustees.

Co-Sale Rights: The right of an existing shareholder to demand pro rata or a prenegotiated percentage of the sale of securities when a founder or other key shareholder wishes to sell shares in the company. This right typically prevents one shareholder from selling stock in a private company that does not have a market for its stock without allowing other shareholders to participate in some manner in the sale of their shares.

Covenant: Typically a protective clause in an agreement, such as a "covenant not to compete," which is intended to protect a company from an individual or entity financially or in other manner competing with the company. Generally, covenants not to compete are not favored and must be supported by adequate consideration for the restriction on someone's actions.

Cram Down: Extraordinary dilution of a nonparticipating investor's percentage of ownership in the company by reason of a subsequent round of financing, also known as a down round. Cram down or down rounds often affected angel investors when venture capitalists came in after the angels financed a company in an earlier round and financed the company at a significantly lower valuation than the valuation paid by the angel investors.

Cumulative Preferred Stock Dividends: A stock having a provision that if one or more dividend payments are omitted, the omitted dividends (arrearage) must be paid before dividends may be paid on the company's common stock.

Cumulative Voting Rights: When shareholders have the right to pool their votes to concentrate them on an election of one or more directors rather than apply their votes to the election of all directors. For example, if the company has twelve openings on the board of directors, in statutory voting, a shareholder with ten shares casts ten votes for each opening (10 x 12 = 120 votes). Under the cumulative voting method, however, the shareholder may opt to cast all 120 votes for one nominee (or any other distribution the shareholder might choose). Compare with statutory voting defined later in this appendix.

Debenture: A debt instrument (basically the same as a promissory note) that obligates a company to repay the loaned amount, typically plus interest. Interest can be paid in cash or stock. See also convertible note or debenture, defined earlier in this appendix.

Debt: Any obligation by person or entity (singular or plural) to pay another (singular or plural). May be a primary (direct) obligation as in a note, or a secondary (contingent) obligation as in a guaranty.

Debt Instrument: Any instrument evidencing the obligation of the maker to pay the holder of the debt instrument. Includes bonds, debentures, and notes of all kinds.

Demand Registration: Resale registration that gives the investor the right to require the company to file a registration statement registering the resale of the securities issued to the investor in a private offering.

Demand Rights: The rights held by an investor related to a demand registration.

Depreciation: An expense recorded to reduce the value of a long-term tangible asset. Since it is a noncash expense, it increases free cash flow while decreasing the amount of a company's reported earnings.

Dilution: A reduction in the ownership percentage of a given shareholder in a company caused by the issuance of new shares, regardless of the class.

Dilution Protection: Provision in private placements of stock that protects the shareholder's ownership percentage in subsequent rounds of financing.

Director: Person with a fiduciary obligation to a company, who is elected by shareholders to serve on the board of directors. The directors appoint the chairman of the board, president, vice president, and all other operating officers, decide when dividends should be paid, determine and approve option issuance, and decide other matters.

Dividend: The payment designated by the Board of Directors to be distributed among the holders of outstanding shares. On preferred shares, it is generally a fixed amount. On common shares, the dividend varies with the fortune of the company and the amount of cash on hand and may be omitted if business is poor or if the directors decide to withhold earnings so as to invest in capital expenditures or research and development.

Down Round: See Cram Down.

Drag-Along Rights: A majority shareholder's right, obligating shareholders whose shares are bound into the shareholders' agreement to sell their shares into an offer the majority wishes to execute.

Due Diligence: A process undertaken by potential investors to analyze and assess the desirability, value, and potential of an investment opportunity. Chapter Eight discusses the due diligence process.

Early Stage: For purposes of comparison with published statistics, this book uses the definitions set out in the MoneyTree Survey, which provides statistics on venture financing through a collaboration of the National Venture Capital Association, PricewaterhouseCoopers, and Thomson Financials. Therefore, the definition of an early-stage company along with the definition of other stages of development are as follows:

Seed/Start-Up Stage

- The initial stage. The company has a concept or product under development, but is probably not fully operational. Usually in existence less than eighteen months.

Early Stage

- The company has a product or service in testing or pilot production. In some cases, the product may be commercially available. May or may not be generating revenues. Usually in business less than three years.

Expansion Stage

- Product or service is in production and commercially available. The company demonstrates significant revenue growth, but may or may not be showing a profit. Usually in business more than three years.

Later Stage

- Product or service is widely available. Company is generating ongoing revenue; probably positive cash flow. More likely to be, but not necessarily profitable. May include spin-outs of operating divisions of existing private companies and established private companies.

EBITDA: Earnings Before Interest, Taxes, Depreciation, and Amortization. A measure of cash flow calculated as revenue minus expenses (excluding interest, tax, depreciation, and amortization).

EBITDA looks at the cash flow of a company. Excluding interest, taxes, depreciation, and amortization makes it easier to understand the actual amount of cash a company brings in and to see if a company has adequate (or inadequate) cash flow for operations and growth.

Elevator Pitch: A concise statement—no more than a few minutes in length (the duration of an elevator ride)—that sets forth an entrepreneur's idea, business model, company solution, marketing strategy, and competition for potential investors.

Employee Stock Option Plan (ESOP): A plan established by a company whereby a certain number of shares is reserved for issuance to employees to allow them to purchase the shares to gain ownership in the company. Such shares usually vest over a certain period of time to serve as an incentive for employees to build long-term value for the company.

Employee Stock Ownership Plan: A trust fund established by a company to purchase stock on behalf of employees.

Equity: Ownership in a company, in numerous forms, generally considered *stock* in a corporation and *member interests* or *member units* in a limited liability company.

Equity Kicker or Sweetener: The option to purchase additional shares (or stock) in a company, typically offered to private equity investors to encourage them to invest. Sometimes used in association with debt financing and differentiated from the debt financing as being in the form of equity.

ERISA: The U.S. Employee Retirement Income Security Act of 1974, as amended, including the regulations promulgated under the Act.

Exchange Act: Or more properly, the Exchange Act of 1934, as amended, which mandates the reporting requirements related to publicly traded securities, companies with more than five hundred shareholders, brokers and dealers in securities, and other activities and securities-related matters, with a primary objective of providing the public generally with full, fair, and complete information related to public companies and governing the actions and obligations of those dealing in the ownership of such companies, among other objectives.

Exercise Price: The price at which an option or warrant can be converted to stock.

Exit Strategy: A company's strategy for providing investors with a liquidity event, which represents an event or time at which the investor can obtain a return on an investment through typically a distribution of cash, publicly tradable stock in the company, or stock in an acquiring company that is publicly traded.

Finder: A person who helps to arrange a transaction. Typically for young companies, this is an individual who finds private equity investors. In nearly all circumstances, if the finder charges a "success fee" or a fee related to the actual cash raised, typically as a percentage of the cash, the individual must be a licensed broker-dealer.

Flipping: The act of buying shares in an IPO and selling them immediately for a profit. Brokerage firms underwriting new stock issues tend to discourage flipping, and will often try to allocate shares to other investment houses in the syndication that intend to hold on to the shares for some time.

Form 10-K: This is the annual report that most reporting companies file with the Securities and Exchange Commission. It provides a comprehensive overview of the registrant's business.

Form S-1: The form can be used to register securities for which no other form is authorized or prescribed, except securities of foreign governments or political subdivisions thereof.

Form S-2: This is a simplified optional registration form that may be used by companies that have been required to report under the 1934 Act for a minimum of three years and have timely filed all required reports during the twelve calendar months and any portion of the month immediately preceding the filing of the registration statement. Unlike Form S-1, it permits incorporation by reference from the company's annual report to stockholders (or annual report on Form 10-K) and periodic reports. The company may be required to deliver these incorporated documents, as well as the prospectus, to investors.

Form S-4: Type of registration statement under which public company mergers and security exchange offers may be registered with the SEC.

Form SB-2: This form may be used by "small business issuers" to register securities to be sold for cash. This form requires less detailed information about the issuer's business than Form S-1.

Formal Financing: Primarily refers to venture capital funds managed by professional venture capital firms. This contrasts with "informal financing," which generally refers to funds that come from the founder's savings, as well as money from friends and family. Many still consider angel investors as a source of informal financing. Angel investors are becoming sophisticated and organized, however, and thus taking on attributes of sources of formal financing such as venture capitalists.

Founders' Shares: Shares issued to a company's founders upon establishment of the company.

Fully Diluted Outstanding Shares: The number of shares representing total company ownership, including common shares and the current number of shares that would result from the conversion or exercise of any instrument that has the ability to convert into common shares—preferred shares, options, warrants, and other convertible securities.

Fund Focus: Most if not all venture capital funds have an industry focus or a stage of company development focus for the fund, or both. Such a focus is important for many reasons including providing the limited partners (VC investors) with an understanding of investment preference for the fund and the fund's risk profile.

Fund Size: The total amount of capital committed by investors into a venture capital fund.

GAAP: Generally Accepted Accounting Principles. The common set of accounting principles, standards, and procedures. GAAP is a combination of authoritative standards set by standard-setting bodies as well as accepted ways of doing accounting.

General Partner (GP): The partner in a limited partnership responsible for all management decisions of the partnership. The GP has fiduciary responsibility to act for the benefit of the limited partners (LPs), and is fully liable for the partnership's actions. Nearly all venture funds are set up as limited partnerships, with the GPs making the investment decisions and the LPs remaining passive as to these investment decisions (which is required to maintain limited partner status).

Golden Parachute: Employment contract for upper management that provides a large payout upon the occurrence of certain control transactions, such as a certain percentage share purchase by an outside entity or a tender offer for a certain percentage of a company's shares.

Holding Company: A corporation that owns the securities of another, in most cases with voting control.

Holding Period: The amount of time an investor has held, or must hold, an investment. The period begins on the date of purchase and ends on the date of sale, and determines whether a gain or loss is considered short term or long term for capital gains tax purposes.

Hot Issue: A newly issued stock that is in great public demand. Technically, an issue is referred to as *hot* when the secondary market price on the effective date is above the new issue offering price. Hot issues usually experience a dramatic rise in price at their initial public offering because the market demand outweighs the supply.

Informal Financing: Generally refers to financing from the founders' savings as well as those of their friends and family. Many would include angel investors in the definition of informal financing. This contrasts with "formal financing," which refers to monies managed by professional venture capital firms.

Information Rights: In private financings, investors articulate the types and frequency of information so desired from the company. These rights can vary across a broad spectrum—from annual reports to quarterly reports to each revised business plan, monthly financials, board minutes, strategic and marketing plans, and board visitation rights.

Initial Public Offering (IPO): The sale or distribution of a stock of a portfolio company to the public for the first time. For the most part, IPOs are conducted by an underwriter (defined later in this appendix).

Institutional Investors: Organizations that professionally invest, including insurance companies, depository institutions, pension funds, investment companies, mutual funds, and endowment funds. Institutional investors are usually mentioned in connection with venture capital funds.

Investor Questionnaire: A questionnaire required of private equity investors to determine their eligibility to invest in a private company. Unless a company has reason to believe that an investor's questionnaire answers are lies or misrepresentations, it may rely on an investor's statement of qualification as an accredited investor for purposes of maintaining the exemption under Regulation D.

IRR: Internal Rate of Return. A typical measure of how VC funds track performance. IRR is technically a discount rate: the rate at which the present value of a series of investments is equal to the present value of the returns on those investments.

Issued Shares: The number of shares in a company actually held by an individual or entity. Issued shares can also include shares, usually common stock, that are designated for distribution under a stock option plan, as well as common stock into which preferred stock or warrants may convert.

Issuer: The organization issuing or proposing to issue a security.

Key Employees: Professionals attracted by the founder to help run the company. Key employees are typically retained with stock options and/or ownership of the company.

Later Stage: The stage of a company's development, defined earlier in this appendix as the stage when its products or services are widely available. The company is generating ongoing revenue; probably positive cash flow. More likely to be profitable, but not necessarily so. May include spin-outs of operating divisions of existing private companies and established private companies. The term can also refer to a venture capital fund investment strategy involving financing the expansion of a company that is producing, shipping, and increasing its sales volume.

Lead Investor: Member of an investment syndicate (or group) of private equity investors, usually investing the largest amount, in charge of negotiating the investment terms with the company and most likely the party engaged with the company after the investment.

Leveraged Buyout (LBO): A takeover of a company using a combination of equity and borrowed funds. Generally, the target company's assets act as the collateral for the loans taken out by the acquiring group. The acquiring group then repays the loan from the cash flow of the acquired company.

Limited Partner (LP): An investor in a limited partnership who has no voice in the management of the partnership. LPs have limited liability and usually have priority over general partners upon liquidation of the partnership. Nearly all venture funds are set up as limited partnerships, with the general partners making the investment decisions and the LPs remaining passive as to these investment decisions (which is required to maintain limited partner status).

Limited Partnership: An organization that consists of a general partner, who manages the organization (usually a venture capital fund for purposes of these definitions), and limited partners, who invest money but have limited liability and are not involved with the day-to-day management of the fund, including its investments. In the typical venture capital fund, the general partner receives a management fee and a percentage of the profits ("carried interest," often referred to as "the carry"). The limited partners receive income, capital gains, and tax benefits.

Liquidation: (1) The process of converting securities into cash. (2) The sale of the assets of a company in order to pay off debts. In the event that a corporation is liquidated, the claims of secured and unsecured creditors and owners of bonds and preferred stock take precedence over the claims of those who own common stock.

Liquidity Event: An event that allows an investor to realize a gain or loss on an investment. The event typically marks the end of a private equity provider's involvement in a business venture with a view to realizing a return on the original investment. Most common liquidity events, or exits, involve (1) a merger of the invested company into another company (preferably a publicly traded company) in return for which the investors and shareholders receive stock in the other company or cash (or a combination); (2) an acquisition by another company, again, preferably a publicly traded company, in return for cash, stock, or a combination of cash and stock; (3) an initial public offering (which is not the typical exit strategy for private companies—see statistics in Chapter Nine), or (4) far less frequently, buybacks, mandatory puts, and other forms of a company purchasing its own shares from an investor-shareholder, whether at the company's discretion or required under the given conditions.

Lockup Period: The period of time that certain stockholders have agreed to waive their right to sell their shares of a public company. Investment banks that underwrite initial public offerings generally insist upon lockups of 180 days or more from at least the large shareholders (1 percent ownership or more) in order to allow an orderly market to develop in the shares. The shareholders subject to lockup usually include the management and directors of the company, strategic partners, and other large investors. These shareholders have typically invested prior to the IPO at a significantly lower price than that offered to the public and therefore stand to gain considerable profits. If a shareholder attempts to sell shares subject to lockup during the lockup period, the transfer agent will not permit the sale to be completed.

Management Fee: Compensation for the management of a venture capital fund typically paid to the general partners or a separate entity the general partners set up to receive the management fee and act as the general partner for the venture capital fund. The fee usually runs between 2 and 3 percent of the total fund amount, on an annual basis.

Management Team: The people responsible for day-to-day operation and direction of a company.

Market Capitalization: The total dollar value of all outstanding tradable shares. Computed as number of shares multiplied by current price per share. Prior to an IPO, market capitalization is arrived at by estimating a company's future growth and by comparing a company with similar public or private corporations. (See also Pre-Money Valuation.)

Merger: Combination of two or more companies for anticipated strategic, marketing, or operational reasons.

Mezzanine Financing: Refers to the stage of venture financing for a company immediately prior to an anticipated IPO. Investors entering in this round have lower risk of loss than those investors who have invested in earlier rounds because of the proximity of an intended IPO.

Mutual Fund: A mutual fund, or an open-end fund, sells as many shares as investor demand requires. As money flows in, the fund grows. If money flows out of the fund the number of the fund's outstanding shares drops. Open-end funds are sometimes closed to new investors, but existing investors can still continue to invest money in the fund. An investor who wishes to sell shares usually sells them back to the fund. An investor who wishes to buy additional shares in a mutual fund must buy newly issued shares directly from the fund.

NASD: The National Association of Securities Dealers, an organization that oversees the registration and operation of brokers and dealers.

NASDAQ: An automated information network that provides brokers and dealers with price quotations on securities traded over the counter.

Net Income: The net earnings of a company after deducting all costs of selling, depreciation, interest expense, and taxes.

Net Present Value: An approach used in capital budgeting where the present value of cash inflow is subtracted from the present value of cash outflows. NPV compares the value of a dollar today to the value of that same dollar in the future after taking inflation and return into account.

Newco: The typical label for any new company prior to actual organization, often used as a term for a hypothetical company in planning stages.

No Shop, No Solicitation Clauses: A type of clause that requires the company to negotiate exclusively with the investor or buyer, and not solicit another investment or acquisition proposal from anyone else for a set period of time. The key provision is the length of time set for the exclusivity period.

Nonaccredited Investor: An investor not considered accredited for a Regulation D offering. (In contrast, see Accredited Investor.)

NYSE: The New York Stock Exchange. Founded in 1792, it is the largest organized securities market in the United States. The exchange itself does not buy, sell, own, or set prices of stocks traded there. The prices are determined by public supply and demand. Also known as the Big Board.

Offering Documents: Documents provided to a potential investor in a private placement transaction (referred to as a *prospectus* in public offerings). Documents can include a combination of agreements and other documents depending on the structure and terms of the investment, such as a private placement memorandum, stock purchase or subscription agreement, investor questionnaire, investor rights agreement, amended and restated articles of incorporation, notes or stock certificates, warrants, registration rights agreement, and other documents required by the particular investment.

Option: A security granting the holder the right to purchase a specified number of a company's securities at a designated price at some point in the future. The term is generally used in connection with employee benefit plans as incentive stock options (ISOs or *statutory options*) and nonqualified stock options (NSOs or *nonquals*) for issuance to employees and nonemployees. Only employees may receive incentive stock options. "Stand-alone options" may be issued outside of any plan. Generally, options are not transferable, in distinction to warrants.

Option Pool: The number of shares set aside for future issuance to employees and nonemployees. A new company, which has not hired key employees other than the founders, may wish to set aside up 20 to 30 percent of its common shares for issuance to employees, board members (fiduciary and advisory), consultants, and other key individuals as part of their compensation and as an incentive to grow the company.

OTC or Over-the-Counter: A market for securities made up of dealers who may or may not be members of a formal securities exchange. The over-the-counter market is conducted over the telephone and is a negotiated market rather than an auction market like the NYSE.

Outside Financing: See Third-Party Financing.

Outstanding Stock: The shares of a company that are in the hands of investors. The total is equal to the number of issued shares less treasury stock (stock held by the company itself).

Oversubscription: Condition that occurs when demand for shares exceeds the supply or number of shares offered for sale. As a result, the underwriters or investment bankers must allocate the shares among investors. In private placements, this occurs when a deal is in great demand because of the company's growth prospects.

Pari Passu: At an equal rate or pace, without preference.

Participating Preferred: A preferred stock in which the holder is entitled to the stated dividend, and also to additional dividends on a specified basis upon payment of dividends to the holders of common stock.

Participating Preferred Stock: Preferred stock that has the right to share on a pro rata basis with any distributions to the common stock upon liquidation, after already receiving the preferred liquidation preference.

Partnership: An entity in which each partner shares in the profits and losses of the partnership. The partners are each responsible for the taxes on their share of profits and losses. In a general partnership, all partners share the liabilities as well; in a limited partnership, the general partners share the liabilities and the limited partners have limited liabilities so long as they do not participate in the day-to-day operations and decisions of the partnership.

Penny Stocks: Low-priced issues, often highly speculative, selling at less than $5/share.

Piggyback Registration: A situation when a securities underwriter allows existing holdings of shares in a company to be sold in combination with an offering of public shares.

PIPE: Private Investment for Public Equity. Private offering by a public entity followed by a resale registration.

PIV: Pooled Investment Vehicle. A legal entity that pools various investors' capital and deploys it according to a specific investment strategy. Although still the minority structure, one form an angel investment group may take is a fund, which can be made up of pooled or committed capital.

Placement Agent: An investment banker, broker, or other person who locates investors to purchase securities from a company in a private offering, in exchange for a commission.

Poison Pill: A right issued by a company as an anti-takeover measure. It allows the rightholders to purchase shares in either their company or in the combined target and bidder entity at a substantial discount, usually 50 percent. This discount may make the takeover prohibitively expensive.

Portfolio Companies: Companies in which a given fund or investor has invested.

Post-Money Valuation: The valuation of a company immediately after the most recent round of financing. This value is calculated by simply adding together the pre-money valuation plus the amount raised in the financing round.

Pre-Money Valuation: The valuation of a company prior to a round of investment. This amount is determined by using various calculation models, such as discounted P/E ratios multiplied by periodic earnings or a multiple times a future cash flow discounted to a present cash value and a comparative analysis to comparable public and private companies.

Preemptive Right: A shareholder's right to acquire an amount of shares in a future offering at the then current price per share paid by new investors, so as to maintain the same ownership percentage as before the offering.

Preferred Dividend: A dividend ordinarily accruing on preferred shares payable where declared and superior in right of payment to common share dividends.

Preferred Stock: A class of capital stock with rights, preferences, and privileges superior to common stock, possibly including preferred rights on liquidation of assets, dividend payments, registration rights, anti-dilution rights, and rights of first refusal. Venture capitalists almost exclusively invest through the use of preferred stock. Preferred stock is almost always convertible into common stock at the investor's discretion, and this right is typically exercised prior to an initial public offering. Historically, angels invested through a number of different vehicles, including common stock. Today, angel investors are becoming sophisticated and require preferred stock, as do venture capitalists. The rights provided to angel investors in early rounds of financing may (or should) differ from later rounds, such as with venture capitalists, to prevent a chilling effect on subsequent rounds by overreaching terms. Investment terms are discussed extensively in Chapter Three.

Private Equity: Equity securities of companies that have not "gone public" (are not listed on a public exchange). Private equities are generally illiquid and thought of as long-term investments. As they are not listed on an exchange, any investor wishing to sell securities in a private company must find a buyer in the absence of a marketplace. In addition, there are many transfer restrictions on private securities. Investors in private securities generally receive their return through a sale or merger, a recapitalization, or an initial public offering.

Private Placement: The sale of unregistered, restricted securities by a company. Can also be a Regulation D exempt offering. The sale of a security (or in some cases, a bond) directly to a limited number of investors. Avoids the need for federal and state securities registration if the securities, issuer, and investors are compliant with the terms of a defined exemption and the shares are purchased for investment as opposed to being resold. See Chapter Three for an extensive discussion of private placement offerings.

Private Placement Memorandum (PPM): Also known as an offering memorandum. A document that outlines the terms of securities to be offered in a private placement. A PPM generally contains risk factors as well as the content similar to that contained in a comprehensive business plan. A PPM is not required for a private placement under Regulation D if all investors are accredited investors, because of the exemption from the information disclosure requirements of Regulation D.

Private Securities: Private securities are securities that are not registered and do not trade on an exchange.

Promissory Note: Debt instrument in which the maker promises to pay the holder according to its terms. Also referred to simply as a *note* or *debenture*.

Prospectus: A formal written offer to sell securities that provides an investor with the information necessary to make an informed decision and typically related to a public offering such as an IPO. A prospectus explains a proposed or existing business enterprise and must disclose any material risks and information according to the securities laws. A prospectus must be filed with the SEC and be given to all potential investors. Companies offering securities, mutual funds, and other investment companies (including business development companies) are required to issue prospectuses describing their history, investment philosophy or objectives, risk factors, and financial statements.

Public Company: A company that has securities that have been sold in a registered offering and that are traded on a stock exchange or NASDAQ; must be a reporting company under SEC rules.

Put option: The right to sell a security at a given price (or range) within a given time period.

QPAM: Qualified professional asset manager as defined by ERISA.

Recapitalization: The reorganization of a company's capital structure. Recapitalization is rarely but can be an alternative exit strategy for private equity investors.

Red Herring: The common name for a preliminary prospectus, derived in part from the red SEC-required legend on the cover. It also retains overtones of the common use of the term: a false lure, like the dead fish sometimes dragged across a trail to confuse hunting hounds. (See Prospectus.)

Redeemable Preferred Stock: Preferred stock that is redeemable at the holder's option after (typically) five years, which in turn gives the holders (potentially converting to creditors) leverage to induce the company to arrange a liquidity event. The threat of creditor status can motivate founders if a liquidity event is not occurring with sufficient rapidity.

Registered Offering: Also known as a "Public Offering." A transaction in which a company sells specified securities to the public under a registration statement that has been declared effective by the SEC.

Registration: The SEC's review process of all securities intended to be sold to the public. The SEC requires that a registration statement be filed in conjunction with any public securities offering. This document includes operational and financial information about the company, its management, and the purpose of the offering. The registration statement and the prospectus are often referred to interchangeably. Technically, the SEC does not "approve" the disclosures in a prospectus.

Registration Obligation: The obligation of a company to register the shares issued to an investor in a private offering for resale to the public through a registration statement that the SEC has declared effective.

Registration Rights: The right to require that a company register restricted shares. Demand registration rights enable the shareholder to request registration at any time, while piggyback registration rights enable the shareholders to request that the company register their shares when the company files a registration statement (for a public offering with the SEC).

Registration Rights Agreement: A separate agreement in which the investor's registration rights are evidenced. Registration rights can also be contained in an investors' rights agreement.

Registration Statement: The document filed by a company with the SEC under the Securities Act in order to obtain approval to sell the securities described in the registration statement to the public; it includes the prospectus. Examples of registration statements include S-1, S-2, S-3, S-4, SB-1, SB-2, and S-8.

Regulation A: An SEC provision for simplified registration for small issues of securities. A Regulation A issue may require a shorter prospectus and carry lesser liability for directors and officers for misleading statements. The conditional small issues securities exemption of the Securities Act of 1933 is allowed if the offering is a maximum of US$5,000,000.

Regulation C: The regulation that outlines registration requirements for the Securities Act of 1933.

Regulation D: A series of rules that allow for the issuance and sale of private securities to purchasers.

Regulation D Offering: (See Appendix 3, as well as Private Placement.)

Regulation S: The rules relating to offers and sales made outside the United States without SEC registration.

Regulation S-B: Regulation S-B of the Securities Act of 1933 governs the Integrated Disclosure System for Small Business Issuers.

Regulation S-K: The standard instructions for filing forms under the Securities Act of 1933, Securities Exchange Act of 1934, and Energy Policy and Conservation Act of 1975.

Regulation S-X: The regulation that governs the requirements for financial statements under the Securities Act of 1933 and the Securities Exchange Act of 1934.

Reporting Company: A company that is registered with the SEC under the Exchange Act or has more than five hundred shareholders, and must now comply with the information disclosure and other requirements applicable to publicly traded companies.

Resale Registration: Registration by a company of the investor's sale of shares purchased by the investor in a private offering.

Restricted Securities: Securities that are not freely tradable due to SEC regulations. (See Securities and Exchange Commission.)

Restricted Shares: Shares acquired in a private placement are considered restricted shares and may not be sold in a public offering absent registration, or after an appropriate holding period has expired for companies currently making a public market for their securities.

Reverse Vesting: Often venture capital investors (and some angel investors) require the founders to essentially give up ownership rights to their stock, and then earn them back over time. The justification or reasoning for investors requiring founders to reestablish their ownership over time is to keep them committed and engaged with the company rather than leaving or coasting after funding is secured. The percentage of shares subject to reverse vesting varies, as does the time period for re-vesting. An example of reverse vesting: Say the founder, Alice Marshal, owns 5,000,000 shares. As a condition to financing, she must agree that 50 percent of her shares are subject to reverse vesting, with a three-year re-vesting period. In other words, if she leaves the company immediately after the financing, then she will own only 2,500,000 shares. However, if she stays for three years, she will re-vest all her shares at the rate of a third of 2,500,000 per year (or possibly a thirty-sixth each month). During re-vesting, founders often do not have voting rights for the shares in question.

Right of First Refusal: The right of first refusal gives a shareholder the right to purchase shares at a designated offering amount prior to new investors or before a subordinate class of shareholders has the right to purchase. The right of first refusal can also be a shareholder right with regard to the purchase of existing interests of other shareholders before the sale to new investors or a subordinate class of shareholders.

Rights Offering: Issuance of rights to current shareholders allowing them to purchase additional shares, usually at a discount from market price. Shareholders who do not exercise these rights are usually diluted by the offering. Rights are often transferable, allowing the holder to sell them on the open market to others who may wish to exercise them.

Risk: The chance of loss on an investment due to many factors—product market, management dependence, operational issues, inflation, interest rates, default, politics, foreign exchange, call provisions, and others. These risks are stated in the company's estimation of priority in a prospectus or private placement memorandum.

Rule 144: Provides for the sale of restricted stock and control stock. Filing with the SEC is required prior to selling restricted and control stock, and the number of shares that may be sold is limited.

Rule 144A: A safe harbor exemption from the registration requirements of Section 5 of the Securities Act for resale of certain restricted securities to qualified institutional buyers, which are commonly referred to as "QIBs." In particular, Rule 144A affords safe harbor treatment for re-offers or re-sales to QIBs—by persons other than issuers—of securities of domestic and foreign issuers that are not listed on a U.S. securities exchange or quoted on a U.S. automated interdealer quotation system. Rule 144A provides that re-offers and re-sales in compliance with the rule are not "distributions" and that the reseller is therefore not an "underwriter" within the meaning of Section 2(a)(11) of the 1933 Act. If the reseller is not the issuer or a dealer, it can rely on the exemption provided by Section 4(1) of the 1933 Act. If the reseller is a dealer, it can rely on the exemption provided by Section 4(3) of the 1933 Act.

Rule 147: Provides an exemption from the registration requirements of the Securities Act for intrastate offerings, if certain requirements are met. One requirement is that 100 percent of the purchasers must be from within one state.

Rule 501: Rule 501 of Regulation D defines *accredited investor* and other key terms.

Rule 505: Rule 505 of Regulation D is an exemption for limited offers and sales of securities not exceeding $5,000,000.

Rule 506: Rule 506 of Regulation D is considered a safe harbor for the private offering exemption of Section 4(2) of the Securities Act. Companies using a Rule 506 exemption can raise an unlimited amount of money if they meet certain exemption requirements.

SBIR: Small Business Innovation Research Program. See Small Business Innovation Development Act of 1982.

Secondary Sale: The sale of private or restricted holdings in a portfolio company to other investors.

Securities: According to Section 2(1) of the Securities Act:

> The term "security" means "any note, stock, treasury stock, security future, bond, debenture, evidence of indebtedness, certificate of interest or participation in any profit-sharing agreement, collateral-trust certificate, pre-organization certificate or subscription, transferable share, investment contract, voting-trust certificate, certificate of deposit for a security, fractional undivided interest in oil, gas, or other mineral rights, any put, call, straddle, option, or privilege on any security, certificate of deposit, or group or index of securities (including any interest therein or based on the value thereof), or any put, call, straddle, option, or privilege entered into on a national securities exchange relating to foreign currency, or, in general, any interest or instrument commonly known as a "security," or any certificate of interest or participation in, temporary or interim certificate for, receipt for, guarantee of, or warrant or right to subscribe to or purchase, any of the foregoing".

Clearly, by this definition, the term *security* is very broadly interpreted and means all types of equity, debt instruments that are convertible into equity, and rights in and to them.

Securities Act of 1933: The federal law covering new issues of securities. It provides for full disclosure of pertinent information relating to the new issue and also contains antifraud provisions. Referred to in this set of definitions as the Securities Act.

Securities Exchange Act of 1934: The federal law that established the Securities and Exchange Commission and regulates the reporting requirements for publicly traded companies. The Act outlaws misrepresentation, manipulation, and other abusive practices in the issuance of securities and under the reporting requirements. Referred to in this set of definitions as the Securities Exchange Act.

Securities and Exchange Commission: The SEC is an independent, nonpartisan, quasi-judicial regulatory agency that is responsible for administering the federal securities laws. These laws protect investors in securities markets and ensure that investors have access to all material information concerning publicly traded securities. Additionally, the SEC regulates firms that trade securities, people who provide investment advice, and investment companies.

Seed Money: The first round of capital for a start-up business. Angel investors are the primary source of first professional seed capital, though there are also a few early-stage venture capital funds.

Senior Securities: Securities that have a preferential claim over other stock on a company's earnings and dividends, and assets in the case of liquidation. Generally, preferred stock and bonds are considered senior securities.

Series A Preferred Stock: The first round of preferred stock offered during a seed or early-stage round of financing. This stock is typically convertible into common stock in certain cases such as an IPO or the sale of the company. Later rounds of preferred stock in a private company are called Series B, Series C, and so on.

Share: An equity ownership vehicle.

Shell Corporation: A corporation with no assets and no business. Typically, shell corporations are designed for the purpose of going public and later acquiring existing businesses. Also known as Specified Purpose Acquisition Companies (SPACs). Shell companies are often companies that remain after the substantial sale of assets of a publicly traded company. Unfortunately, many shell companies still have liabilities from the previous operations, making the acquisition of a shell company a potentially undesirable mechanism for going public.

Small Business Innovation Development Act of 1982: The Small Business Innovation Research Program (SBIR) is a set-aside program (2.5 percent of an agency's extramural budget) for domestic small business concerns to engage in research or research and development (R/R&D) that has the potential for commercialization. The SBIR Program was established under the Small Business Innovation Development Act of 1982 (P.L. 97-219), reauthorized until September 30, 2000, by the Small Business Research and Development Enhancement Act (P.L. 102-564), and reauthorized again until September 30, 2008, by the Small Business Reauthorization Act of 2000 (P.L. 106-554).

Staggered Board: An arrangement whereby the election of directors is split into separate periods so that only a portion (for example, one-third) of the total number of directors come up for election in a given year. It is an antitakeover measure—that is, a step designed to make taking control of the board of directors more difficult.

Statutory Voting: A method of voting for members of the board of directors. Under this method, a shareholder receives one vote for each share and may cast those votes for each of the directorships. For example: An individual owning a hundred shares of stock of a corporation that is electing six directors could cast a hundred votes for each of the six candidates. This method tends to favor the larger shareholders. Compare to cumulative voting, defined earlier in this appendix.

Stock: An equity ownership vehicle.

Stock Options: The right to purchase a stock at a specified price (at or below the market price at the time the option is granted) within a stated period. Options are typically for common stock and are a widely used form of employee incentive and employee and nonemployee compensation.

Stock Option Plan: The actual document approved by the shareholders of a company, representing the establishment of a stock plan and governing the parameters for the issuance of stock options.

Stock Purchase Agreement: The actual agreement witnessing the purchase of shares by an investor, including a founder. Provides the purchaser with notification of any restrictions on the stock and required status of the investor, such as being an accredited investor.

Strategic Investors: Corporate or individual investors that add value to investments they make through industry and personal ties that can assist companies in making connections with possible customers, in the marketing and sales process, as well as raising additional capital.

Subordinated Note or Debt: Debt that by its terms has no right to be paid until another debt holder is paid. Also referred to as junior debt.

Subscription Agreement: An agreement in which an investor formally commits to the purchase of shares in a company. It contains the terms for such purchase and can be combined with the investor questionnaire to qualify the investor as an accredited investor and to state the terms under which stock may be purchased. A company has the right to refuse an investor's offer of a subscription agreement. Differentiated from a "stock purchase agreement," which is the actual purchase rather than the offer to purchase securities.

Syndicate: Underwriters or broker-dealers who sell a security as a group. (See Allocation.)

Tag-Along Rights (see also Co-Sale Rights): A protection affording shareholders the right to include their shares in any sale of control at the offered price.

Term Sheet: A nonbinding but agreed-upon outline of the principal points for investment between the investor and company. The actual investment documents are then created consistent with the term sheet and cover the terms in detail.

Third-Party Financing: Investment in a company by an individual or entity not related to or personally known by the founders. Typically describes investment rounds other than founders' initial investment or any investments by employees or friends and family. Also known as "outside financing."

Time Value of Money: The basic principle that money can earn interest, therefore $1 today will be worth more in the future, if invested. This is also referred to as future value.

Treasury Stock: Stock issued by a company but later reacquired. It may be held in the company's treasury indefinitely, reissued to the public, or retired. Treasury stock receives no dividends and does not carry voting power while held by the company.

Underwriter: The underwriters are the investment bankers who sell securities in an underwritten registered public offering. But beware, under the Securities Act, the class of persons who are considered "underwriters" is far more expansive and problematic.

Underwritten Offering: Registered offering that is sold through a consortium of investment banks assembled by one or more lead investment bank.

Unit Offering: Private or public offering of securities in groups of more than one security. Most often a share of stock and a warrant to purchase some number of shares of stock, but could be two shares of stock, a note and a share of stock, or other arrangement. Also used in some cases to refer to the sale of LP and LLC interests, since those interests are composed of more than one right.

Venture Capital Financing: An investment in a start-up business that is perceived to have excellent growth prospects but does not have access to capital markets. Statistics show that venture capital financing typically follows angel financing, although it can be the first round of professional financing.

Voting Agreements: Majority shareholders or a specific group agrees to vote their stock in a particular manner or consistent with choices made by a designated shareholder.

Voting Right: Shareholders' right to vote their stock in the affairs of the company. The right to vote may be delegated by a stockholder to another person, often referred to as a proxy.

Warrant: A type of security that entitles the holder to buy a proportionate amount of common or preferred stock at a specified price for a period of years. Warrants are often issued together with a loan, a bond, or preferred stock—and act as sweeteners, to induce people to become investors.

Weighted Average Anti-dilution: The investor's conversion price is reduced, and thus the number of common shares received on conversion increased, in the case of a down round; it takes into account both the reduced price and the number of shares (or rights) issued in the dilutive financing.

Workout: A negotiated agreement between debtors and creditors outside the bankruptcy process.

Write-off: The act of changing the value of an asset to an expense or a loss. A write-off is used to reduce or eliminate the value of an asset and reduce profits.

Write-up and Write-down: An upward or downward adjustment of the value of an asset for accounting and reporting purposes. These adjustments are estimates and tend to be subjective, although they are usually based on events affecting the company or its securities beneficially or detrimentally.

Non-Disclosure Agreement (Mutual)

*N*ote: Non-disclosure agreements can contain many other terms and conditions including non-competes and non-interference, depending on your needs and consideration provided. All agreements should be reviewed and approved by your legal counsel for compliance with state law and alignment with your needs. This agreement is set up to protect disclosure by both parties. The definition of "Confidential Information" is quite extensive and can be shortened, but does give you a good idea of possible information that may be included in this type of document.

This Agreement governs the disclosure of information by and between Great Starts, Inc., and _____ [second party to agreement], as of _____ [date] (the "Effective Date").

As used herein, "Confidential Information" shall mean any and all technical and nontechnical information provided by either party to the other, including but not limited to (a) patents and patent applications, (b) trade secrets, and (c) proprietary information—mask works, ideas, media, techniques, sketches, drawings, works of authorship, models, inventions, know-how, equipment, software programs, software source documents, and formulae related to the current, future, and proposed products and services of each of the parties, and including, without limitation, their respective information concerning research, experimental work, development, design details and specifications, engineering, financial information, procurement requirements, purchasing, manufacturing, customer lists, investors, employees, business and contractual relationships, business forecasts, sales and merchandising, marketing plans, and information the disclosing party provides regarding third parties.

[*Optional:* If you anticipate receipt of confidential information of any significance, you may wish to add the following language to ensure you understand what is confidential. Of course, these terms will also apply to any information you communicate, in writing or orally. Even without this additional, optional language, always mark your confidential information as such to ensure clear understanding of confidentiality by the receiving party. "If the Confidential Information is embodied in tangible material (including without limitation software, hardware, drawings, graphs, charts, disks, tapes, prototypes, and samples), it shall be labeled as "Confidential" or bear a similar legend. If the Confidential Information is disclosed orally or visually, it shall be identified as such at the time of disclosure and be confirmed in writing to the receiving party within thirty (30) days of such disclosure, referencing the place and date of oral or visual disclosure and the names of the employees of the receiving party to whom such oral or visual disclosure was made, and including therein a brief description of the Confidential Information disclosed."]

Each party agrees that at all times and notwithstanding any termination or expiration of this Agreement it will hold in strict confidence and not disclose to any third party Confidential Information of the other, except as approved in writing by the other party to this Agreement, and will use the Confidential Information for no purpose other than _____
[Define the permitted use, which is usually "evaluating or pursuing a business relationship with the other party to this Agreement."] Notwithstanding the above, the party to whom Confidential Information was disclosed (the "Recipient") shall not be in violation of this Section 2 with regard to a disclosure that was in response to a valid order by a court or other governmental body, provided that the Recipient provides the other party with prior written notice of such disclosure in order to permit the other party to seek confidential treatment of such information. Each party shall permit access to Confidential Information of the other party only to those of its employees or authorized representatives who have a need to know and who have signed confidentiality agreements or are otherwise bound by confidentiality obligations at least as restrictive as those contained herein.

Each party shall immediately notify the other upon discovery of any loss or unauthorized disclosure of the Confidential Information of the other party.

Each party's obligations under this Agreement with respect to the relevant portion of the other party's Confidential Information shall terminate when the Recipient can document that: (a) it was in the public domain at the time it was communicated to the Recipient by the other party; (b) it entered the public domain subsequent to the time it was communicated to the Recipient by the other party through no fault of the Recipient; (c) it was in the Recipient's possession free of any obligation of confidence at the time it was communicated to the Recipient by the other party; (d) it was rightfully communicated to the Recipient free of any obligation of confidence subsequent to the time it was communicated to the Recipient by the other party; or (e) it was developed by employees or agents of the Recipient independently of and without reference to any information communicated to the Recipient by the other party.

Upon termination or expiration of the Agreement, or upon written request of the other party, each party shall promptly return to the other all documents and other tangible materials representing the other's Confidential Information and all copies thereof.

The parties recognize and agree that nothing contained in this Agreement shall be construed as granting any property rights, by license or otherwise, to any Confidential Information of the other party disclosed pursuant to this Agreement, or to any invention or any patent, copyright, trademark, or other intellectual property right that has issued or that may issue, based on such Confidential Information. Neither party shall make, have made, use, or sell for any purpose any product or other item using, incorporating, or derived from any Confidential Information of the other party.

Confidential Information shall not be reproduced in any form except as required to accomplish the intent of this Agreement. Any reproduction of any Confidential Information of the other party by either party shall remain the property of the disclosing party and shall contain any and all confidential or proprietary notices or legends that appear on the original, unless otherwise authorized in writing by the other party.

This Agreement shall terminate _____ ( ) years [often one to two years] after the Effective Date, or may be terminated by either party at any time upon thirty (30) days' written notice to the other party. The Recipient's obligations under this Agreement shall survive termination of the Agreement between the parties and shall be binding upon the Recipient's heirs, successors, and assigns. The Recipient's obligations hereunder shall continue in full force and effect with respect to all Confidential Information for _____ ( ) years [often three to five years or indefinitely] from the date of disclosure of such Confidential Information. The protection period for Confidential Information marked or otherwise identified as trade secret shall be for so long as such trade secret information remains secret and confidential and is protected under applicable laws.

This Agreement shall be governed by and construed in accordance with the laws of the State of _____ without reference to conflict of laws principles. This Agreement may not be amended except by a writing signed by both parties hereto.

If any provision of this Agreement is found by a proper authority to be unenforceable or invalid, such unenforceability or invalidity shall not render this Agreement unenforceable or invalid as a whole, and in such event, such provision shall be changed and interpreted so as to best accomplish the objectives of such unenforceable or invalid provision within the limits of applicable law or applicable court decisions.

Neither party will assign or transfer any rights or obligations under this Agreement without the prior written consent of the other party.

All notices or reports permitted or required under this Agreement shall be in writing and shall be delivered by personal delivery, electronic mail, facsimile transmission, or by certified or registered mail, return receipt requested, and shall be deemed given upon personal delivery, five (5) days after deposit in the mail, or upon acknowledgment of receipt of electronic transmission. Notices shall be sent to the addresses set forth at the end of this Agreement or such other address as either party may specify in writing.

Each of the parties agrees that the software programs of the other party contain valuable confidential information and each party agrees it will not modify, reverse engineer, decompile, create other works from, or disassemble any software programs contained in the Confidential Information of the other party without the prior written consent of the other party.

In Witness Whereof, the parties hereto have caused this Non-Disclosure Agreement to be executed as of the Effective Date.

By: _____   By: _____

Title: _____   Title: _____

Date: _____   Date: _____

Address: _____   Address: _____

U.S. Securities and
Exchange Commission
Washington, D.C. 20549

Regulation D
Rules Governing the Limited Offer and Sale of Securities Without Registration Under the Securities Act of 1933

PRELIMINARY NOTES

1. The following rules relate to transactions exempted from the registration requirements of section 5 of the Securities Act of 1933 (the "Act") [15 U.S.C. 77a et seq., as amended]. Such transactions are not exempt from the antifraud, civil liability, or other provisions of the federal securities laws. Issuers are reminded of their obligation to provide such further material information, if any, as may be necessary to make the information required under this regulation, in light of the circumstances under which it is furnished, not misleading.

2. Nothing in these rules obviates the need to comply with any applicable state law relating to the offer and sale of securities. Regulation D is intended to be a basic element in a uniform system of federal-state limited offering exemptions consistent with the provisions of sections 18 and 19(c) of the Act.

In those states that have adopted Regulation D, or any version of Regulation D, special attention should be directed to the applicable state laws and regulations, including those relating to registration of persons who receive remuneration in connection with the offer and sale of securities, to disqualification of issuers and other persons associated with offerings based on state administrative orders or judgments, and to requirements for filings of notices of sales.

3. Attempted compliance with any rule in Regulation D does not act as an exclusive election; the issuer can also claim the availability of any other applicable exemption. For instance, an issuer's failure to satisfy all the terms and conditions of Rule 506 shall not raise any presumption that the exemption provided by section 4(2) of the Act is not available.

4. These rules are available only to the issuer of the securities and not to any affiliate of that issuer or to any other person for resales of the issuer's securities. The rules provide an exemption only for the transactions in which the securities are offered or sold by the issuer, not for the securities themselves.

5. These rules may be used for business combinations that involve sales by virtue of Rule 145(a) (17 CFR 230.145(a)) or otherwise.

6. In view of the objectives of these rules and the policies underlying the Act, Regulation D is not available to any issuer for any transaction or chain of transactions that, although in technical compliance with these rules, is part of a plan or scheme to evade the registration provisions of the Act. In such cases, registration under the Act is required.

7. Securities offered and sold outside the United States in accordance with Regulation S need not be registered under the Act. See Release No. 33–6863. Regulation S may be relied upon for such offers and sales even if coincident offers and sales are made in accordance with Regulation D inside the United States. Thus, for example, persons who are offered and sold securities in accordance with Regulation S would not be counted in the calculation of the number of purchasers under Regulation D. Similarly, proceeds from such sales would not be included in the aggregate offering price. The provisions of this note, however, do not apply if the issuer elects to rely solely on Regulation D for offers or sales to persons made outside the United States.

DEFINITIONS AND TERMS USED IN REGULATION D

Reg. § 230.501. As used in Regulation D [§§ 230.501–230.508], the following terms shall have the meaning indicated:

(a) *Accredited investor.* "Accredited investor" shall mean any person who comes within any of the following categories, or who the issuer reasonably believes comes within any of the following categories, at the time of the sale of the securities to that person:

Potential persons who are to respond to the collection of information contained in this form are not required to respond unless the form displays a currently valid OMB control number.

(1) Any bank as defined in section 3(a)(2) of the Act, or any savings and loan association or other institution as defined in section 3(a)(5)(A) of the Act whether acting in its individual or fiduciary capacity; any broker or dealer registered pursuant to section 15 of the Securities Exchange Act of 1934; any insurance company as defined in section 2(13) of the Act; any investment company registered under the Investment Company Act of 1940 or a business development company as defined in section 2(a)(48) of that Act; any Small Business Investment Company licensed by the U.S. Small Business Administration under section 301(c) or (d) of the Small Business Investment Act of 1958; any plan established and maintained by a state, its political subdivisions, or any agency or instrumentality of a state or its political subdivisions, for the benefit of its employees, if such plan has total assets in excess of $5,000,000; any employee benefit plan within the meaning of the Employee Retirement Income Security Act of 1974 if the investment decision is made by a plan fiduciary, as defined in section 3(21) of such Act, which is either a bank, savings and loan association, insurance company, or registered adviser, or if the employee benefit plan has total assets in excess of $5,000,000 or, if a self-directed plan, with investment decisions made solely by persons that are accredited investors;

(2) Any private business development company as defined in section 202(a)(22) of the Investment Advisers Act of 1940;

(3) Any organization described in section 501(c)(3) of the Internal Revenue Code, corporation, Massachusetts or similar business trust, or partnership, not formed for the specific purpose of acquiring the securities offered, with total assets in excess of $5,000,000;

(4) Any director, executive officer, or general partner of the issuer of the securities being offered or sold, or any director, executive officer, or general partner of a general partner of that issuer;

(5) Any natural person whose individual net worth, or joint net worth with that person's spouse, at the time of his purchase exceeds $1,000,000;

(6) Any natural person who had an individual income in excess of $200,000 in each of the two most recent years or joint income with that person's spouse in excess of $300,000 in each of those years and has a reasonable expectation of reaching the same income level in the current year;

(7) Any trust, with total assets in excess of $5,000,000, not formed for the specific purpose of acquiring the securities offered, whose purchase is directed by a sophisticated person as described in § 230.506(b)(2)(ii); and

(8) Any entity in which all of the equity owners are accredited investors.

(b) *Affiliate.* An "affiliate" of, or person "affiliated" with, a specified person shall mean a person that directly, or indirectly through one or more intermediaries, controls or is controlled by, or is under common control with, the person specified.

(c) *Aggregate offering price.* "Aggregate offering price" shall mean the sum of all cash, services, property, notes, cancellation of debt, or other consideration to be received by an issuer for issuance of its securities. Where securities are being offered for both cash and non-cash consideration, the aggregate offering price shall be based on the price at which the securities are offered for cash. Any portion of the aggregate offering price attributable to cash received in a foreign currency shall be translated into United States currency at the currency exchange rate in effect at a reasonable time prior to or on the date of the sale of the securities. If securities are not offered for cash, the aggregate offering price shall be based on the value of the consideration as established by bona fide sales of that consideration made within a reasonable time, or, in the absence of sales, on the fair value as determined by an accepted standard. Such valuations of non-cash consideration must be reasonable at the time made.

(d) *Business combination.* "Business combination" shall mean any transaction of the type specified in paragraph (a) of Rule 145 under the Act (17 CFR 230.145) and any transaction involving the acquisition by one issuer, in exchange for all or a part of its own or its parent's stock, or stock of another issuer if, immediately after the acquisition, the acquiring issuer has control of the other issuer (whether or not it had control before the acquisition).

(e) *Calculation of number of purchasers.* For purposes of calculating the number of purchasers under §§ 230.505(b) and 230.506(b) only, the following shall apply:

(1) The following purchasers shall be excluded:

(i) Any relative, spouse or relative of the spouse of a purchaser who has the same principal residence as the purchaser;

(ii) Any trust or estate in which a purchaser and any of the persons related to him as specified in paragraph (e)(1)(i) or (e)(1)(iii) of this § 230.501 collectively have more than 50 percent of the beneficial interest (excluding contingent interests);

(iii) Any corporation or other organization of which a purchaser and any of the persons related to him as specified in paragraph (e)(1)(i) or (e)(1)(ii) of this § 230.501 collectively are beneficial owners of more than 50 percent of the equity securities (excluding directors' qualifying shares) or equity interests; and

(iv) Any accredited investor.

(2) A corporation, partnership or other entity shall be counted as one purchaser. If, however, that entity is organized for the specific purpose of acquiring the securities offered and is not an accredited investor under paragraph (a)(8) of this section, then each beneficial owner of equity securities or equity interests in the entity shall count as a separate purchaser for all provisions of Regulation D (§§ 230.501–230.508), except to the extent provided in paragraph (e)(1) of this section.

(3) A non-contributory employee benefit plan within the meaning of Title I of the Employee Retirement Income Security Act of 1974 shall be counted as one purchaser where the trustee makes all investment decisions for the plan.

Note: The issuer must satisfy all the other provisions of Regulation D for all purchasers whether or not they are included in calculating the number of purchasers. Clients of an investment adviser or customers of a broker or dealer shall be considered the "purchasers" under Regulation D regardless of the amount of discretion given to the investment adviser or broker or dealer to act on behalf of the client or customer.

(f) *Executive officer.* "Executive officer" shall mean the president, any vice president in charge of a principal business unit, division or function (such as sales, administration or finance), any other officer who performs a policy making function, or any other person who performs similar policy making functions for the issuer. Executive officers of subsidiaries may be deemed executive officers of the issuer if they perform such policy making functions for the issuer.

(g) *Issuer.* The definition of the term "issuer" in section 2(4) of the Act shall apply, except that in the case of a proceeding under the Federal Bankruptcy Code [11 U.S.C. 101 et seq.], the trustee or debtor in possession shall be considered the issuer in an offering under a plan or reorganization, if the securities are to be issued under the plan.

(h) *Purchaser representative.* "Purchaser representative" shall mean any person who satisfies all of the following conditions or who the issuer reasonably believes satisfies all of the following conditions:

(1) Is not an affiliate, director, officer or other employee of the issuer, or beneficial owner of 10 percent or more of any class of the equity securities or 10 percent or more of the equity interest in the issuer, except where the purchaser is:

(i) A relative of the purchaser representative by blood, marriage or adoption and not more remote than a first cousin;

(ii) A trust or estate in which the purchaser representative and any persons related to him as specified in paragraph (h)(1)(i) or (h)(1)(iii) of this § 230.501 collectively have more than 50 percent of the beneficial interest (excluding contingent interest) or of which the purchaser representative serves as trustee, executor, or in any similar capacity; or

(iii) A corporation or other organization of which the purchaser representative and any persons related to him as specified in paragraph (h)(1)(i) or (h)(1)(ii) of this § 230.501 collectively are the beneficial owners of more than 50 percent of the equity securities (excluding directors' qualifying shares) or equity interests;

(2) Has such knowledge and experience in financial and business matters that he is capable of evaluating, alone, or together with other purchaser representatives of the purchaser, or together with the purchaser, the merits and risks of the prospective investment;

(3) Is acknowledged by the purchaser in writing, during the course of the transaction, to be his purchaser representative in connection with evaluating the merits and risks of the prospective investment; and

(4) Discloses to the purchaser in writing a reasonable time prior to the sale of securities to that purchaser any material relationship between himself or his affiliates and the issuer or its affiliates that then exists, that is mutually understood to be contemplated, or that has existed at any time during the previous two years, and any compensation received or to be received as a result of such relationship.

Note 1: A person acting as a purchaser representative should consider the applicability of the registration and antifraud provisions relating to brokers and dealers under the Securities Exchange Act of 1934 ("Exchange Act") [15 U.S.C. 78a *et seq.,* as amended] and relating to investment advisers under the Investment Advisers Act of 1940.

Note 2: The acknowledgment required by paragraph (h)(3) and the disclosure required by paragraph (h)(4) of this § 230.501 must be made with specific reference to each prospective investment. Advance blanket acknowledgment, such as for "all securities transactions" or "all private placements," is not sufficient.

Note 3: Disclosure of any material relationships between the purchaser representative or his affiliates and the issuer or its affiliates does not relieve the purchaser representative of his obligation to act in the interest of the purchaser.

GENERAL CONDITIONS TO BE MET

Reg. § 230.502. The following conditions shall be applicable to offers and sales made under Regulation D (§§ 230.501–230.508):

(a) *Integration.* All sales that are part of the same Regulation D offering must meet all of the terms and conditions of Regulation D. Offers and sales that are made more than six months before the start of a Regulation D offering or are made more than six months after completion of a Regulation D offering will not be considered part of that Regulation D offering, so long as during those six month periods there are no offers or sales of securities by or for the issuer that are of the same or a similar class as those offered or sold under Regulation D, other than those offers or sales of securities under an employee benefit plan as defined in Rule 405 under the Act [17 CFR 230.405].

Note: The term "offering" is not defined in the Act or in Regulation D. If the issuer offers or sells securities for which the safe harbor rule in paragraph (a) of this § 230.502 is unavailable, the determination as to whether separate sales of securities are part of the same offering (i.e., are considered "integrated") depends on the particular facts and circumstances. Generally, transactions otherwise meeting the requirements of an exemption will not be integrated with simultaneous offerings being made outside the United States in compliance with Regulation S. See Release No. 33–6863. The following factors should be considered in determining whether offers and sales should be integrated for purposes of the exemptions under Regulation D:

(a) whether the sales are part of a single plan of financing;

(b) whether the sales involve issuance of the same class of securities;

(c) whether the sales have been made at or about the same time;

(d) whether the same type of consideration is being received; and

(e) whether the sales are made for the same general purpose.

See Release No. 33–4552 (November 6, 1962) [27 F.R. 11316].

(b) *Information requirements.*

(1) *When information must be furnished.*

If the issuer sells securities under § 230.505 or § 230.506 to any purchaser that is not an accredited investor, the issuer shall furnish the information specified in paragraph (b)(2) of this section to such purchaser a reasonable time prior to sale. The issuer is not required to furnish the specified information to purchasers when it sells securities under § 230.504, or to any accredited investor.

Note: When an issuer provides information to investors pursuant to paragraph (b)(1), it should consider providing such information to accredited investors as well, in view of the anti-fraud provisions of the Federal securities laws.

(2) *Type of information to be furnished.*

(i) If the issuer is not subject to the reporting requirements of section 13 or 15(d) of the Exchange Act, at a reasonable time prior to the sale of securities, the issuer shall furnish to the purchaser, to the extent material to an understanding of the issuer, its business, and the securities being offered:

(A) *Non-financial statement information.* If the issuer is eligible to use Regulation A (§ 230.251–263), the same kind of information as would be required in Part II of Form 1-A (§ 239.90 of this chapter). If the issuer is not eligible to use Regulation A, the same kind of information as required in Part I of a registration statement filed under the Securities Act on the form that the issuer would be entitled to use.

(B) *Financial Statement Information.*

(1) *Offerings up to $2,000,000.* The information required in Item 310 of Regulation S-B [§ 228.310 of this chapter], except that only the issuer's balance sheet, which shall be dated within 120 days of the start of the offering, must be audited.

(2) *Offerings up to $7,500,000.* The financial statement information required in Form SB-2 [§ 239.10 of this chapter]. If an issuer, other than a limited partnership, cannot obtain audited financial statements without unreasonable effort or expense, then only the issuer's balance sheet, which shall be dated within 120 days of the start of the offering, must be audited. If the issuer is a limited partnership and cannot obtain the required financial statements without unreasonable effort or expense, it may furnish financial statements that have been prepared on the basis of Federal income tax requirements and examined and reported on in accordance with generally accepted auditing standards by an independent public or certified accountant.

(3) *Offerings over $7,500,000.* The financial statement as would be required in a registration statement filed under the Act on the form that the issuer would be entitled to use. If an issuer, other than a limited partnership, cannot obtain audited financial statements without unreasonable effort or expense, then only the issuer's balance sheet, which shall be dated within 120 days of the start of the offering, must be audited. If the issuer is a limited partnership and cannot obtain the required financial statements without unreasonable effort or expense, it may furnish financial statements that have been prepared on the basis of Federal income tax requirements and examined and reported on in accordance with generally accepted auditing standards by an independent public or certified accountant.

(C) If the issuer is a foreign private issuer eligible to use Form 20-F (§ 249.220f of this chapter), the issuer shall disclose the same kind of information required to be included in a registration statement filed under the Act on the form that the issuer would be entitled to use. The financial statements need be certified only to the extent required by paragraph (b)(2)(i)(B)*(1), (2)* or *(3)* of this section, as appropriate.

(ii) If the issuer is subject to the reporting requirements of section 13 or 15(d) of the Exchange Act, at a reasonable time prior to the sale of securities, the issuer shall furnish to the purchaser the information specified in paragraph (b)(2)(ii)(A) or (B) of this section, and in either event the information specified in paragraph (b)(2)(ii)(C) of this section:

(A) The issuer's annual report to shareholders for the most recent fiscal year, if such annual report meets the requirements of § 240.14a-3 or 240.14c-3 under the Exchange Act, the definitive proxy statement filed in connection with that annual report, and, if requested by the purchaser in writing, a copy of the issuer's most recent Form 10-K and 10-KSB [17 CFR 249.310 and 249.310b] under the Exchange Act.

(B) The information contained in an annual report on Form 10-K (§ 249.310 of this chapter) or 10-KSB(§ 249.310b of this chapter) under the Exchange Act or in a registration statement on Form S-1 (§ 239.11 of this chapter), SB-1 (§ 239.9 of this chapter), SB-2 (§ 239.10 of this chapter) or S-11 (§ 239.18 of this chapter) under the Act or on Form 10 (§ 249.210 of this chapter) or Form 10-SB (§ 249.210b of this chapter) under the Exchange Act, whichever filing is the most recent required to be filed.

(C) The information contained in any reports or documents required to be filed by the issuer under sections 13(a), 14(a), 14(c), and 15(d) of the Exchange Act since the distribution or filing of the report or registration statement specified in paragraph (A) or (B), and a brief description of the securities being offered, the use of the proceeds from the offering, and any material changes in the issuer's affairs that are not disclosed in the documents furnished.

(D) If the issuer is a foreign private issuer, the issuer may provide in lieu of the information specified in paragraph (b)(2)(ii)(A) or (B) of this section, the information contained in its most recent filing on Form 20-F or Form F-1 (§ 239.31 of this chapter).

(iii) Exhibits required to be filed with the Commission as part of a registration statement or report, other than an annual report to shareholders or parts of that report incorporated by reference in a Form 10-K and Form 10-KSB report, need not be furnished to each purchaser that is not an accredited investor if the contents of material exhibits are identified and such exhibits are made available to a purchaser, upon his written request, a reasonable time prior to his purchase.

(iv) At a reasonable time prior to the sale of securities to any purchaser that is not an accredited investor in a transaction under § 230.505 or § 230.506, the issuer shall furnish to the purchaser a brief description in writing of any material written information concerning the offering that has been provided by the issuer to any accredited investor but not previously delivered to such unaccredited purchaser. The issuer shall furnish any portion or all of this information to the purchaser, upon his written request a reasonable time prior to his purchase.

(v) The issuer shall also make available to each purchaser at a reasonable time prior to his purchase of securities in a transaction under § 230.505 or § 230.506 the opportunity to ask questions and receive answers concerning the terms and conditions of the offering and to obtain any additional information which the issuer possesses or can acquire without unreasonable effort or expense that is necessary to verify the accuracy of information furnished under paragraph (b)(2)(i) or (ii) of this § 230.502.

(vi) For business combinations or exchange offers, in addition to information required by Form S-4 [17 CFR 239.25], the issuer shall provide to each purchaser at the time the plan is submitted to security holders, or, with an exchange, during the course of the transaction and prior to sale, written information about any terms or arrangements of the proposed transactions that are materially different from those for all other security holders. For purposes of this subsection, an issuer which is not subject to the reporting requirements of section 13 or 15(d) of the Exchange Act may satisfy the requirements of Part I.B or C of Form S-4 by compliance with paragraph (b)(2)(i) of this § 230.502.

(vii) At a reasonable time prior to the sale of securities to any purchaser that is not an accredited investor in a transaction under § 230.505 or § 230.506, the issuer shall advise the purchaser of the limitations on resale in the manner contained in paragraph (d)(2) of this section. Such disclosure may be contained in other materials required to be provided by this paragraph.

(c) *Limitation on manner of offering.* Except as provided in § 230.504(b)(1), neither the issuer nor any person acting on its behalf shall offer or sell the securities by any form of general solicitation or general advertising, including, but not limited to, the following:

(1) Any advertisement, article, notice or other communication published in any newspaper, magazine, or similar media or broadcast over television or radio; and

(2) Any seminar or meeting whose attendees have been invited by any general solicitation or general advertising. *Provided, however,* that publication by an issuer of a notice in accordance with § 230.135c shall not be deemed to constitute general solicitation or general advertising for purposes of this section. *Provided further,* that, if the requirements of § 230.135e are satisfied, providing any journalist with access to press conferences held outside of the United States, to meetings with issuer or selling security holder representatives conducted outside of the United States, or to written press-related materials released outside the United States, at or in which a present or proposed offering of securities is discussed, will not be deemed to constitute general solicitation or general advertising for purposes of this section.

(d) *Limitations on resale.* Except as provided in § 230.504(b)(1), securities acquired in a transaction under Regulation D shall have the status of securities acquired in a transaction under section 4(2) of the Act and cannot be resold without registration under the Act or an exemption therefrom. The issuer shall exercise reasonable care to assure that the purchasers of the securities are not underwriters within the meaning of section 2(11) of the Act, which reasonable care may be demonstrated by the following:

Provided, however, that publication by an issuer of a notice in accordance with § 230.135c shall not be deemed to constitute general solicitation or general advertising for purposes of this section.

(1) Reasonable inquiry to determine if the purchaser is acquiring the securities for himself or for other persons;

(2) Written disclosure to each purchaser prior to sale that the securities have not been registered under the Act and, therefore, cannot be resold unless they are registered under the Act or unless an exemption from registration is available; and

(3) Placement of a legend on the certificate or other document that evidences the securities stating that the securities have not been registered under the Act and setting forth or referring to the restrictions on transferability and sale of the securities. While taking these actions will establish the requisite reasonable care, it is not the exclusive method to demonstrate such care. Other actions by the issuer may satisfy this provision. In addition, § 230.502(b)(2)(vii) requires the delivery of written disclosure of the limitations on resale to investors in certain instances.

Filing of Notice of Sales
Reg. § 230.503.

(a) An issuer offering or selling securities in reliance on § 230.504, § 230.505 or § 230.506 shall file with the Commission five copies of a notice on Form D (17 CFR 239.500) no later than 15 days after the first sale of securities.

(b) One copy of every notice on Form D shall be manually signed by a person duly authorized by the issuer.

(c) If sales are made under § 230.505, the notice shall contain an undertaking by the issuer to furnish to the Commission, upon the written request of its staff, the information furnished by the issuer under § 230.502(b)(2) to any purchaser that is not an accredited investor.

(d) Amendments to notices filed under paragraph (a) of this § 230.503 need only report the issuer's name and the information required by Part C and any material change in the facts from those set forth in Parts A and B.

(e) A notice on Form D shall be considered filed with the Commission under paragraph (a) of this § 230.503:

(1) As of the date on which it is received at the Commission's principal office in Washington, D.C.; or

(2) As of the date on which the notice is mailed by means of United States registered or certified mail to the Commission's principal office in Washington, D.C., if the notice is delivered to such office after the date on which it is required to be filed.

Exemption for Limited Offerings and Sales of Securities Not Exceeding $1,000,000

Reg. § 230.504.

(a) *Exemption.* Offers and sales of securities that satisfy the conditions in paragraph (b) of this § 230.504 by an issuer that is not:

(1) subject to the reporting requirements of section 13 or 15(d) of the Exchange Act;

(2) an investment company; or

(3) a development stage company that either has no specific business plan or purpose or has indicated that its business plan is to engage in a merger or acquisition with an unidentified company or companies, or other entity or person, shall be exempt from the provisions of section 5 of the Act under section 3(b) of the Act.

(b) *Conditions to be met.*

(1) To qualify for exemption under this § 230.504, offers and sales must satisfy the terms and conditions of § 230.501 and § 230.502(a),(c) and (d), except that the provisions of § 230.502(c) and (d) will not apply to offers and sales of securities under this § 230.504 that are made:

(i) Exclusively in one or more states that provide for the registration of the securities, and require the public filing and delivery to investors of a substantive disclosure document before sale, and are made in accordance with those state provisions;

(ii) In one or more states that have no provision for the registration of the securities or the public filing or delivery of a disclosure document before sale, if the securities have been registered in at least one state that provides for such registration, public filing and delivery before sale, offers and sales are made in that state in accordance with such provisions, and the disclosure document is delivered before sale to all purchasers (including those in the states that have no such procedure); or

(iii) Exclusively according to state law exemptions from registration that permit general solicitation and general advertising so long as sales are made only to "accredited investors" as defined in § 230.501(a).

(2) The aggregate offering price for an offering of securities under this § 230.504, as defined in § 230.501(c), shall not exceed $1,000,000, less the aggregate offering price for all securities sold within the twelve months before the start of and during the offering of securities under this § 230.504, in reliance on any exemption under section 3(b) of the Act, or in violation of section 5(a) of the Securities Act.

Note 1: The calculation of the aggregate offering price is illustrated as follows:

If an issuer sold $900,000 on June 1, 1987 under this § 230.504 and an additional $4,100,000 on December 1, 1987 under § 230.505, the issuer could not sell any of its securities under this § 230.504 until December 1, 1988. Until then the issuer must count the December 1, 1987 sale towards the $1,000,000 limit within the preceding twelve months.

Note 2: If a transaction under § 230.504 fails to meet the limitation on the aggregate offering price, it does not affect the availability of this § 230.504 for the other transactions considered in applying such limitation. For example, if an issuer sold $1,000,000 worth of its securities on January 1, 1988 under this § 230.504 and an additional $500,000 worth on July 1, 1988, this § 230.504 would not be available for the later sale, but would still be applicable to the January 1, 1988 sale.

Exemption for Limited Offers and Sales of Securities Not Exceeding $5,000,000

Reg. § 230.505.

(a) *Exemption.* Offers and sales of securities that satisfy the conditions in paragraph (b) of this § 230.505 by an issuer that is not an investment company shall be exempt from the provisions of section 5 of the Act under section 3(b) of the Act.

(b) *Conditions to be met.*

(1) *General conditions.* To qualify for exemption under this section, offers and sales must satisfy the terms and conditions of § 230.501 and § 230.502.

(2) *Specific conditions.*

(i) *Limitations on aggregate offering price.* The aggregate offering price for an offering of securities under this § 230.505, as defined in § 230.501(c), shall not exceed $5,000,000, less the aggregate offering price for all securities sold within the twelve months before the start of and during the offering of securities under this § 230.505 in reliance on any exemption under section 3(b) of the Act or in violation of section 5(a) of the Act.

Note: The calculation of the aggregate offering price is illustrated as follows:

Example 1. If an issuer sold $2,000,000 of its securities on June 1, 1982 under this § 230.505 and an additional $1,000,000 on September 1, 1982, the issuer would be permitted to sell only $2,000,000 more under this § 230.505 until June 1, 1983. Until that date the issuer must count both prior sales towards the $5,000,000 limit. However, if the issuer made its third sale on June 1, 1983, the issuer could then sell $4,000,000 of its securities because the June 1, 1982 sale would not be within the preceding twelve months.

Example 2. If an issuer sold $500,000 of its securities on June 1, 1982 under § 230.504 and an additional $4,500,000 on December 1, 1982 under this § 230.505, then the issuer could not sell any of its securities under this § 230.505 until June 1, 1983. At that time it could sell an additional $500,000 of its securities.

(ii) *Limitation on number of purchasers.* There are no more than or the issuer reasonably believes that there are no more than 35 purchasers of securities from the issuer in any offering under this section § 230.505.

Note: See § 230.501(e) for the calculation of the number of purchasers and § 230.502(a) for what may or may not constitute an offering under this section.

(iii) *Disqualifications.* No exemption under this section shall be available for the securities of any issuer described in § 230.262 of Regulation A, except that for purposes of this section only:

(A) The term "filing of the offering statement required by § 230.252" as used in § 230.262(a), (b) and (c) shall mean the first sale of securities under this section;

(B) The term "underwriter" as used in § 230.262(b) and (c) shall mean a person that has been or will be paid directly or indirectly remuneration for solicitation of purchasers in connection with sales of securities under this section; and

(C) Paragraph (b)(2)(iii) of this § 230.505 shall not apply to any issuer if the Commission determines, upon a showing of good cause, that it is not necessary under the circumstances that the exemption be denied. Any such determination shall be without prejudice to any other action by the Commission in any other proceeding or matter with respect to the issuer or any other person.

Exemption for Limited Offers and Sales Without Regard to Dollar Amount of Offering

Reg. § 230.506.

(a) *Exemption.* Offers and sales of securities by an issuer that satisfy the conditions in paragraph (b) of this § 230.506 shall be deemed to be transactions not involving any public offering within the meaning of section 4(2) of the Act.

(b) *Conditions to be met.*

(1) *General conditions.* To qualify for exemption under this section, offers and sales must satisfy all the terms and conditions of § 230.501 and § 230.502.

(2) *Specific conditions.*

(i) *Limitation on number of purchasers.* There are no more than or the issuer reasonably believes that there are no more than 35 purchasers of securities from the issuer in any offering under this § 230.506.

Note: See § 230.501(e) for the calculation of the number of purchasers and § 230.502(a) for what may or may not constitute an offering under this section 230.506.

(ii) *Nature of purchasers.* Each purchaser who is not an accredited investor either alone or with his purchaser representative(s) has such knowledge and experience in financial and business matters that he is capable of evaluating the merits and risks of the prospective investment, or the issuer reasonably believes immediately prior to making any sale that such purchaser comes within this description.

Disqualifying Provision Relating to Exemptions Under § 230.504, § 230.505 and § 230.506

Reg. § 230.507.

(a) No exemption under § 230.504, § 230.505 or § 230.506 shall be available for an issuer if such issuer, any of its predecessors or affiliates have been subject to any order, judgment, or decree of any court of competent jurisdiction temporarily, preliminarily or permanently enjoining such person for failure to comply with § 230.503.

(b) Paragraph (a) of this section shall not apply if the Commission determines, upon a showing of good cause, that it is not necessary under the circumstances that exemption be denied.

Insignificant Deviations From a Term, Condition or Requirement of Regulation D

Reg. § 230.508.

(a) A failure to comply with a term, condition or requirement of § 230.504, § 230.505 or § 230.506 will not result in the loss of the exemption from the requirements of section 5 of the Act for any offer or sale to a particular individual or entity, if the person relying on the exemption shows:

(1) The failure to comply did not pertain to a term, condition or requirement directly intended to protect that particular individual or entity; and

(2) The failure to comply was insignificant with respect to the offering as a whole, provided that any failure to comply with paragraph (c) of § 230.502, paragraph (b)(2) of § 230.504, paragraphs (b)(2)(i) and (ii) of § 230.505 and paragraph (b)(2)(i) of § 230.506 shall be deemed to be significant to the offering as a whole; and

(3) A good faith and reasonable attempt was made to comply with all applicable terms, conditions and requirements of § 230.504, § 230.505 or § 230.506.

(b) A transaction made in reliance on § 230.504, § 230.505 or § 230.506 shall comply with all applicable terms, conditions and requirements of Regulation D. Where an exemption is established only through reliance upon paragraph (a) of this section, the failure to comply shall nonetheless be actionable by the Commission under section 20 of the Act.

Angel Organizations in the United States and Canada

*N*otes: This appendix is provided as reference material. Contact information is based on what was found on the Web sites. Information provided is directly from each respective Web site.

This is not an exhaustive list of operating angel organizations. Some choose not to have a Web presence. Those groups without Web sites that have been identified have been listed with location, but no information.

Some groups require an application fee to submit business plans, which can range between $100 and $250, with some rare exceptions of higher fees.

ALABAMA

Huntsville Angel Network
Huntsville, Alabama

The Huntsville Angel Network, or HAN, was established in 2005 by a group of Huntsville, Alabama area active angel investors, teamed with the area's leading professional services firms and BizTech, Huntsville's technology-focused business incubator. The group has approximately 40 members and meets monthly to hear presentations from entrepreneurs seeking capital of $250,000 to $750,000. The group's strengths are in information technology, biotechnology and energy, but opportunities are considered in any area where the membership of the HAN has some domain expertise.

Contact:
The Huntsville Angel Network
515 Sparkman Drive
Huntsville, AL 35816
Phone: 256-704-6000
Fax: 256-704-6002
Dick Reeves, Executive Director
Phone: 256-489-0103
E-mail: director@huntsvilleangels.com
Web site: http://huntsville.angelgroups.net

ALASKA

Alaska InvestNet
Anchorage, Alaska

Alaska InvestNet is a statewide non-profit corporation helping entrepreneurs access investors by providing them with the tools and resources they need to succeed.

Alaska InvestNet brings entrepreneurs, investors and service providers together at educational events that provide technical assistance and facilitate business relationships. Alaskan private equity investments keep entrepreneurial talent and businesses in state; our entrepreneurs build fresh economic infrastructure creating wealth with sales and new jobs. Strengthening the startup economy provides the competitive jobs so vital to Alaska's 25 to 35-year old population.

Contact:
Kevin Wiley, Executive Director
Alaska InvestNet
P.O. Box 241126
Anchorage, AK 99524
Phone: 907-569-2123
E-mail: kevinw@alaskainvestnet.org
Web site: www.alaskainvestnet.org

ARIZONA

Arizona Angels
Scottsdale, Arizona

The Arizona Angels Investor Network was formed in 1999 and has grown to over 100 individual and institutional (VC funds, incubators and other angel groups) investor members. To date, members have invested over $3.5M in six companies with over $16M in additional capital raised by these companies from co-investors in the same or subsequent rounds.

Contact:
2415 East Camelback Road
Suite 700
Phoenix, AZ 85016
Phone: 602-508-6055
E-mail: info@arizona-angels.org
Web site: www.arizonaangels.com

Desert Angels
Tucson, Arizona

Desert Angels, formed in 2000, is a Tucson-based non-profit organization of accredited investors who seek opportunities to invest in regional startup or early stage no tech, low tech, or high tech companies. Today, the organization has over 70 members of which many have invested in a significant portfolio of companies.

Contact:
Bob Morrison
Executive Director
E-mail: morrisonr@qwest.net
Phone: 520-490-8137
Web site: www.arizonaangels.com

ARKANSAS

Fund for Arkansas' Future
Little Rock, Arkansas

Companies targeted for investment are seed and start-up stage Arkansas-based firms that provide an opportunity for rapid growth. Companies with an emphasis on technology or biotechnology will be targeted, but other companies with significant growth potential will also be considered.

Contact:
Jeff Stinson
Executive Director
Fund for Arkansas' Future
P.O. Box 17107
Little Rock, AR 72222

Phone: 501-227-7767
E-mail: jeff@arkansasfund.com
Web site: www.arkansasfund.com

CALIFORNIA

12 Angels
Los Angeles, California

The mission of 12 Angels is to create jobs and increase productivity for men and women recovering from alcoholism and addiction. 12 Angels requires that its services and investment are used to provide jobs, improve productivity, prevent or treat individuals affected by alcoholism, addiction and other addictive disorders. The organization supports businesses that reduce the harm addictive disorders cause to individuals, their families and our society.

Contact:
Phone: 888-233-1411
E-mail: info@12angels.org
Web site: www.12angels.org

Acorn Angels
Cupertino, California

Acorn Angels is a group of Silicon Valley Angel Investors who provide early stage investment capital for hi-tech companies. Our network of Angels consists of highly successful professionals who all bring invaluable knowledge and experience to our ongoing commitment to support innovation and creativity in the information technology industry.

Contact:
6 Results Way
Cupertino, CA 95014
Phone: 408-777-8090
Fax: 408-777-8091
E-mail: info@AcornAngels.com
Web site: www.AcornAngels.com

Angels Corner
Santa Clara, California

Angels Corner is primarily focused on investing into private companies with strong teams, proprietary solutions, and high potentials. Through Angels

Corner, entrepreneurs can access critical resources of seed capital and management guidance from experienced business veterans.

Contact:
Web site: www.angelscorner.com

Angel Capital Network
Sausalito, California

A venture capital and investment banking firm focused on finding, developing and financing early stage companies with revolutionary new technologies. In addition to capital, we offer entrepreneurs mentoring and development support from our management team and network members who, collectively, have decades of investment and operational experience in a wide variety of industries.

Contact:
Angel Capital Network, Inc.
1 Harbor Drive, Suite 112
Sausalito, CA 94965
Phone: 415-289-8701
Fax: 415-331-3978
Web site: www.angelcapitalnetwork.com

Aztec Venture Network, LLC
San Diego, California

AVN focuses on start-up or early-stage companies—primarily headquartered in Southern California—that need less than $2 million seed capital to move the company and its business plan closer to institutional financing. Generally, AVN will seek those companies operating in the technology sectors of communications, telecommunications, Internet, computer hardware, software, or peripherals. AVN will typically invest in two to six ventures per year.

Contact:
Joseph Sullivan
3104 Fourth Avenue
San Diego, CA 92103
Phone: 619-725-4947
E-mail: info@aztecventurenetwork.com
Web site: www.rjwatkins.com/venture

Band of Angels
Menlo Park, California

The Band of Angels is Silicon Valley's oldest organization still dedicated exclusively to funding and advising seed stage startups. The Band is a formal group of more than 100 former and current high tech executives who are interested in investing in seed stage high technology companies with strong teams, proprietary technology, and big markets. We invest in the range of $300K to $750K, but often lead a syndication of $2-3M.

Contact:
Band of Angels
275 Middlefield Road
Menlo Park, CA 94025
E-mail: contact@bandangels.com
Web site: www.bandangels.com

European-American Angel Club
San Francisco, California

The European-American Angel Club is a San Francisco-based group of Angel Investors helping start-ups in Silicon Valley. Its goal is to support entrepreneurs from the European community, to help them jump start their business so that they can address the U.S. market faster. This club is mainly (but not exclusively) focused on deals from Europe or with a European connection.

Contact:
E-mail: info@euroamericanangels.com
Web site: www.euroamericanangels.com

Film Angels
San Francisco, California

Angel investment group focused on providing funding for independent film projects.

Contact:
E-Mail: team@filmangels.org
Web site: www.filmangels.org

Golden Gate Angels
San Francisco, California

Contact:
E-mail: ggangel@ggangels.com

InvestIN Forum of Angel Investors
Los Angeles, Santa Barbara, and Westlake, California

The InvestIN Forum is an association of angel investor communities operating with the same goals and best practices under a common brand. We
are concerned with helping fuel the local entrepreneurial ecosystem and
try to be helpful to all entrepreneurs providing useful resources whilst at
the same time we are looking for early stage investment opportunities for
our members.

Contact:
John Dilts
Phone: 818-706-7686
E-mail: info@maverickangels.com
Web site: www.theinvestINforum.com

Coachella Valley Angel Network
Palm Desert, California

The CV Angel Network is a Coachella Valley-based angel investment group
that meets to hear presentations from companies seeking angel funding.
CV Angel Network meets monthly, and each meeting features presentations
from 2-4 companies interested in obtaining investment funding. CV Angel
Network is interested in entrepreneurial opportunities with strong sales
growth and profit potential, with a preference for early-stage investment
situations. Companies should be seeking capital within the range of
$100,000 to $500,000. CV Angel Network members invest in prospective
companies as individuals, and make their investment decisions on a deal-
by-deal basis.

Contact:
E-mail: info@CVAngelNetwork.com
Web site: www.CVAngelNetwork.com

Idealflow Angel Fund LLC
Beverly Hills, California

The Idealflow Angel Fund LLC is an early stage venture capital group composed of and run solely by angel investors. This organized group of angels
focuses on nurturing high-growth businesses that are developing innovative
products and services in the information and electronic technology areas.
Our geographical focus is on North America and Greater China and we have
the expertise and connections to bridge the two continents.

Contact:
Dominic K. Chan, Managing Director
317 S. Rexford Drive, Suite 306
Beverly Hills, CA 90212
E-mail: select@idealflowfund.com
Web site: www.idealflowfund.com

Imporium Angel Network
San Diego, California

Members of Imporium Angels consist of successful entrepreneurs who have
founded their own companies. They want to lend their capital and, more
importantly, their experience to high-risk startups. Companies that receive
capital from Imporium Angels get much more than money. The extensive
personal networks built by our members in their respective careers will be
available to deals we finance.

Contact:
Imporium Angel Network
113 West G Street, #137
San Diego, CA 92101
Fax: 619-243-1453
E-mail: info@ImporiumAngels.com
Web site: www.ImporiumAngels.com

Keiretsu Forum
Lafayette, California

Keiretsu Forum is an investment community of accredited private equity
investors, venture capitalists and corporate/institutional investors. We are
a North America network of capital, resources and deal flow with chapters
in Northern California (San Francisco East Bay and Silicon Valley), Southern
California (Westlake Village, Los Angeles, San Diego and Orange County),
Chicago/Midwest, Boston/New England, Dallas/Fort Worth, and Calgary,
Canada.

Contact:
3466 Mt. Diablo Boulevard, Suite C-205
Lafayette, CA 94549
E-mail: randy@keiretsuforum.com
Web site: www.keiretsuforum.com

Keiretsu Forum
Los Angeles/San Diego

> *Contact:*
> 12230 El Camino Real, Suite 300
> San Diego, CA 92130-2090
> Phone: 310-991-4309
> Chip Parker
> Chapter President, Keiretsu Forum OC & San Diego
> E-mail: chip@keiretsuforum.com
> Web site: www.k4forum.com/chapters/los_angeles

Keiretsu Forum Orange County
Newport Beach, California

After a very successful launch in November 2005, Keiretsu Forum Orange County is emerging as one of the fastest growing angel investment groups in Southern California. Keiretsu Forum Orange County is now providing local opportunities for entrepreneurs in Southern California to access resources and capital and increase their chances for success in a competitive global economy.

> *Contact:*
> Keiretsu Forum Orange County & San Diego
> 4533 MacArthur, Suite 280
> Newport Beach, CA 92660
> Phone: 714-444-1414
> Fax: 714-444-1914
> Chip Parker
> Chapter President, Keiretsu Forum OC & San Diego
> E-mail: chip@keiretsuforum.com
> Web site: www.k4forum.com/chapters/orange_county

Keiretsu Forum—San Francisco
San Francisco, California

> *Contact:*
> One California Street, Suite 2630
> San Francisco, CA 94111
> Colin Wiel
> Chapter President, Keiretsu Forum San Francisco
> E-mail: colin@keiretsuforum.com
> Web site: www.k4forum.com/chapters/san_francisco

ANGEL FINANCING FOR ENTREPRENEURS

ANGEL FINANCING FOR ENTREPRENEURS
ANGEL FINANCING FOR ENTREPRENEURS
ANGEL FINANCING FOR ENTREPRENEURS
ANGEL FINANCING FOR ENTREPRENEURS
ANGEL FINANCING FOR ENTREPRENEURS
ANGEL FINANCING FOR ENTREPRENEURS
ANGEL FINANCING FOR ENTREPRENEURS
ANGEL FINANCING FOR ENTREPRENEURS
ANGEL FINANCING FOR ENTREPRENEURS
ANGEL FINANCING FOR ENTREPRENEURS
ANGEL FINANCING FOR ENTREPRENEURS
ANGEL FINANCING FOR ENTREPRENEURS
ANGEL FINANCING FOR ENTREPRENEURS
ANGEL FINANCING FOR ENTREPRENEURS

ANGEL FINANCING FOR ENTREPRENEURS

ANGEL FINANCING FOR ENTREPRENEURS

Keiretsu Forum—Westlake Village/Ventura County
San Diego, California

Contact:
Keiretsu Forum San Diego
12230 El Camino Real, Suite 300
San Diego, CA 92130-2090
Phone: 310-991-4309
Chip Parker
E-mail: chip@keiretsuforum.com
Web site: www.k4forum.com/chapters/westlake

Life Science Angels, Inc.
Menlo Park, California

Life Science Angels, Inc. was founded in 2004 by senior life science executives and experienced angel investors as a vehicle to bring angel capital to worthy early-stage biotech and medical device companies. Formally launched in January 2005 with backing of 15 industry sponsors, LSA follows a rigorous due diligence process before presenting investment opportunities to its membership. LSA also works with select angel groups, venture capitalists and outside investors to syndicate opportunities requiring larger investments. We hold membership meetings approximately every other month, with one or two companies presenting. Members make their own individual investment decisions and are afforded an opportunity for additional due diligence if they wish. The investments are made through an LLC so the funded companies see a single investor. LSA typically takes a seat on the company's board.

Contact:
Web site: www.lifescienceangels.com

North Bay Angels
San Francisco, California

The North Bay Angels (NBA) has been formed by a group of San Francisco, North Bay Area executives and professionals to fill a growing need to provide a forum for learning about and making early stage investment capital (seed capital) and advisory assistance (mentoring) available to entrepreneurial companies in the North Bay.

Contact:
Web site: www.northbayangels.com

Pasadena Angels
Altadena, California

Founded in 2000, the Pasadena Angels invests in early-stage companies in a broad range of industries including, but not limited to technology, that have the potential to build sustainable and successful businesses. The Pasadena Angels charges no fees for its services.

> *Contact:*
> 2400 North Lincoln Ave.
> Altadena, CA 91001
> E-mail: info@pasadenaangels.com
> Web site: www.pasadenaangels.com

Sacramento Angels
Roseville, California

The Sacramento Angels is a group of individuals who invest in early-stage Northern California companies. The group meets once a month over dinner and listens to presentations from candidate companies. Members act on their own behalf and make individual investment decisions.

> *Contact:*
> Web site: www.sacangels.org

Sand Hill Angels
Los Altos, California

The key distinctions of Sand Hill Angels are our professional and well defined process, our open approach to working with others in the startup financing ecosystem, our investor-only membership, and our investments are made as a single legal entity. We invest in private companies at all stages and favor investments in the Internet, Information Technology, and Life Sciences. In Information Technology, we are particularly active in Semiconductors, Software, Storage, and Communications. In the Life Sciences, our interests primarily include medical devices and diagnostics. Our operating model is to work collaboratively with venture capital firms and other Bay Area angel organizations to lend early stage capital and guidance so that a startup may accomplish the critical milestones necessary to achieve its next stage growth and financing objectives.

> *Contact:*
> E-mail: info@sandhillangels.com
> Web site: www.sandhillangels.com

Silicom Ventures
Los Altos, California

Silicom Ventures is one of the largest organized groups of Angel Investors in the United States, linking experienced investors with entrepreneurs from around the globe. Based in Silicon Valley, California, Silicom Ventures' investments range from life sciences and medical technology to semiconductors, software and media. The group is comprised of Venture Capital and Angel Investors who are high tech executives in leading Bay Area companies. Since its founding in 1999, the Silicom Ventures has invested in more than 50 companies, among them WebAppoint (acquired by Microsoft), InterVideo (second best IPO in 2003), BindKey Technologies (acquired by DuPont Photomasks), Sparta Systems (acquired by AIG Healthcare Partners, L.P.) and Sensant Corp. (acquired by Siemens).

> *Contact:*
> 1442 Fowler Lane
> Los Altos, CA 94024
> Phone: 650-961-8877 (Line 1)
> Phone: 650-964-2858 (Line 2)
> Fax: 650-988-1888
> E-mail: info@silicomventures.com
> Web site: www.silicomventures.com

Tech Coast Angels
Los Angeles, Orange County, San Diego and Westlake/
Santa Barbara, California

Tech Coast Angels (TCA) is helping fuel the growth of the most innovative companies and entrepreneurs in Southern California. TCA's 270 members have invested more than $65 million in more than 100 companies and have helped attract more than $650 million of additional capital, mostly from venture capital firms. TCA operates four networks in Los Angeles, Orange County, San Diego and Westlake/Santa Barbara.

> *Contact:*
> E-mail: jeff@techcoastangels.com
> Web site: www.techcoastangels.com

Tenex Medical Investors
Burlingame, California

The mission of Tenex Medical is to provide a nonprofit forum for private investors who are successful entrepreneurs in the life sciences to meet entrepreneurs who have developed innovative concepts, procedures, products or services and who are seeking both advice and capital. The Tenex investment focus is primarily early stage ventures, whether they are product or company concepts, which can achieve a meaningful business benchmark with a capital infusion of between $250,000 and $750,000 from Tenex. These would include medical devices, healthcare information systems and services, clinical diagnostics, research products, medical equipment, hospital products and biotechnology.

Contact:
Silicon Valley, CA
E-mail: info@tenxmedical.com
Web site: www.tenxmedical.com

The Angels' Forum, LLC
Palo Alto, California

The Angels' Forum (TAF) is a private, closed group of 25 investors, including individuals and small corporate and family venture funds. The TAF group reviews 20+ new deals per week and on average makes 5-15 new A round investments per year, as well as follow on B and C round investments in existing portfolio companies. When TAF members invest, TAF creates a special LLC entity to make the investment, making the administration process vastly simpler for the entrepreneur and protecting the privacy of the investors.

Contact:
2458 Embarcadero Way
Palo Alto, CA 94303
Phone: 650-857-0700
Fax: 650-857-0773
E-mail: businessplans@angelsforum.com
Web site: www.angelsforum.com

US Angel Investors
San Francisco, California

US Angel Investors is a newly formed investment community of angel investors including former and current executives and entrepreneurs, venture capitalists, corporate investors, institutional investors, and Boston Consulting Group alumni. They meet once a month, alternating between Silicon Valley and San Francisco. US Angel Investors works closely with Bay Area Startup Network (www.basn.org), a sister organization whose goal is to provide networking opportunities for early-stage startups.

Contact:
E-mail: info@usangelinvestors.com
Web site: www.usangelinvestors.com

COLORADO

CTEK Angels
Denver, Colorado

CTEK Angels was launched in January 2002 and is now the largest organized group of individual private investors in Colorado. CTEK Angels have made 25 investments in 20 companies. The CTEK Angels meet once a month to listen to a series of presentations from companies seeking funding. Prior to presenting before the CTEK Angels, a company is screened to ensure the presentation meets the CTEK Angels investment criteria and to provide the entrepreneur with valuable feedback to most effectively address the angel audience.

Contact:
Christina James
E-mail: Christina.James@CTEK.biz
CTEK Angels
One World Trade Center
1625 Broadway, Suite 950
Denver, CO 80202
Phone: 303-546-9595
Fax: 303-546-9494
Web site: www.CTEKAngels.biz

Rockies Venture Club
Denver, Colorado

Founded in 1985, RVC is the Rocky Mountain region's premier networking organization that links entrepreneurs, service professionals, and funding sources.

Contact:
Art Harrison
Arthur Harrison & Company
4290 S. Hudson Pkwy.
Englewood, CO 80110
Phone: 303-753-6410
E-mail: aharr83679@aol.com

Jim Arkebauer
Venture Associates
Denver, Colorado

> *Contact:*
> 4950 E. Evans Avenue, Suite 105
> Denver, CO 80222
> Phone: 303-58-8710
> E-mail: jarkebauer@ventureA.com
> Web site: www.rockiesventureclub.org

CONNECTICUT

Angel Investor Forum
Hartford, Connecticut

The Angel Investor Forum was founded in 2004 in response to the growing
need for an organized angel effort in Connecticut. AIF members invest their
time, talent, and money in supporting companies with solid business models
and their efforts to grow successfully. We present monthly reviews of two targeted, prescreened companies that are matched to investor's interests. Each
month we target one of the four investment types: medical devices, financial
services, software and consumer products.

> *Contact:*
> CityPlace I
> 37th Floor
> 185 Asylum Street
> Hartford, CT 06103-3495
> Reggie Babcock
> Managing Director
> Phone: 860-430-1257
> E-mail: rbabcock@angelinvestorforum.com
> Elizabeth Karter
> Managing Director
> Phone: 203-376-7958
> E-mail: ekarter@angelinvestorforum.com

Golden Seeds
Cos Cob, Connecticut

We identify and invest in women-led ventures with the potential to grow into
multi-million dollar businesses, and provide women entrepreneurs with
strategic business advice and the tools they need for growth. We provide

access to capital on terms that enable women to be honest about the requirements they have to enable integration in their work and family lives. We are
keen to support all women entrepreneurs, even those we are not able to invest
in. We regularly provide advice and mentoring on an ad hoc, and sometimes
more structured basis. Often we refer companies to other resources that we
think will be best able to provide the support they need.

Contact:
Golden Seeds LLC
665 River Road
Cos Cob, CT 06807
Web site: www.goldenseeds.com

DISTRICT OF COLUMBIA

WomenAngels.net
Washington, D.C.

WomenAngels.net is an angel investment club designed to help women
investors capitalize on the explosive growth in entrepreneurial activity and
venture financing in Maryland, Washington, D.C. and Virginia. WomenAn-
gels.Net is a group of highly successful women who have invested their
money, talent, expertise and experience, to select investments and to assist in
the growth of the club's portfolio companies.

Contact:
Web site: www.womenangels.net

FLORIDA

Emergent Growth Fund
Gainesville, Florida

Emergent Growth Fund, LLC (Emergent) is a member-managed angel investment group, focusing on early-stage companies developing unique, leading-
edge products, or proprietary technologies that possess the potential for rapid
growth in significant markets.

Contact:
Stephanie George
Emergent Growth Fund, LLC
101 SE 2nd Place, Suite 201-C
Gainesville, FL 32601
Phone: 352-335-3021
E-mail: sgeorge@emergentgrowth.com
Web site: www.emergentgrowth.com/public/index.asp

New World Angels
Boca Raton, Florida

New World Angels (NWA) is a group of private investors dedicated to providing equity capital to early and mid-stage entrepreneurial companies. Our primary focus is on companies based in South Florida. NWA works closely with other regional and national venture firms. In addition, it is supported by such leading institutions as The Enterprise Development Corporation, Florida Atlantic University, and Florida International University.

> *Contact:*
> New World Angels, Inc.
> 3701 FAU Boulevard, Suite 210
> Boca Raton, FL 33431
> Phone: 561-620-8494
> Fax: 561-620-8493
> E-mail: info@newworldangels.com
> Web site: www.newworldangels.com

Springboard Capital
Jacksonville, Florida

Springboard Capital is a member-managed, early stage, private equity fund. Comprised exclusively of individual accredited investors, Springboard seeks investment opportunities in emerging companies in their pre-revenue and early revenue stages. Springboard Capital I, LLC was formed in May 2002, and Springboard Capital II, LLC was formed in July 2005.

> *Contact:*
> Alan Rossiter, Administrator
> 4905 Belfort Road, Suite 110
> Jacksonville, FL 32256
> Phone: 904-861-2400
> Fax: 904-332-9925
> Web site: www.springboardcapllc.com

Startup Florida
Sarasota, Florida

Startup Florida promotes the creation and acceleration of early-stage technology businesses by providing capital, mentoring and a supportive community for entrepreneurs. Startup Florida brings an innovative and proven model of angel investing which combines the collective intellect and experience of the investors with a sophisticated due diligence process led by the managing partners. Startup Florida believes the key to a successful Angel Fund is investing both time and capital throughout the life of the investment. The target investments for Startup Florida are early-stage companies in the Information Technology, Communications and Internet markets.

Contact:
1605 Main Street, Suite 1100
(Bank of America Building)
Sarasota, FL 34236
Web site: www.startupflorida.com

Lovett Miller
Jacksonville/Tampa, Florida

Lovett Miller & Co., based in Florida, provides equity capital to rapidly grow-ing, privately-held companies. The Firm manages $175 million in commit-ted capital and invests in a broad range of financings including (1) early stage, (2) growth capital, and (3) growth buyouts. Lovett Miller & Co. typically invests $2 million to $10 million per company, although it is willing to con-sider both smaller and larger equity investments.

Contact:
Mr. W. Radford Lovett II
One Independent Drive
Suite 1600
Jacksonville, FL 32202
Phone: 904-634-0077
E-mail: rad@lovettmiller.com
Mr. W. Scott Miller
100 North Tampa Street
Suite 2675
Tampa, FL 33602
Phone: 813-222-1477
E-mail: scott@lovettmiller.com
Web site: www.lovettmiller.com

Winter Park Angels
Winter Park, Florida

Winter Park Angels is a group of accredited investors who provide equity capital to early-stage entrepreneurial companies located in Florida. Members are entrepreneurs and successful business leaders who have founded and built some of the nation's best companies. Winter Park Angels helps others succeed by mentoring and coaching those entrepreneurs in whose businesses they invest; serve on their boards, provide contacts and assist with strategic planning. Winter Park Angels looks for companies which are in the early stage of rolling out a unique, preferably proven, product or concept.

Contact:
Winter Park Angels
601 N. New York Avenue, Suite 110
Winter Park, FL 32789
Phone: 407-745-1354
E-mail: info@WinterParkAngels.com
Web site: www.WinterParkAngels.com

GEORGIA

Ariel Savannah Angel Partners
Savannah, Georgia

Ariel Savannah Angel Partners (ASAP) is a member-driven organization composed of experienced business, medical, legal and educational professionals from a wide range of industries working together to review, analyze, and invest in early-stage high-growth potential companies. Our objectives are to improve member investment portfolios and financial returns relative to what an individual could accomplish working alone, to promote regional economic development in Georgia, South Carolina and the Southeast region, and to provide a satisfying professional, personal, and social experience.

Contact:
Investor Relations
Robert Franklin
Phone: 912-598-9820
Web site: www.savannahangelpartners.com

Atlanta Technology Angels
Atlanta, Georgia

The Atlanta Technology Angels (ATA) is a private investing group, founded in 1998, that actively seeks investments in early-stage technology companies based in Atlanta. ATA is an active source of private capital and business experience to local technology entrepreneurs. ATA, as a group, has invested more than $20,000,000 in 32 Atlanta technology companies between 1999 and 2006.

Contact:
Atlanta Technology Angels
75 5th Street, NW
Suite 311
Atlanta, GA 30308
E-mail: director@angelatlanta.com
Web site: www.angelatlanta.com/default.asp

HAWAII

Hawai'i Angels
Honolulu, Hawaii

Hawai'i Angels was founded as UH Angels by Robert Robinson Ph.D., in February 2002. It attracted high net worth individuals from a variety of professions including chief executives, attorneys, physicians, and scientists, who share an enthusiasm for entrepreneurship. The number of members has grown to nearly 100. Maui and Big Island chapters were founded in 2006. Individual members have invested $14 million in various companies and have played a significant role in Hawaii's startup community. Members often mentor entrepreneurs and provide new companies with valuable business advice and important contacts.

Contact:
Robert Robinson, Ph.D.
900 Fort Street Mall, Suite 1800
Honolulu, HI 96813
Phone: 808-447-9372
E-mail: info@HawaiiAngels.org
Web site: www.HawaiiAngels.org

IDAHO

Boise Angel Alliance
Boise, Idaho

The Boise Angel Alliance is an organization of accredited angel investors that meet to hear presentations from emerging companies seeking capital. Volunteers in the Boise, Idaho area founded the BAA in 2004. Idaho's Boise Angel Alliance exists to help Boise's angel investors find more deals in their own backyard.

Contact:
P.O. Box 1845
Boise, ID 83701

E-mail: info@boiseangelalliance.com
Web site: www.boiseangelalliance.com

Northwest Angel Network, Inc.
Boise, Idaho

Northwest Angel Network, Inc. founded theAngelPeople.com to build strong associations with companies and accredited investors. TheAngelPeople.com supports a significantly detailed financing database for new start-up companies seeking capital investment or companies that need next round financing to improve their product or service. The Angel Investors associated with theAngelPeople.com generally commit between $50,000.00 and $1,000,000.00 to a single business.

Contact:
Northwest Angel Network, Inc.
3350 Americana Terrace
Suite 350
Boise, ID 83706
Phone: 208-424-8438
Fax: 208-426-8838
E-mail: info@theAngelPeople.com
Web site: www.theAngelPeople.com

ILLINOIS

BioAngels
Lake Bluff, Illinois

BioAngels is a not-for-profit corporation whose mission is to facilitate investment in startup and early-stage medical and life sciences businesses in the Midwest. Companies must be early-stage life science or medical device businesses located in the Midwest which are seeking seed investment, meaning generally up to $1 million.

Contact:
BioAngels
402 Greenbay Road
Lake Bluff, IL 60044
Samantha Borland
Phone: 847-235-5150
E-mail: sborland@bioangels.com
Web site: www.bioangels.com

Bluestem Ventures
Springfield, Illinois

Bluestem Ventures was started from a recognized need to provide nontradi-
tional capital to local companies and entrepreneurs in need of financing. We
do not limit our focus to one market or technology, but seek diversified
opportunities in a variety of sectors. Similarly, we do not specialize in a particular stage of financing, but rather seek both mature and early-stage business opportunities.

Contact:
Bluestem Ventures
P.O. Box 7446
Springfield, IL 62791
Phone: 603-828-8249
Fax: 603-868-2450
E-mail: info@bluestemventures.com
Web site: www.bluestemventures.com

DePaul Blue Angel Network (DBAN)
Chicago, Illinois

The DePaul Blue Angel Network (DBAN) is a membership-based network
of accredited investors who invest in early-stage ventures. Although not
required, many of these investors are affiliated with DePaul University (fac-
ulty, alumni, and students).

Contact:
1 E. Jackson
Chicago, IL 60604
Phone: 312-362-8625
Web site: http://cec.depaul.edu/dban/entrepreneurs/index.php

Heartland Angels, Inc.
Skokie, Illinois

Heartland Angels, Inc. is a private equity network that brings together
accredited investors with start-up and early stage start-up companies and
real estate opportunities looking for equity and debt investments. Potential
investment opportunities are presented to the network investors monthly.

Contact:
Heartland Angels, Inc.
c/o Ronald L. Kirschner
7650 N. La Vergne

Skokie, IL 60077
Phone: 847-675-3057
Fax: 847-675-3057
E-mail: info@heartlandangels.com

Prairie Angels, LLC
Chicago, Illinois

Our goal is to match funding for seed stage (angel round) investors with start up entrepreneurs and their businesses in the Midwest. A committee then recommends two to three companies to present at the group's dinner meeting every other month. Business from all verticals including non high technology areas are welcome. Presenting companies can be pre revenue and need not have a full management team in place.

Contact:
Barry Moltz
Prairie Angels, LLC
600 West Jackson, Suite 400
Chicago, IL 60661
Phone: 773-837-8250
E-mail: info@prairieangels.org
Web site: www.prairieangels.org

INDIANA

Indiana Seed Fund I
Indianapolis, Indiana

The formation of the Indiana Seed Fund I, a $6 million venture pre-venture capital fund designed to promote business formation and growth in the state's life sciences sector. The $4 million Seed Fund, which is return-driven, will provide working capital in the range of $50,000-$500,000 to promising Indiana life sciences companies at the preliminary stages of operation. Under the leadership of BioCrossroads, the Indiana Seed Fund I is a seed-stage private investment fund designed to be a source of critical pre-venture investment capital for emerging Indiana life sciences companies. The term 'life sciences' encompasses, but is not limited to, the fields of biotechnology, pharmaceuticals, nutraceuticals, agbiotech and biomedical diagnostics and devices. The Indiana Seed Fund is a return-driven fund that anticipates making direct equity investments of $50,000—$500,000. The Fund anticipates making investments over a three year period, but the time period will vary depending on the quantity and quality of the submissions received.

Contact:
300 N. Meridian Street, Suite 950
Indianapolis, IN 46204
Phone: 317-238-2450
E-mail: biocrossroads@biocrossroads.com
Web site: www.biocrossroads.com/entrepreneur/isf.htm

Irish Angels
Notre Dame, Indiana

One of the missions of Irish Angels is to support aspiring entrepreneurs within the Notre Dame community by providing mentoring and networking assistance, as well as access to funding networks for those plans that demonstrate strong business potential.

Contact:
Phone: 574-631-3042
E-mail: entrep@nd.edu
Web site: www.irishangels.com

IOWA

Cedar Valley Venture Fund (RAIN fund)
Cedar Falls, Iowa

The Cedar Valley Venture Fund is a $1.61 million fund comprised of investors from Black Hawk and its contiguous counties. The fund is a partnership of local investors, Buchanan County Economic Development, Cedar Valley Economic Development, and the John Pappajohn Entrepreneurial Center. The fund will consider investing in post-family and friends start-ups with an established product and proven sales, follow-on deals, mergers and acquisitions, and succession-based opportunities.

Contact:
John Pappajohn Entrepreneurial Center
University of Northern Iowa
Curris Business Building 5 & 264
Cedar Falls, IA 50614-0130
Phone: 319-273-7350
Fax: 319-273-7512
E-mail: katherine.cota@uni.edu
Web site: www.jpec.org/cvvf.htm

Northern Iowa Venture Capital Fund
Mason City, Iowa

This fund is a member of the multi-state network of RAIN® funds that works with angel investors who are interested in supporting growing companies.

Contact:
RAIN Source Capital
1600 University Avenue West, Suite 401
St. Paul, MN 55104
Phone: 651-632-2140
Fax: 651-632-2145
Web site: www.rainsourcecapital.com

Rock River Capital, LLC
Rock Rapids, Iowa

Rock River Capital, formed in August 2005, is a member of the multi-state network of RAIN® funds that works with angel investors who are interested in supporting growing companies.

Contact:
RAIN Source Capital
1600 University Avenue West, Suite 401
St. Paul, MN 55104
Phone: 651-632-2140
Fax: 651-632-2145
Web site: www.rainsourcecapital.com

KANSAS

Mid America Angels
Lawrence, Kansas

Founded in 2006, Mid America Angels (MAA) is a regional network of angel investors dedicated to identifying and funding the most promising start up business opportunities in the Kansas – Missouri Region. MAA members fund deals in the investment range of $250,000 to $2,000,000.

Contact:
8527 Blue Jacket Street
Lenexa, KS 66214
Phone: 913-438-2282

or
1617 St. Andrew Drive
Lawrence, KS 66047
Phone: 785-832-2110
E-mail: info@midamericaangels.com
Web site: www.midamericaangels.com

Midwest Venture Alliance
Wichita, Kansas

Founded in 2005, Midwest Venture Alliance (MVA), including its affiliate, the Southeast Kansas Venture Alliance (SEKVA), is a network of accredited investors committed to investing in high-growth seed and early-stage technology companies in Kansas and surrounding states. MVA members provide seed and early-stage capital in the range of $250K-$2M.

Contact:
Carrie Miller, MVA Administrator
7829 E. Rockhill Road, Suite 307
Wichita, KS 67206
Phone: 316-651-5900
Fax: 866-810-6671
Ric Ferrell, SEKVA Administrator
1501 S. Joplin, Shirk Hall
Pittsburg State University
Pittsburg, KS 66762
Phone: 620-235-4927
Fax: 620-235-4030

KENTUCKY

Bluegrass Angels
Lexington, Kentucky

An important, although not exclusive, focus of the BGA is to develop start-up companies through the commercialization of the ongoing research of the University of Kentucky.

Contact:
Dean E. Harvey
E-mail: harvey@uky.edu

Phone: 859-257-1930
Fax: 859-323-2333
Web site: www.lexicc.com

LOUISIANA

Louisiana Angel Network
Baton Rouge, Louisiana

The Louisiana Angel Network is a registered Louisiana Nonprofit Corporation headquartered in Baton Rouge, Louisiana governed by its Board of Directors. LAN is a select network of accredited investors across Louisiana that provides early-stage investment capital to viable start-up companies ready for angel-round funding.

Contact:
7912 Wrenwood Boulevard, Suite A
Baton Rouge, LA 70809
Phone: 225-927-3331
E-mail: administration@louisianaangelnetwork.com
Web site: www.louisianaangelnetwork.com

MAINE

First Run Angel Group
Maine

First Run acts as a conduit to find and screen business proposals for the investors. Once an angel investor(s) takes an interest in a company the investor(s) and business owners work out the terms and conditions of the investment together.

Contact:
Web site: www.firstrunangelgroup.com

Maine Angels
Maine

While MAINE ANGELS intends to make many of its investments within Maine, it will consider and may participate in opportunities elsewhere through direct company application and/or collaboration with other Angel or Venture groups. All investments are made individually. Many MAINE ANGELS members are interested in actively mentoring the companies in which they invest, and this is encouraged. Investments by individuals are usually $10,000 or more per deal.

Contact:
E-mail: info@maineangels.org
Web site: www.maineangels.org

MARYLAND

Chesapeake Emerging Opportunities Club
Columbus, Maryland

The Club is a manager-led Maryland limited liability company angel investing fund. The primary focus of the Club is to invest in early-stage companies with significant growth potential that operate in large markets, are run by talented management and are located within a two-hour drive of Columbia, Maryland. The Club initially invests an average of $150,000 to $200,000 in a portfolio company, with the possibility of follow-on investments. The Club generally invests in the form of preferred stock or equity-enhanced subordinated debt.

Contact:
Rick Kohr
Phone: 410-997-6000
or
Steve Dubin
Phone: 410-442-2521
8808 Centre Park Drive, Suite 204
Columbia, MD 21045
Phone: 443-367-0101
E-mail: jlinsert@ecapitalllc.com
Web site: www.ceopportunities.com

MASSACHUSETTS

Angel Healthcare Investors LLC
Newton, Massachusetts

Angel Healthcare Investors, LLC was founded in 1999 to leverage the expertise and resources of their colleagues in response to healthcare investment opportunities. Angel Healthcare has committed over $18 million to more than 30 opportunities as part of transactions with an aggregate value of over $500 million.

Contact:
Angel Healthcare Investors, LLC
One Gateway Center, Suite 902
Newton, MA 02458
Phone: 617-630-0777
Fax: 617-663-6081
E-mail: info@hcangels.com
Web site: www.hcangels.com/index.html

Bay Angels
Boston, Massachusetts

Bay Angels is a Cape Cod-based angel investment group that provides funding to early-stage companies in Cape Cod and The Islands, Southeastern Massachusetts and Rhode Island. We are looking for innovative, technology driven startup companies addressing a significant market opportunity where our investment can make a difference. Bay Angels is looking to invest in "startup" businesses. Our typical investment is between $100,000 and $500,000.

Contact:
Robert "Bob" Lamkin
E-mail: bob@bayangels.net
Web site: www.bayangels.net

Beacon Angels
Boston, Massachusetts

Beacon Angels is a Boston-based angels' group that makes investments in start-up companies in the $100,000 to $300,000 range.

Contact:
E-mail: candidates@beaconangels.com.
Web site: http://beaconangels.com

Boston Harbor Angels
Boston, Massachusetts

Boston Harbor Angels is a group of successful business leaders from the Boston area committed to providing capital and assistance to passionate entrepreneurs aspiring to build "The Next Big Thing".

Contact:
Web site: www.bostonharborangels.com

CommonAngels
Lexington, Massachusetts

Named after the city's historic public meeting grounds, CommonAngels® is a group of 70 leading private investors and several dozen limited partners in two co-investment funds. We have rich expertise in over 58 specific sectors; have founded over 115 companies; sold over 100; and participated in over 34 IPOs. We finance the region's most innovative high-tech ventures with a focus on capital efficiency: Series A rounds of $500K-$5M with total capital less than $20M.

> Contact:
> James Geshwiler
> Managing Director
> One Cranberry Hill
> Lexington, MA 02421
> Phone: 781-274-9124
> E-mail: inquiry@commonangels.com
> Web site: www.commonangels.com/home.html

HubAngels
Brookline, Massachusetts

The HubAngels began meeting in March 2000 with the notion of matching active, early stage investors with technology-driven, start-up companies. With a focus on the greater Boston area—known as the "Hub" by Boston locals—the Hub Angel Investment Group developed its present methodology and structure of investing which includes a fund with co-investment rights for the individual Members of the Fund. Currently there are more than 50 Members in Hub Fund I and Hub Fund II. Hub does not accept unsolicited business plans.

> Contact:
> E-mail: info@hubangels.com
> Web site: www.hubangels.com

InvestIN Forum of Angel Investors
Boston, Massachusetts

The InvestIN Forum is an association of angel investor communities operating with the same goals and best practices under a common brand. We are concerned with helping fuel the local entrepreneurial ecosystem and try to be helpful to all entrepreneurs providing useful resources whilst at the same time we are looking for early stage investment opportunities for our members.

Contact:
Mic Williams
Phone: 617-742-7887
Fax: 617-429-1786
E-mail: harborangels@aol.com
Web site: www.theinvestINforum.com

Investors' Circle
Brookline, Massachusetts

Since our inception in 1992, over $100 million has been invested by Investors' Circle members into 163 companies or small venture funds. The IC Mission is to galvanize the flow of capital to entrepreneurial companies that enhance bioregional, cultural and economic health and diversity. IC supports investing in minority and women entrepreneurs and companies that support organic agriculture and sustainable forestry.

Contact:
320 Washington Street, 4th Floor
Brookline, MA 02445
Phone: 617-566-2600
Fax: 617-739-3550
E-mail: inbox@investorscircle.net
Web site: www.investorscircle.net

Launchpad Venture Group
Wellesley, Massachusetts

Launchpad Venture Group, with over 45 active investors, is looking for innovative, technology-driven startup companies addressing a significant market opportunity where our investment can make a difference. In a typical situation, Launchpad will invest between $100,000 and $500,000 and work with the company to proceed to the next stage.

Contact:
E-mail: info@launchpadventuregroup.com
Web site: www.launchpadventuregroup.com

River Valley Investors
Springfield, Massachusetts

River Valley Investors is centered around Springfield, Massachusetts but looks at investment opportunities throughout New England and, in select cases, throughout the United States.

> *Contact:*
> Paul G. Silva, Co-Manager
> 100 Venture Way, Suite 4
> Hadley, MA 01035
> Phone: 413-303-1268
> E-mail: paul@rivervalleyinvestors.com
> Web site: www.rivervalleyinvestors.com

Walnut Venture Associates
Wellesley Hills, Massachusetts

Walnut Venture Associates is a group of experienced entrepreneurs and investors seeking investment opportunities in seed and early-stage companies in the New England area. We only invest in companies in the New England area. We are focused on information technology companies with significant technology addressing rapidly growing markets. We can commit $250,000 to $1,000,000 to a single financing. Our objective is to help talented entrepreneurs build lasting businesses of significant value and to participate as active investors. Individuals in the group have been the founders of 20 companies, the CEOs of more than 20 companies, have invested in over 225 private companies, and have been members of the Board of Directors of over 125 companies.

> *Contact:*
> E-mail: info@walnutventures.com
> Web site: www.walnutventures.com

MICHIGAN

Ann Arbor Angels
Ann Arbor, Michigan

The Ann Arbor Angels (A2A) is dedicated to bringing together angel investors and early stage technology-based companies in Southern Michigan. A2A Advisory Group's members are leaders in Michigan's technology business community.

Contact:
E-mail: webmaster@annarborangels.org
Web site: http://annarborangels.org

Aurora Angels
Petoskey, Michigan

Aurora Angels is a newly formed seed/early-stage angel capital group focused on nurturing high-growth businesses that are developing innovative products and services in cleantech (environmental, alternate energy), alternate energy (wind, solar, biomass), advanced materials, automation, telecommunications, and information technology. Our primary geographical focus is on northwestern lower and the eastern upper peninsulas of Michigan, although we will address outstanding opportunities throughout the state of Michigan.

Contact:
Bruce Woodry, Managing Member
Aurora Angels
2255 Summit Park Drive
Petoskey, MI 49770
E-mail: woodry@auroraangels.com
Web site: www.auroraangels.com

Grand Angels
Holland, Michigan

The mission of the Grand Angels is to utilize its financial, intellectual and networking capital to promote the success of young growing companies and to enhance the economic development of West Michigan. While Grand Angels investments are not geographically limited, the major focus is Kent, Ottawa and Muskegon counties.

Contact:
Vickie Morgan
10720 Adams Street
Holland, MI 49423
Phone: 616-546-4559
Fax: 616-396-2424
E-mail: info@grandangels.org
Web site: www.grandangels.org

Great Lakes Angels, Inc.
Bloomfield Hills, Michigan

The Great Lakes Angels focus on investments in life science, IT, MEMS, advanced manufacturing, and various other technologies.

> *Contact:*
> David P. Weaver, President
> Great Lakes Angels, Inc.
> 568 Woodway Court, Suite 1
> Bloomfield Hills, MI 48302-1572
> Phone: 248-540-3758
> E-mail: dweaver@glangels.org
> Web site: www.glangels.org

Southwest Michigan First Angel Network
Kalamazoo, Michigan

> *Contact:*
> Office Location: 491 W. South Street, Kalamazoo, MI 49007
> Mailing Address: PO Box 50827, Kalamazoo, MI 49005-0827
> Phone: 269-553-9588
> Fax: 269-553-6897
> Web site: www.southwestmichiganfirst.com

MINNESOTA

Central Minnesota Growth and Transition Fund, LLC (RAIN fund)
Willmar, Minnesota

> *Contact:*
> RAIN Source Capital
> 1600 University Avenue West, Suite 401
> St. Paul, MN 55104
> Phone: 651-632-2140
> Fax: 651-632-2145
> Web site: www.rainsourcecapital.com

Lakes Venture Group, LLC (RAIN fund)
Alexandria, Minnesota

Lakes Venture Group is an investment fund that focuses on making equity investments in companies primarily in the Alexandria area.

Contact:
Keith Anderson
Phone: 320-762-1709
or
Minnesota Investment Network
Phone: 651-632-2140

Lakes Venture Group II, LLC (RAIN fund)
Alexandria, Minnesota

Lakes Venture Group II is an investment fund that focuses on making equity investments in companies primarily in the Alexandria area.

Contact:
Keith Anderson
Phone: 320-762-1709
or
Minnesota Investment Network
Phone: 651-632-2140

North Star Fund, LLC (RAIN fund)
Grand Rapids, Minnesota

Contact:
RAIN Source Capital
1600 University Avenue West, Suite 401
St. Paul, MN 55104
Phone: 651-632-2140
Fax: 651-632-2145
Web site: www.rainsourcecapital.com

Prairie Capital, LLC (RAIN fund)
Worthington, Minnesota

Contact:
RAIN Source Capital
1600 University Avenue West, Suite 401
St. Paul, MN 55104
Phone: 651-632-2140
Fax: 651-632-2145
Web site: www.rainsourcecapital.com

RAIN Source Capital
St. Paul, Minnesota

RAIN Source Capital is a multi-state network of RAIN® funds that works with angel investors who are interested in supporting growing companies. RAIN funds range in size from seven to 61 members, who have pooled anywhere from $500,000 to $2 million. Each individual RAIN fund determines what industry it will focus on, and the type and level of financing to provide, based on the interests and expertise of its members.

> *Contact:*
> RAIN Source Capital
> 1600 University Avenue West, Suite 401
> St. Paul, MN 55104
> Phone: 651-632-2140
> Fax: 651-632-2145
> Web site: www.rainsourcecapital.com

River Valley Capital, LLC (RAIN fund)
Montevideo, Minnesota

> *Contact:*
> RAIN Source Capital
> 1600 University Avenue West, Suite 401
> St. Paul, MN 55104
> Phone: 651-632-2140
> Fax: 651-632-2145
> Web site: www.rainsourcecapital.com

Sofia Angel Fund, LLC (RAIN fund)
Minneapolis, Minnesota

> *Contact:*
> RAIN Source Capital
> 1600 University Avenue West, Suite 401
> St. Paul, MN 55104
> Phone: 651-632-2140
> Fax: 651-632-2145
> Web site: www.rainsourcecapital.com

St. Cloud RAIN Fund, LLC (RAIN fund)
St. Cloud, Minnesota

> *Contact:*
> RAIN Source Capital

1600 University Avenue West, Suite 401
St. Paul, MN 55104
Phone: 651-632-2140
Fax: 651-632-2145
Web site: www.rainsourcecapital.com

Two Rivers Angel Investment Network, LLC (RAIN fund)
Mankato, Minnesota

> *Contact:*
> RAIN Source Capital
> 1600 University Avenue West, Suite 401
> St. Paul, MN 55104
> Phone: 651-632-2140
> Fax: 651-632-2145
> Web site: www.rainsourcecapital.com

MISSOURI

Centennial Investors
Columbia, Missouri

Centennial Investors was created to meet the early capital needs of university and private sector entrepreneurs. It will assist in bringing to market exciting ideas generated in university labs and private businesses.

> *Contact:*
> 300 S. Providence Rd
> Columbia, MO 65203-1016
> Phone: 573-884-0467
> E-mail: info@centennialinvestors.com

St. Louis Arch Angels
St. Louis, Missouri

Arch angel members provide seed and early-stage capital in the range of $250K-$1M to early-stage companies with high growth potential in the St. Louis region. Members do not invest in a pooled fund, but rather commit to invest a minimum of $50,000 a year directly in a startup in partnership with other members of the network.

> *Contact:*
> St. Louis Arch Angels
> One Metropolitan Square, Suite 1300
> St. Louis, MO 63102

Phone: 314-444-1151
Fax: 314-206-3277
E-mail: cwalsh@stlrcga.org
Web site: www.stlouisarchangels.com

MONTANA

Bridger Private Capital Network
Bozeman, Montana

Since its inception in April, 2002, the Bridger Private Capital Network has invested over $3 million dollars into five Gallatin and Park County businesses, entertained presentations from eleven businesses, and recruited over 100 members, with a core group of 25.

Contact:
John O'Donnell, Executive Director
910 Technology Boulevard, Suite A
Bozeman, MT 59718
Phone: 406-556-0272
Fax: 406-556-0969
E-mail: jodonnell@techranch.org
Web site: www.techranch.org

Frontier Angel Fund (RAIN fund)
Kalispell, Montana

The Frontier Fund invests primarily in early- to mid-stage private companies located in northwestern Montana. It may also invest in late-stage private companies, and in private companies that are undergoing generational or other ownership transitions.

Contact:
Liz Marchi
Phone: 406-257-7711
or
RAIN Source Capital
1600 University Avenue West, Suite 401
St. Paul, MN 55104
Phone: 651-632-2140
Fax: 651-632-2145
Web site: www.rainsourcecapital.com

NEVADA

Sierra Angels
Incline Village, Nevada

The Sierra Angels is the premier angel investment group in the Northern Sierra region. We provide seed-stage investments in promising local technology ventures and support the entrepreneurs we fund with mentoring and connections. The Sierra Angels meet at regular intervals to review opportunities that have been sponsored by one or more of our members.

Contact:
Web site: www.sierraangels.com

Vegas Valley Angels
Las Vegas, Nevada

The Vegas Valley Angels (VVA) is focused on companies based in southern Nevada. We provide seed and early-stage capital in the range of $150,000 to $1 million. Since 2003, members of the Vegas Valley Angels have invested more than $5 million dollars in eight companies.

Contact:
Web site: www.vegasvalleyangels.com

NEW HAMPSHIRE

1st Run Angel Group
Conway, New Hampshire

1st Run Angel Group's goal is to identify investors from within the group who will evaluate business proposals brought forth by qualified business candidates in order to make individual investment decisions.

This group will help solve the problem of where to obtain injection capital for desirable business startups, expansions or recruitment opportunities to bring businesses to our area.

Contact:
Web site: www.firstrunangelgroup.com

eCoast Angels
Portsmouth, New Hampshire

The eCoast Angels Network was formed in July 2000 to focus on early-stage companies involved with advanced technology, e-commerce, healthcare, and industrial products and services, principally located in the New Hampshire coastal region. The group is most interested in companies requiring $250K-$2 million at pre-money valuations of less than $5 million, who have a credible multi-option exit strategy and are led by an experienced core management team. In keeping with the group's purpose, we have offered advice and counsel to many companies that were not funded by the network. In fact, several of these companies have gone on to receive funding based on the network's referrals.

Contact:
E-mail: ecoastangels@comcast.net
Web site: www.ecoastangels.com

Granite State Angels
Hanover, New Hampshire

Granite State Angels (GSA) brings together over 15 successful and experienced entrepreneurs who are active in making early-stage and seed investments in companies located in the northeastern United States. Members of GSA make individual decisions about investments. Many are interested in taking active roles in the development of a venture, from management and board activities to helping structure financially sound investment placements.

Contact:
Fred Wainwright
E-mail: wainwright@granitestateangels.com
Web Site: www.granitestateangels.com

NEW JERSEY

Jumpstart New Jersey Angel Network
Mt. Laurel, New Jersey

Jumpstart is a private, member-led angel group that invests in early-stage technology companies in the Mid-Atlantic region. Jumpstart was formed in November of 2002 with the active support of New Jersey Technology Council (NJTC) and New Jersey Economic Development Authority (EDA). In the last two years, Jumpstart angels invested $4.5 million.

Contact:
Jumpstart New Jersey Angel Network
1001 Briggs Road
Suite 280

Mt. Laurel, NJ 08054
Phone: 856-813-1440
Fax: 856-787-9800
E-mail: info@jumpstartnj.com.
Web site: www.jumpstartnj.com

Silicon Garden Angels & Investors Network
Somerset, New Jersey

Silicon Garden Angels & Investors Network helps entrepreneurs think long-term, and create with them win + win + win + win capital solutions. With Dan Conley working as your OnCallCFO + Venture Catalyst you will be nominated or sponsored into the highest quality and most prestigious east coast venture fairs, forums, and angel networks.

Contact:
Web site: www.njangels.net

NEW MEXICO

New Mexico Private Investors
Albuquerque, New Mexico

New Mexico Private Investors (NMPI) seeks to invest in companies with world class potential from technology based on patented/proprietary products or processes. Advice and attention are provided before investments are made, and on a continuing basis after money is put into a company.

Contact:
Jerry Mattingly
E-mail: jmattingly@nmprivateinvestors.com
or
John Rice
E-mail: ricejohnr@earthlink.net
New Mexico Private Investors, Inc.
One Technology Center
1155 University Boulevard SE
Albuquerque, NM 87106
Phone: 505-843-4206
Web site: www.nmprivateinvestors.com

NEW YORK

12Angels
New York, New York

Our organization's mission is to create jobs and increase productivity for men and women recovering from alcoholism and addiction. We believe that business is a vehicle of social change. We support businesses that reduce the harm addictive disorders cause to individuals, their families and our society.

> *Contact:*
> 94 Mercer Street
> New York, NY 10012
> Phone: 212-625-2094
> Web site: www.12angels.org

Blue Angel Ventures, Inc.
Manhasset, New York

We provide value-added business advisory, strategic and business development, interim executive management, and seed funding to promising young companies—companies that are commercializing innovative products or disruptive processes based on the use of advanced materials, IT/telecommunications, orbiosciences. We have a special interest in helping technologists-turned-entrepreneurs who are developing compelling solutions backed by an extremely strong patent portfolio.

> *Contact:*
> P.O. Box 566
> Manhasset, NY 11030
> Phone: 919-201-3798
> E-mail: Contact@BlueAngelVentures.com
> Web site: www.BlueAngelVentures.com

Central New York Angel Forum
Syracuse, New York

We can connect your business with the right source of funding. From Angel Capital to later stage growth financing, a range of organizations are interested in supporting Central New York business ventures.

> *Contact:*
> E-mail: info@growsyracuse.com
> Web site: www.cnyangel.com

Ivy Plus Network
New York, New York

Ivy Plus is a private network of elite business professionals and investors from the alternative investment industry including hedge funds, private equity and real estate. Members must be invited to gain access to Ivy Plus Investor Forums and Educational Conferences. Membership is limited to graduates of elite universities working in the industry or investing in alternative investment strategies.

> *Contact:*
> Marty Secada
> Ivy Plus Alternative Investment Network
> P.O. Box 443
> New York, NY 10185-0443
> E-mail: marty.secada@ivyplus.biz
> Web site: www.ivyplus.biz

New York Angels, Inc.
New York, New York

NYA's members are focused on investing in early-stage technology and new media companies in the New York City area and accelerating them to market leadership. Members of the group have invested in more than 20 companies since 2003, committing more than $14 million in capital.

> *Contact:*
> New York Angels
> 599 Lexington Avenue
> New York, NY 10022
> E-mail: info@newyorkangels.com
> Web site: www.newyorkangels.com

Orange County Angel Network
Orange County, New York

The Orange County Angel Network was founded in March of 2005 as a d/b/a of the Orange County Capital Development Corp. to provide early-stage capital in the range of $100K-$1M. Our mission is to provide opportunities for our members to obtain outstanding financial returns by investing in early-stage companies located in, or willing to relocate to, Orange County, New York.

Contact:
Robert P. Hannan, Managing Director
40 Matthews St., Suite 108
Goshen, NY 10924
Phone: 845-294-4295
E-mail: rhannan@orangecountyangelnetwork.com
Web site: www.orangecountyangelnetwork.com

Rochester Angel Network
Rochester, New York

The Rochester Angel Network is a private group of accredited investors in the Greater Rochester, NY region with an interest in investing in seed and early stage startup companies. Founded in 2005, the group meets monthly to listen to presentations by one or two selected entrepreneurs, and is actively seeking applications from entrepreneurs who are seeking funding.

Contact:
Web site: www.rochesterangels.com

Softbank Capital
Buffalo, New York

We invest primarily in companies addressing information technology, communications, and financial services opportunities in the northeastern U.S., southeastern Canada, and Israel. We don't "invest" in companies, we "build" them—and we build a very select number of companies. We are unequivocally active investors and always take board seats. However, we do not define active investing as simply showing up every six weeks to monitor our investment at a board meeting. We continuously help build early stage companies by recruiting top-tier management and board members; solving strategic problems; identifying and securing key channels and partners; defining organizational structure; and raising additional capital. We will also take interim operating roles when appropriate.

Contact:
Kim Borowski
E-mail: kim@softbank.com
Web site: www.softbank.com

Tech Valley Angel Network
Albany, New York

TVAN seeks growth-oriented, technology companies that are located within 150 miles of Albany, New York and are seeking $1 million or less in investments—though there are always exceptions to this standard.

Contact:
63 State Street
Albany, NY 12207
Phone: 518-465-8975
Fax: 518-465-6681
Web site: www.techvalleyangels.com

Tri-State Private Investors Network
New York, New York

The Tri-State Private Investors Network is a private, angel investor membership network based in New York City that serves the interests of early stage
entrepreneurs who are too small, too early or inappropriate for venture capital financing.

Contact:
Ellen Sandles
Executive Director
E-mail: ellen@angelinvestorfunding.com
Web site: www.angelinvestorfunding.com

TriState Ventures, LLC
New York, New York

TriState Ventures is a leading organization of Angel Investors in the Tri-State
area. Founded in 1999, we meet on a monthly basis and view prescreened
investment opportunities from various sectors. Companies that we have
funded include healthcare wireless, energy, as well as consumer products. We
are not geographically limited and will participate with other angel groups
in other areas.

Contact:
E-mail: Execsummary@tristateventures.com
Web site: www.tristateventures.com

Wharton Angel Network
New York, New York

The group aims to bring together Wharton alumni active in the greater angel
network and early stage investment community, which includes professionals working as angel investors, members of angel networks, early stage fund
raisers and marketers, members of venture capital firms, fund marketers, private equity investors, lawyers, accountants, foundations and other service
providers active in the early stage investment space.

Contact:
Marty Secada, Manager
Wharton Business School Club of New York
603 West 115th Street, Box 300
New York, NY 10025-2803
Phone: 212-463-5559
Fax: 917-464-5977
E-mail: WAN@whartonny.com

NORTH CAROLINA

Atlantis Group
Raleigh, North Carolina

The Atlantis Group, LLC is an angel investment group designed to capitalize on the explosive growth in the entrepreneurial activity and venture financing primarily in North Carolina.

Contact:
2530 Meridian Parkway, 3rd floor
Durham, NC 27713
Phone: 919-806-4340
Fax: 919-806-4739
E-mail: info@TheAtlantisGroup.net
Web site: www.TheAtlantisGroup.net

Blue Angel Ventures, Inc.
Morrisville, North Carolina

We provide value-added business advisory, strategic and business development, interim executive management, and seed funding to promising young companies—companies that are commercializing innovative products or disruptive processes based on the use of advanced materials, IT/telecommunications, or biosciences. We have a special interest in helping technologists-turned-entrepreneurs who are developing compelling solutions backed by an extremely strong patent portfolio.

Contact:
P.O. Box 12482
Research Triangle Park, NC 27709
Phone: 919-201-3798
E-mail: Contact@BlueAngelVentures.com
Web site: www.BlueAngelVentures.com

Blue Ridge Angel Investor Network (BRAIN)
Fletcher, North Carolina

> *Contact:*
> Jim Roberts
> E-mail: jroberts@awnc.org
> Web site: www.ncmtns.biz

Inception Micro Angel Fund
Greensboro, North Carolina

The Inception Micro Angel Fund, LLC (IMAF) is a member-managed seed stage angel capital fund operating primarily in the Piedmont Triad area of North Carolina, greater North Carolina and in selective areas of Virginia and South Carolina.

> *Contact:*
> Inception Micro Angel Fund
> 1959 N. Peace Haven Road
> Suite 111
> Winston Salem, NC 27106
> E-mail: funddirector@inceptionmicroangelfund.com
> Web site: www.inceptionmicroangelfund.com

Piedmont Angel Network
Greensboro, North Carolina

PAN seeks to create and protect an entrepreneur friendly (helpful) environment. We are not in the business of terrorizing entrepreneurs. Many of us have been on their side of the fence before becoming investors. And it is not always fun. Growth company opportunities include service companies, technology opportunities, and life sciences.

> *Contact:*
> 2007 Yanceyville Street, Box 69
> Greensboro, NC 27405
> Phone: 336-235-0941
> Lou Anne Flanders-Stec
> E-mail: lafstec@piedmontangelnetwork.com
> or
> Troy Knauss
> E-mail: tknauss@piedmontangelnetwork.com
> Web site: www.piedmontangelnetwork.com

Triangle Accredited Capital Forum
Wake Forest, North Carolina

The purpose of the Triangle Accredited Capital Forum is to enable local private investors to review high quality investment opportunities across multiple industries, in the company of other investors. Capital-Forum directors screen all business plans and work with the entrepreneurs to assure the quality of the plans and presentations.

> *Contact:*
> E-mail: chairman@capital-forum.com
> Web site: www.capital-forum.com

Tri-State Investment Group
Chapel Hill, North Carolina

Tri-State Investment Group (TIG) is a group of investors dedicated to providing equity capital to early and mid-stage entrepreneurial companies that are based in Virginia, North Carolina and South Carolina. TIG seeks investment opportunities in private companies with explosive growth potential. Companies that are attempting to capitalize on new technologies or changing market conditions are of highest interest. Typical investments range from $150,000 to $500,000 with a targeted exit in three to five years. Exits can include sale, IPO or repurchase of TIG's investment by management.

> *Contact:*
> 405 Tramore Drive
> Chapel Hill, NC 27516
> E-mail: contact@tignc.com
> Web site: www.tignc.com

WED3
Charlotte, North Carolina

This members-only group reviews business summaries and real estate development plans submitted by companies and individuals. Selected groups then have the opportunity to present their presentations to a Wed3 regular membership meeting.

> *Contact:*
> 1523 Elizabeth Avenue, Suite 210
> Charlotte, NC 28204
> E-mail: info@wed3.org
> Web site: www.wed3.org

Wilmington Investor Network
Wilmington, North Carolina

Wilmington Investor Network (WIN) provides capital to early-stage companies in eastern North and South Carolina. Our investors focus on technology, biotechnology, and medical device companies, but will consider other business ventures with high-return potential.

> *Contact:*
> 1802 South Churchill Drive
> Wilmington, NC 28403
> Phone: 910-538-6641
> E-mail: info@wilmingtoninvestor.com
> Web site: www.wilmingtoninvestor.com

NORTH DAKOTA

CEO Praxis (RAIN fund)
Grand Forks, North Dakota

> *Contact:*
> RAIN Source Capital
> 1600 University Avenue West, Suite 401
> St. Paul, MN 55104
> Phone: 651-632-2140
> Fax: 651-632-2145
> Web site: www.rainsourcecapital.com

Northern Plains Investment (RAIN fund)
Bismarck, North Dakota

> *Contact:*
> RAIN Source Capital
> 1600 University Avenue West, Suite 401
> St. Paul, MN 55104
> Phone: 651-632-2140
> Fax: 651-632-2145
> Web site: www.rainsourcecapital.com

OHIO

Akron Arch Angels
Akron, Ohio

ARCH Angel Network is led by the University of Akron Research Foundation and is a loose collection of around two dozen investors and community leaders.

Contact:
E-mail: schorr@uakron.edu
Web site: www.uakron.edu/research/archangels

C-Cap / Queen City Angels
Cincinnati, Ohio

C-CAP members have made most of their investments as individual private investors, without a fund. It is possible for a group of our investors to form a single legal entity and pool their investment, or for a group to invest on a single term sheet. However, in 2003 several investors and others formed the QCA First Fund, to invest smaller amounts, in earlier deals, than they invest as individuals.

Contact:
Phone: 513-618-6440
E-mail: c-cap@thecircuit.net
Web site: www.qca.net

CoreNetwork
Toledo, Ohio

Companies seeking investment who submit their material along with paying the review fee ($200), will have the initial material reviewed by two committees (and need their approval) before being asked to make a presentation to the CoreNetwork Investor Group. Companies should expect to hear feedback from the first committee within 30 days.

Contact:
Bob Savage
CoreNetwork
101 Main Street
Toledo, OH 43605
Fax: 419-698-1260
E-mail: submitplan@core-network.org
Web site: www.core-network.org

Jumpstart, Inc.
Cleveland, Ohio

JumpStart funds high-growth businesses and ideas, works with their founders to develop the businesses into venture-ready entities and simultaneously celebrates Northeast Ohio's early-stage company successes. JumpStart is organized and operated exclusively for charitable and educational purposes, including combating community deterioration and lessening the burden of government in the Northeast Ohio area. On average, we invest $300,000 in our portfolio companies. About ten to twelve companies per year receive a JumpStart investment.

Contact:
JumpStart, Inc.
737 Bolivar Road, Suite 3000
Cleveland, OH 44115
Phone: 216-363-3400
Fax: 216-363-3401
E-mail: Ask@JumpStartInc.org
Web site: www.JumpStartInc.org

NCIC Capital Fund
Dayton, Ohio

NCIC Capital Fund is an early stage investment company. We invest in emerging, growth-oriented, technology-based companies. Since June of 1995, NCIC Capital Fund has made 59 rounds of investments in 29 companies totaling over $15 million. Our investments have been leveraged with an additional $60 million in co-investments. Our investments have ranged from $200,000 to $1,000,000 with an average of $500,000 per company.

Contact:
NCIC Capital Fund
3155 Research Boulevard, Suite 203
Dayton, OH 45420
Phone: 937-253-1777
Fax: 937-253-2634
E-mail: rbowman@ncicfund.com
Web site: www.ncicfund.com

North Coast Angel Fund
Cleveland, Ohio

North Coast Angel Fund (NCAF) is a newly established contributed capital and "sidecar" pre-seed investment fund with a focus on early-stage technology investments. Its membership consists of a number of the region's leading investors, entrepreneurs, and business leaders who are dedicated to accelerating early-stage ventures.

Contact:
North Coast Angel Fund, LLC
737 Bolivar Road, Suite 3000
Cleveland, OH 44115
Phone and fax: 800-975-5846
Web site: www.northcoastangelfund.com

Ohio TechAngel Fund, LLC
Columbus, Ohio

The Fund is seeking Ohio-based opportunities in life sciences, information technology, and physical sciences but will also consider investing in consumer retail, distribution and innovative service businesses.

Contact:
E-mail: manager@ohiotechangels.com
Web site: www.ohiotechangels.com

OKLAHOMA

i2E
Tulsa, Oklahoma

i2E, Inc. is focused on growing the technology-based entrepreneurial economy in Oklahoma. Originally founded as the Oklahoma Technology Development Corporation in September 1997, i2E was founded to respond to an Oklahoma Center for the Advancement of Science and Technology (OCAST) initiative.

Contact:
Tom Walker, Executive VP and COO
Phone: 918-582-5592, Ext. 1455
E-mail: twalker@i2E.org
Web site: www.i2E.org

OREGON

Portland Angel Network
Portland, Oregon

The Portland Angel Network (PAN) meets bimonthly, and each event features 2-4 selected companies. Early stage deals are preferred. Companies should be seeking capital within the range of $500,000 to $2,000,000.

Contact:
309 SW Sixth Avenue, Suite 212
Portland, OR 97204
Phone: 503-222-2270
Fax: 503-241-0827
Web site: www.oef.org/programs/pan

Women's Investment Network (Oregon)
Portland, Oregon

The Women's Investment Network (WIN) is a forum for women who are active angels or would like to learn more about becoming an angel investor. WIN's mission is to provide an environment that promotes education, networking, leadership, and investment opportunities to women for the purpose of helping early stage companies successfully grow in Oregon's entrepreneurial community. Early stage deals are preferred. Companies should be seeking capital within the range of $500,000 to $2,000,000.

Contact:
309 SW Sixth Avenue, Suite 212
Portland, OR 97204
Phone: 503-222-2270
E-mail: applytoWIN@oef.org
Web site: https://www.oef.org/programs/win

PENNSYLVANIA

BlueTree Allied Angels
Wexford, Pennsylvania

BlueTree Allied Angels meet on a monthly basis to evaluate and consider preinstitutional, early-stage investments. Although the membership works together as a group to efficiently and effectively evaluate investment opportunities, each member makes his/her own individual decisions to invest.

Contact:
Catherine Mott
Phone: 724-699-1076
E-mail: cvmott@bluetreecapital.com
or
Tom Jones
Phone: 724-493-4944
E-mail: tjones@bluetreecapital.com
Web site: www.bluetreealliedangels.com

Central Pennsylvania Angel Network
Mechanicsburg, Pennsylvania

The Central Pennsylvania Angel Network (CPAN) is an angel group comprised of successful business people from the greater Harrisburg area. The organization meets the first Thursday of every month to hear about promising companies in the region. Preferred industry segments include information technology, manufacturing and biotech. Generally three companies make presentations at each meeting.

> *Contact:*
> Jan Rumberger
> Phone: 717-766-9208
> E-mail: mateer@epix.net

Delaware Crossing Investor Group
Warrington, Pennsylvania

Members of Delaware Crossing Investor Group are typically private investors who have founded or run successful high-growth companies. Members join Delaware Crossing Investor Group to fund and aid the development of local companies through their collective business experience and contacts.

> *Contact:*
> Delaware Crossing Investor Group
> P.O. Box 1493
> Doylestown, PA 18901
> Phone: 215-918-3614
> E-mail: info@delawarecrossing.org
> Web site: www.delawarecrossing.org

Great Valley Pennsylvania Angel Network
Scranton, Pennsylvania

The group meets on a quarterly basis to review business plans, and to network with firms looking for Angel investments.

> *Contact:*
> Kenneth G. Okrepkie
> Vice President
> Scranton Enterprise Center
> 201 Lackawanna Avenue
> Scranton, PA 18503
> Phone: 570-341-8099
> Phone: 570-408-9810
> E-mail: kokrepkie@greatvalleyalliance.com

Innovation Works
Pittsburgh, Pennsylvania

The Innovation Works team specializes in helping seed stage technology ventures by providing them with access to risk capital, business expertise, and third-party resources.

> *Contact:*
> Innovation Works
> 2000 Technology Drive, Suite 250
> Pittsburgh, PA 15219-3109
> Phone: 412-681-1520
> Fax: 412-681-2625
> E-mail: info@innovationworks.org
> Web site: www.innovationworks.org

Investors Circle of York
York, Pennsylvania

The mission of ICY is to create a source of financial capital to help facilitate entrepreneurship, new business development and growth in the York County. Companies need to contact York County Economic Development Corporation (YCEDC) for information required to be presented with their request.

> *Contact:*
> Carole J. Swope, Projects Coordinator
> York County Economic Development Corporation
> 144 Roosevelt Avenue, Suite 100
> York, PA 17401
> Phone: 717-846-8879 ext 3034
> Fax: 717-843-8837
> E-mail: cswope@ycedc.org
> Web site: www.ycedc.org

Lancaster Angel Network
Lancaster, Pennsylvania

The Lancaster Angel Network is a group of successful business people that meets monthly to review companies in a wide variety of industries and businesses of all sizes. The meeting is held over dinner and is preceded with a cocktail mixer. Businesses interested in making a presentation should e-mail executive summaries to:

Contact:
Michael A. Shoemaker
c/o Wellspring FV LLC
128 East Grant Street, Fourth Floor
Lancaster, PA 17602
Phone: 717-293-5151
Fax: 717-293-1611
E-mail: mas@wellspringfv.com

LORE Associates
Malvern, Pennsylvania

Since its founding in 1988, the principal mission of the LORE ("Loosely Organized Retired Executives") group is to provide investment capital and mentoring to early stage companies principally in the Greater Philadelphia Area.

Contact:
Ginger Cutlip
Phone: 610-964-8452
E-mail: verus@tpinv.com

Mid-Atlantic Angel Group Fund I (part of Science Center)
Philadelphia, Pennsylvania

The Mid-Atlantic Angel Group Fund I, LP (MAG) provides its investors with
an opportunity for active involvement in diversified venture capital investments throughout Southeastern Pennsylvania, Central and Southern New
Jersey, and Delaware. MAG is the first formally structured angel capital venture fund in the Greater Philadelphia Region and seeks to leverage various
public and private funding resources and networks by providing equity capital to seed and early-stage, technology-based, high-growth companies.

Contact:
Chris Starr, Managing Director and Vice President of Investments
Science Center
3701 Market Street
Third Floor
Philadelphia, PA 19104
Phone: 215-966-6147
E-mail: cstarr@sciencecenter.org
Web site: www.magfund.com

Minority Angel Investor Network
Philadelphia, Pennsylvania

MAIN is the nation's first and only formalized angel network with a minority investment focus. MAIN is sponsored by the Ben Franklin Technology Partners of Southeastern Pennsylvania with support from The Kauffman Foundation and the Commonwealth of Pennsylvania.

> *Contact:*
> Minority Angel Investor Network (MAIN)
> 1835 Market Street, Suite 1100
> Philadelphia, PA 19103
> Sushma Raj
> Phone: 215-972-6700 ext 3240
> E-mail: sushma@sep.benfranklin.org
> Terry Hicks
> Phone: 215-972-6700 ext 3799
> E-mail: terry@sep.benfranklin.org
> Gloria Sanchious
> Phone: 215-972-6700 ext 3330
> E-mail: gloria@sep.benfranklin.org
> Web site: www.main-usa.com

Private Investors Forum
Philadelphia, Pennsylvania

The Private Investors Forum (PIF) is a nonprofit organization of accredited private investors dedicated to providing education and stimulating investment in the Greater Philadelphia Region, including New Jersey, Delaware and Maryland.

> *Contact:*
> Valerie S. Gaydos
> Executive Director
> 224 Pine Street, Third Floor
> Harrisburg, PA 17101
> Phone: 717-238-1222
> Fax: 717-238-9512
> E-mail: vgaydos@51st.com
> Web site: www.privateinvestorsforum.com

Robin Hood Ventures
Wayne, Pennsylvania

Robin Hood Ventures, founded in 1999, is a group of experienced entrepreneurs and accredited investors interested in investing and taking an active role in early stage companies with high return on investment potential. We can invest $250K to $500K for a single financing, and will co-invest with other angels or institutions. Robin Hood Ventures invests as a single entity and considers business opportunities that represent the diverse interests and experience of our members.

> *Contact:*
> 200 Musket Lane
> Wayne, PA 19087
> Phone: 610-993-9060
> Fax: 484-214-0114
> E-mail: info@robinhoodventures.com

Southwest Pennsylvania Angel Network
Pittsburgh, Pennsylvania

SPAN is an organization that connects angel investors seeking early-stage investment opportunities with the region's most promising startup technology companies. Each quarter, two companies are selected to present their business plans to SPAN members who then have the opportunity to evaluate the organizations for potential investment.

> *Contact:*
> Innovation Works
> 2000 Technology Drive, Suite 250
> Pittsburgh, PA 15219-3109
> Phone: 412-681-1520
> E-mail: info@innovationworks.org
> Web site: www.innovationworks.org

Susquehanna Investment Network
Lewisburg, Pennsylvania

The Susquehanna Investment Network (SIN) is a group of 57 highly successful angel investors who represent 11 counties in Central PA. The group meets the third Wednesday of each month. Meetings start with a networking reception followed by presentations during dinner. The average investment range is from $25,000 to $500,000.

Contact:
Bill Metzger, Sr.
Susquehanna Investment Network
One Kelly Square
Route 15 North
Lewisburg, PA 17837
Phone: 570-568-2000
Fax: 570-568-9000
E-mail: csi@uplink.net

Winners Investment Network
Altoona, Pennsylvania

WIN is made up of a regional network of highly successful entrepreneurs and businessmen.

Contact:
Winners Investment Network For ABCD Corp.
3900 Industrial Park Drive
Devorris Center for Business Development
Altoona, PA 16602
Phone: 814-944-6113
E-mail: abcd@abcdcorp.org

Women's Investment Network (Pennsylvania)
Pottstown, Pennsylvania

Women's Investment Network (WIN) is the Greater Philadelphia region's only organization specifically for women who are leaders of and investors in high-growth businesses. WIN promotes the expansion of women-led and women-owned businesses with high growth potential through education, networking, mentoring, and exposure to investment resources.

Contact:
WIN
P.O. Box 543
Pottstown, PA 19464
Phone: 484-945-2108
Fax: 610-970-7520
E-mail: info@winwomen.org
Web site: www.winwomen.org

RHODE ISLAND

Cherrystone Angel Group
Providence, Rhode Island

Cherrystone Angel Group, founded in 2004 with more than 30 members, is Rhode Island's first organized angel investment group. All our members are experienced and qualified investors who have either built their own companies or have extensive experience launching new business ventures. While we recognize that it is the entrepreneur who drives the company—and on whom ultimate success depends—we also understand that good advice and focused expertise are vital to the success of any business venture. That's what we provide.

> *Contact:*
> E-mail: info@cherrystoneangelgroup.com
> Web site: www.cherrystoneangelgroup.com

SOUTH CAROLINA

Charleston Angel Partners
Charleston, South Carolina

CHAP members share the common objective of supporting economic development in the Charleston area and surrounding region, particularly in growth oriented early stage companies (not pure start-ups) that have the potential to become $50 million companies in 3-5 years.

> *Contact:*
> E-mail: roozen@charlestonangelpartners.com
> Web site: www.charlestonangelpartners.com/default.htm

Columbia Angel Partners
Columbia, South Carolina

Columbia Angel Partners (CAP-SC) was formed in early 2004 to create an angel network in Columbia, South Carolina. Its members are Columbia area investors, leaders, and business professionals possessing strong expertise in business and entrepreneurship across a variety of industries.

> *Contact:*
> Neil McLean
> E-mail: nmclean@cap-sc.com
> Web site: www.cap-sc.com

SOUTH DAKOTA

Enterprise Angels
Brookings, South Dakota

A network of accredited angel investors and angel associations with support services provided by the Enterprise Institute.

> *Contact:*
> 815 Medary Avenue, Suite 201
> Brookings, SD 57006
> Phone: 605-275-2833 (Marcia)
> Phone: 605-275-8013 (Mari Beth)
> Phone: 605-697-5015 (Main)
> E-mail: info@sdei.org
> Web site: www.sdei.org/enterprise_angels.shtml

TENNESSEE

Nashville Capital Network
Nashville, Tennessee

The Nashville Capital Network (NCN) is a collaborative initiative of Vanderbilt University, the Nashville Technology Council, Nashville Health Care Council, local investors, as well as local business and professional leaders. The NCN strives to promote entrepreneurial education and economic growth by becoming the hub for early stage capital formation in middle Tennessee.

> *Contact:*
> T. Sidney Chambless, Jr., Executive Director
> Nashville Capital Network
> 1207 17th Avenue South, Suite 303,
> Nashville, TN 37212
> Phone: 615-322-3154
> Fax: 615-343-6900
> E-mail: schambless@nashvillecapital.com
> Web site: www.nashvillecapital.com

TEXAS

Camino Real Angels
El Paso, Texas

The Camino Real Angels provide seed and early-stage capital up to $2M.

Our member angels work closely with the new entrepreneur to refine his or her strategy and positioning, help clarify their business plan, prepare a presentation, and resolve issues related to financing. We are able to assist in structuring the terms of a deal and provide extensive help to the entrepreneur after making an investment. Our members may serve as directors or in an advisory capacity, and are available to provide coaching to the management team. We maintain close relationships with venture capital firms, service providers and universities, and can facilitate access to talent, technology and other resources needed to build a successful venture.

Our members collaborate on due diligence, but make individual investment decisions.

Contact:
E-mail: contactus@caminorealangels.com
Web site: www.caminorealangels.com

Central Texas Angel Network
Austin, Texas

The Central Texas Angel Network (CTAN) is a not-for-profit corporation dedicated to providing quality early-stage investment opportunities for accredited Central Texas angel investors, and to assisting, educating and connecting early stage growth companies in Central Texas with information and advisors for the purpose of raising money and assisting in their growth.

Contact:
Hall Martin
Phone: 512-322-5600
E-mail: director@centexangels.org
Web site: www.centexangels.org

Houston Angel Network
Houston, Texas

HAN was founded in late 2001 and is the largest and most active angel network in Texas: HAN members have provided twenty-seven rounds of funding for nineteen companies.

Contact:
Kala Marathi, Managing Director
Houston Angel Network
410 Pierce
Houston, TX 77002
Phone: 832-476-9291
E-mail: kmarathi@houstonangelnetwork.org
Web site: www.houstonangelnetwork.org/home.htm

InvestIN Forum of Angel Investors
Dallas, Forth Worth, and Austin, Texas

The InvestIN Forum is an association of angel investor communities operating with the same goals and best practices under a common brand. We are concerned with helping fuel the local entrepreneurial ecosystem and try to be helpful to all entrepreneurs providing useful resources whilst at the same time we are looking for early stage investment opportunities for our members.

> *Contact:*
> The InvestIN Forum—DFW chapter
> 4245 North Central Expressway, Suite 465
> Dallas, TX 75206
> Phone: 214-329-1244
> Laurence D. Briggs
> E-mail: laurence@theinvestINforum.com
> Cindy Bailey
> E-mail: cindy@theinvestINforum.com
> Paul Briggs
> E-mail: paul@theinvestINforum.com
> Web site: www.theinvestINforum.com

North Dallas Investment Group
Dallas, Texas

NDIG is a group of Angel Investors who meet and listen to presentations from companies needing capital of $2M or less. There are currently ninety "Accredited Angel Investors" in the group. Every month NDIG meets to hear from four start-up companies who have been selected to present. Each investor can then decide whether they would like to meet with the companies to explore and invest.

> *Contact:*
> Mary Ann Sadowski
> Chapman, Hext & Co., P.C.
> 301 South Sherman, Suite 200
> Richardson, TX 75081-4176
> Phone: 972-644-7112 ext 307
> E-mail: maryann@chapmanhext.com
> Web site: www.nd-ig.com

San Antonio Capital Alliance
San Antonio, Texas

The San Antonio Capital Alliance focuses on developing capital resources for San Antonio's emerging technology sectors. This Alliance is absolutely critical to overcoming a severe deficiency in our San Antonio entrepreneurial market—the lack of an organized network for assisting startup and early-stage ventures with high-performance growth potential. The Alliance is extended to qualified investors who have an interest in San Antonio equity investment opportunities, who offer access to capital for entrepreneurs with high-performance ventures, or who provide services for early-stage companies. The Alliance is targeted to accredited corporate or individual investors and lenders who have a work history of serving this market.

> *Contact:*
> Anne Thompson
> Phone: 210-458-2585
> E-mail: Anne.vanhorn@satai-network.com
> Web site: www.satai-network.com

Technology Tree Group
Houston, Texas

Our constituents include investors looking for cutting edge technology investment opportunities and private research organizations / early stage companies bringing new technologies to market.

> *Contact:*
> Technology Tree Group, Inc.
> 410 Pierce Street, Suite 307
> Houston, TX 77002
> Phone: 832-476-9226
> E-mail: info@technology-tree.com
> Web site: www.technology-tree.com

Texas Women Ventures Fund
Dallas, Texas

Texas Women Ventures Fund, LP was created with the mission to invest a majority of its capital in women-led companies located in Texas and the Southwest. The TWVF offers Dequity©, which is debt that performs a lot like equity. You get the money in the form of a loan and you keep control of your company. In addition to prominent institutional investors, the fund has over forty successful women entrepreneurs and executives as investors and mentors.

Contact:
Texas Women Ventures Fund
2435 North Central Expressway, Suite #200
Richardson, TX 75080
Phone: 972-725-0323
Fax: 972-991-1647
E-mail: info@texaswomenventures.com
Web site: www.texaswomenventures.com

UTAH

Olympus Angel Investors
Salt Lake City, Utah

Our investment profile is a product or service with at least phase 1 development suitable for immediate revenue generation. The maximum collective investment parameters are $500,000.

Contact:
E-mail: contactus@olympusangelinvestors.org
Web site: www.olympusangelinvestors.org

Top of Utah Angels
Salt Lake City, Utah

Top of Utah Angels assists each entrepreneur by providing mentoring, advice and seed capital, all of which increase the likelihood that the venture will be successful. The overall objective of the Top of Utah Angels is to support and fund businesses at the emerging stage where more traditional means of business financing are not likely.

Contact:
T. Craig Bott
Grow Utah Ventures
P.O. Box 764
Kaysville, UT 84037
Phone: 801-479-5525
E-mail: info@growutahventures.com
Web site: www.growutahventures.com/touamain.asp

Utah Angels
Salt Lake City, Utah

The Utah Angels are fifteen private investors backing Utah entrepreneurs. We collaborate, but invest individually. Since formation in May 1998, Utah Angels have invested $16 million in thirty nine companies. Previously, among us we have made private investments in hundreds of companies. We are all knowledgeable active investors, and former or current entrepreneurs ourselves. We invest from $50,000 to $2,000,000 as equity or convertible debt. We assist in securing next stage financing from a venture capital firm, from private sources, or from an IPO.

> *Contact:*
> E-mail: info@utahangels.org
> Web site: www.utahangels.org

VERMONT

North Country Angels
Vermont

North Country Angels (NCA) brings together over 20 successful and experienced entrepreneurs who are active in making early-stage and seed investments in companies located in the northeastern United States. Members of NCA make individual decisions about investments. Many are interested in taking active roles in the development of a venture, from management and board activities to helping structure financially sound investment placements.

> *Contact:*
> Fred Wainwright
> E-mail: wainwright@northcountryangels.com
> Web site: www. northcountryangels.com

VIRGINIA

Active Angel Investor Network
Vienna, Virginia

Active Angel Investors is a membership network of accredited investors who desire to invest in seed-stage opportunities in the Mid-Atlantic region. The Active Angel membership meets ten or eleven times over the year to consider two or three investment opportunities per meeting. The network considers exclusively pre-institutional, early-stage investments, and typically lead the financing rounds.

Contact:
New Vantage Group
402 Maple Avenue West
Vienna, VA 22180
Phone: 703-255-4930
Fax: 703-255-4931
Web site: www.activeangelinvestors.com

The eMedia Club
Vienna, Virginia

The eMedia Club is an early stage venture fund administered by New Vantage Group (NVG). The Club finances high technology companies by participating in the Series A and B rounds of financing alongside other venture funds. A primary geographic screen of the East coast of the U.S. is employed, but the Club does consider opportunities outside of that area on a case by case basis. The Club's focus is on the telecommunications industry, especially wireless technology and products and services for the burgeoning CLEC and broadband industries. The Club also focuses on Internet commerce and content opportunities, business to business and Internet infrastructure, as well as multimedia technologies particularly those utilizing the Internet for delivery of both content and services.

Contact:
The eMedia Club, LLC
402 Maple Avenue West
Vienna, VA 22180
Phone: 703-255-4930
Fax: 703-255-4931
E-mail: info@emediaclub.com
Web site: www.newvantagegroup.com/site/emclub.asp

Virginia Active Angel Network
Charlottesville, Virginia

Virginia Active Angel Network (VAAN) is a member-led, professionally managed club of angel investors who gather for ten dinner meetings from September through July in Charlottesville, Virginia. Started in 2005 by a group of local University of Virginia alumni, and joined by New Vantage Group of McLean, Virginia, VAAN seeks to bring energy, expertise and entrepreneurs together to create opportunities to invest and network with other like-minded angel investors throughout Virginia.

Contact:
VAAN
c/o TJ Capital Group, LLC
P.O. Box 5767
Charlottesville, VA 22905
Phone: 434-409-3383
E-mail: info@tjcapitalgroup.com
Web site: www.virginiaactiveangelnetwork.com

Washington Dinner Club
Vienna, Virginia

The Washington Dinner Club is an early stage venture fund administered by New Vantage Group (NVG). The primary focus of the Club is to discover and invest in those companies located in and around the expanding Washington, D.C. area. After primary attention on the region, a secondary screen is used for the states of Virginia and Maryland.

Contact:
New Vantage Group
402 Maple Avenue West
Vienna, VA 22180
Phone: 703-255-4930
Fax: 703-255-4931
E-mail: info@washingtondinnerclub.com
Web site: www.washingtondinnerclub.com

WASHINGTON

Alliance of Angels
Seattle, Washington

The Alliance of Angels (AoA) is a regionally-focused group of about 140 individual investors and representatives of investment corporations. The goal of the Alliance of Angels is to nurture the growth of technology-based businesses in the Pacific Northwest by improving the interactions among angel investors and emerging local technology companies seeking funding.

Contact:
Alliance of Angels
1301 5th Avenue, Suite 2500
Seattle, WA 98101
Phone: 206-389-7261

Fax: 206-903-3423
E-mail: info@allianceofangels.com
Web site: www.allianceofangels.com

Bellingham Angel Group
Bellingham, Washington

We review and screen company business plans on a regular basis and select three to four companies to make a 15-minute presentation to our members during our scheduled quarterly (or semi-monthly) member meetings. The angels may collaborate on due diligence, but make individual investment decisions; we do not have a fund and do not necessarily invest as a group.

Typically, the Bellingham Angels will invest between $25,000 and $250,000 to help companies grow to the next stage.

Contact:.
Web site: www.bellinghamangels.com

Delta Angel Group
Spokane, Washington

Established February 2003, the Delta Angel Group is a nonprofit alliance of accredited investors who have a common interest in investing with technology-centric businesses in Eastern Washington, Idaho, and Montana who are seeking early stage funding. The group is very interested in northwest technology companies that have good prospects for growth and promise generous returns to stakeholders and the community.

Contact:
120 N. Pine, Suite 152
Spokane, WA 99202
Phone: 509-979-5308
Fax: 509-838-0505
Web site: www.deltaangelgroup.org

Keiretsu Forum Seattle/Northwest
Seattle, Washington

Keiretsu stands for collaboration, the culture in which our forum thrives. Keiretsu Forum is the largest network of accredited angel investors in North America. We are a part of the greater Keiretsu network which, since 2000, has monetized over 90 companies with over $60 million amid chapters located throughout the United States.

Contact:
M. Todd Dean, Seattle/Northwest Chapter President
One Convention Place
701 Pike Street, Suite 2250
Seattle, WA 98101
Phone: 206-334-5300
E-mail: todd@keiretsuforum.com
Web site: www.k4seattle.com

Seraph Capital Forum
Seattle, Washington

Seraph Capital Forum is the foremost woman's organization of active angels in the Puget Sound region individually providing capital and board level expertise to early stage companies.

Contact:
E-mail: seraph-info@seraphcapital.com
Web site: www.seraphcapital.com

TacomaAngel Network
Tacoma, Washington

Established in June 2006, the TacomaAngel Network is a non-profit alliance of accredited investors. The ultimate goal is to help investors make profitable investments in the high risk/high return private equity market, while fueling the growth of early stage companies in the Pacific Northwest.

Contact:
Paul Ellis
950 Pacific Avenue, Suite 300
P.O. Box 1933
Tacoma, WA 98401-1933
Phone: 253-627-2175
Fax: 253-597-7305
E-mail: paulellis@tacomaangelnetwork.com

Zino Society
Seattle, Washington

ZINO Society roundtable meetings showcase exceptional investment opportunities from multiple business sectors. Though preference is given to strong companies with a focus on the wine industry and lifestyle/consumer products and services investment offerings, ZINO Society and its members are also interested in seeing investment opportunities in technology, bio-technology, real estate, retail, education, travel and hospitality, etc.

Applications must be accompanied by an application fee ($150/$300—latter for Private Reserve Presentation). Companies who are accepted and agree to present are responsible for $1,500 presentation fee ($5,000 for the Private Reserve Presentation)

> *Contact:.*
> 411 University Street, Suite 1200
> Seattle, WA 98101
> Phone: 206-621-0466
> E-mail: info@zinosociety.com
> Web site: www.zinosociety.com/roundtable

WISCONSIN

Badger AgVest, LLC
Wausau, Wisconsin

A membership organization formed by Wisconsin farmers and agribusinesses to better identify and support businesses that may add value to agricultural commodities and industries and that might spur rural economic development.

> *Contact:*
> James Hanke, Executive Director
> Badger AgVest, LLC
> 210 McClellan Street, Suite 210
> Wausau, WI 54403
> Phone: 715-849-5510, Ext. 306
> E-mail: jhanke@ncwrpc.org
> Web site: www.badgeragvest.com

Central Wisconsin Business Angels, LLC
Wisconsin

This fund was formed to assist in equity financing of business start-ups and expansions that produce a product or service that is exported beyond the Central Wisconsin area.

Contact:
Connie Loden
E-mail: cloden@heartofwi.com
Phone: 715-423-1830
or
Jeff Landin
E-mail: jlandin@portagecountybiz.com
Phone: 715-344-1940
Web site: www.progressinitiative.com/breaking82.html

Chippewa Valley Angel Investors Network
Chippewa Falls, Wisconsin

The Chippewa Valley Angel Investors Network, LLC began operating in April, 2003 in an effort to provide a one-stop resource for entrepreneurs seeking equity financing in the Chippewa Valley. The Chippewa Valley Angel Investors Network is operated in a manner that allows each investor to make his or her own decision on each company seeking equity, which results in a high degree of autonomy for the investors.

Contact:
Pete Marsnik, Manager
Phone: 715-878-9791
E-mail: cvangels@execpc.com

Golden Angels Network
Milwaukee, Wisconsin

The Golden Angels Network was formed at Marquette University in early 2003. The network considers business opportunities primarily from Illinois and Wisconsin, as well as from the Midwest. It has invested $3.2 million in seven companies since 2003. Our members provide early-stage capital in the range of $250,000—$750,000. Since 2003, we have invested over $3.2 million in 7 ventures companies.

Contact:
Tim Keane, Golden Angels Network Director
Marquette University College of Business Administration
P.O. Box 1881
Milwaukee, WI 53201-1881
Phone: 414-288-5722
Fax: 262-364-2311
E-mail: tim.keane@mu.edu

or

Nels Larsen, Golden Angels Network Graduate Assistant
Marquette University College of Business Administration
P.O. Box 1881
Milwaukee, WI 53201-1881
Phone: 414-288-0673
Fax: 262-288-1668
E-mail: nels.larsen@mu.edu
Web site: www.goldenangelsnetwork.org

IQ Corridor Angel Network
Waukesha, Wisconsin

Members focus on making investments that would lead to the development of high-wage jobs in the Waukesha, Wisconsin area.

Contact:
Bill Mitchell, Executive Director
Waukesha County Economic Development Corporation
Phone: 262-695-7900
E-mail: bmitchell@wctc.edu
Web site: www.wisconsintechnologycouncil.com/i-q_corridor

Marshfield Investment Partners, LLC
Wausau, Wisconsin

Established to fund local medical technology ventures in the greater Marshfield region and throughout Wisconsin.

Contact:
James Hanke, Director
Marshfield Investment Partners, LLC
210 McClellan Street, Suite 210
Wausau, WI 54403
Phone: 715-849-5510, Ext. 306
E-mail: jhanke@ncwrpc.org
Web site: www.marshfieldchamber.com/angels/main.htm

NEW Capital Fund, LP
Appleton, Wisconsin

NEW Capital Fund, LP is a private equity limited partnership with nearly $10 million of committed capital. The NEW Capital Fund has 75 investors, most of who live and work in the New North. In the next five years, the fund will focus on investing in 10 to 12 early-stage companies located in and around the New North that have the potential for rapid growth and can be certified as qualified businesses under Wisconsin's Act 255.

> *Contact:*
> Charlie Goff
> Phone: 920-731-5777
> E-mail: Charlie@newcapitalfund.com
> Web site: www.newcapitalfund.com

Origin Investment Group
La Crosse, Wisconsin

Origin Investment Group was established in 2001. Monthly meetings are held on the UW-La Crosse campus to review proposals and discuss investment actions. There are 19 investor-members; three projects have been funded.

> *Contact:*
> Small Business Development Center
> UW-La Crosse
> 120 W. Carl Wimberly Hall
> La Crosse, WI 54601
> Phone: 608-785-8782
> Fax: 608-785-6919
> Web site: www.uwlax.edu/sbdc/origin_investment_group.htm

Pennies From Heaven
Wisconsin

This Angel group focuses on manufacturing technology, information technology, and medical technology in the Racine / Kenosha / Metro Milwaukee area.

> *Contact:*
> Attorney David Barnes
> Phone: 262-657-6000
> E-mail: dbarnes@vonbriesen.com

Phenomenelle Angels Fund I, LP
Madison, Wisconsin

Phenomenelle Angels Fund I, LP is a new, early stage fund that invests in women and minority owned or managed businesses in Wisconsin and the

Midwest. Qualifying businesses must have at least one woman or an ethnic minority holding substantial ownership or in an executive (C-level) position. Investors are limited to women who are accredited investors, and select entities. We invest in exceptional management teams that exploit proprietary technology to create breakthrough applications in the following market sectors: Information Technology, Life Sciences, Communications and Consumer Goods and Services. The Phenomenelle Angels Fund is expected to help fill special unmet investment opportunities in women and minority owned and/or managed businesses.

> *Contact:*
> Phenomenelle Angels Fund I, LP
> University Research Park
> 510 Charmany, Suite 1758
> Madison, WI 53719
> Phone: 608-441-8315
> E-mail: info@phenomenelleangels.com
> Web site: www.phenomenelleangels.com

Silicon Pastures
Milwaukee, Wisconsin

Silicon Pastures is a premier local network of angel investors and strategic partners for emerging businesses, especially those based in the Midwest. We consider numerous technology and industry sectors, including traditional manufacturing, high-tech, and biotech. Our members have participated in deals ranging from $60K to $1.9M.

> *Contact:*
> Silicon Pastures
> 10437 Innovation Drive, Suite 146
> Milwaukee, WI 53226
> Managing Director: Pehr Anderson
> Phone: 414-433-4982
> E-mail: pehr@siliconpastures.com
> Web site: www.siliconpastures.com

The St. Croix Valley Angel Network, Inc.
River Falls, Wisconsin

Members of this network seek to foster economic development in the St. Croix Valley by connecting candidate companies with prospective angel investors.

Contact:
Steven DeWald
410 S. 3rd Street
River Falls, WI 54022
Phone: 715-425-3398
E-mail: steven.e.dewald@uwrf.edu
Web site: www.stcroixedc.com/services.htm#StCroixValleyAngelNetwork

Wisconsin Investment Partners, LLC
Wisconsin

We are a life science-oriented angel investment network with a Wisconsin-focused investment strategy.

Contact:
Richard H. Leazer
Phone: 608-832-6365
E-mail: rleazer@facstaff.wisc.edu
or
Terry Sivesind
Phone: 608-238-7674
E-mail: siv@itis.com

Women Angels
Milwaukee, Wisconsin

Women Angels is a Milwaukee angel group of women who invest in women-owned businesses.

Contact:
Barbara Boxer
Phone: 414-298-8173
E-mail: bboxer@reinhartlaw.com

CANADA

Alberta Deal Generator
Calgary, Alberta

Alberta Deal Generator (ADG) has established the largest network of accredited investors in Canada who are actively pursuing opportunities in Alberta's early and growth-stage companies.

Contact:
Northern Alberta (Red Deer and north):
Warren Bergen, Executive Director
Alberta Deal Generator
TEC Edmonton
Research Transition Facility (RTF)
8308-114 Street, Suite 4000
Edmonton, AB T6G 2E1
Phone: 780-492-8977 or (toll free) 888-492-8977
Fax: 780-492-7876
E-mail: director@dealgenerator.com
Southern Alberta (south of Red Deer):
Ivan Sierralta, Ph.D., Southern Alberta Manager
Alberta Deal Generator
Calgary Technologies Inc.
3553 31 Street NW
Calgary, AB T2L 2K7
Phone: 403-284-6408
Fax: 403-282-1238
E-mail: isierralta@calgarytechnologies.com
Web site: www.dealgenerator.com/aboutadg.asp

Angel Forum
Vancouver, British Columbia

Started in 1997, the Angel Forum-Vancouver introduces emerging companies to private equity investors, each spring and fall. It is the oldest angel group in Canada with 100+ investors and its sponsors include leading companies and industry associations in BC. 30+ pre-screened technology, service and industrial companies seeking equity funding up to $1 million, present "in- person" and demonstrate their products/services to 70+ pre-screened investors in one day.

Contact:
E-mail: bob@angelforum.org
Web site: www.angelforum.org

Fundamental Technologies II
Coquitlam, British Columbia

Fundamental Technologies II (FTII) is a corporation that allows investors to participate in the returns from a portfolio of actively managed synergistic investments in emerging technology companies.

Contact:
E-mail: BusinessPlans@FundamentalTechnologies2.com
Web site: www.FundamentalTechnologiesII.com

InvestIN Forum of Angel Investors
Calgary, Alberta

The InvestIN Forum is an association of angel investor communities operating with the same goals and best practices under a common brand. We are concerned with helping fuel the local entrepreneurial ecosystem and try to be helpful to all entrepreneurs providing useful resources whilst at the same time we are looking for early stage investment opportunities for our members.

Contact:
Randy Thompson
VentureAlberta
3553 31st NW
Calgary, AB T2L 2K7
Phone: 403-313-2697
E-mail: Thompson@venturealberta.com
Web site: www.theinvestINforum.com

InvestIN Forum of Angel Investors
Edmonton, Alberta

The InvestIN Forum is an association of angel investor communities operating with the same goals and best practices under a common brand. We are concerned with helping fuel the local entrepreneurial ecosystem and try to be helpful to all entrepreneurs providing useful resources whilst at the same time we are looking for early stage investment opportunities for our members.

Contact:
Randy Thompson
Phone: 403-313-2697
E-mail: Thompson@venturealberta.com
Web site: www.theinvestINforum.com

First Angel Network Association
Halifax, Nova Scotia

The goal of the First Angel Network Association is to identify and invest in, and help grow promising companies. FAN is a member-based organization which offers a forum for Angel investors to increase their exposure to quality, pre-screened investment opportunities and expand their network of like-minded investors.

> *Contact:*
> First Angel Network Association
> 5162 Duke Street, Suite 402
> Halifax, NS B3J 1N7
> Phone: 902-425-5162
> Fax: 902-425-0354
> E-mail: info@firstangelnetwork.ca
> Brian Lowe
> Phone: 902-483-6689
> E-mail: bl@firstangelnetwork.ca
> or
> Ross Finlay
> Phone: 902-499-2355
> E-mail: rf@firstangelnetwork.ca
> Web site: www.firstangelnetwork.ca

Kingston Angel Network
Kingston, Ontario

This group of private investors is interested in investment opportunities in the Kingston area, particularly those related to biotech.

> *Contact:*
> E-mail: angels@kingstoncanada.com

Okanagan Angel Network
Salmon Arm, British Columbia

This Network consists of experienced technology entrepreneurs who meet monthly to hear a selected number of short business presentations by nascent technology entrepreneurs. Between 20 and 30 angels typically attend each meeting. The objective is to make initial introductions with a view to having interested parties subsequently meet in private.

> *Contact:*
> E-mail: mikeb@techbrew.com
> Web site: www.ostec.ca/angels

Ottawa Angel Alliance
Ottawa, Ontario

The Ottawa Angel Alliance (OAA) is an alliance of individual angel investors and venture capital firms, which are committed to investing in early stage companies in the Ottawa area.

> Contact:
> E-mail: info@ottawaangels.ca
> Web site: www.ottawaangels.ca

Purple Angel
Ottawa, Ontario

Formed in early 2001, Purple Angel is a group of mostly former Nortel Networks executives. Its mission is to invest, mentor, and guide start-up companies in the Ottawa area. Given the technology and business breadth of the group, the focus is to communications and infrastructure investment.

> Contact:
> E-mail: information@purple-angel.com
> Web site: www.purple-angel.com

Saskatchewan Angel Investor Network
Saskatchewan

The Saskatchewan Angel Investor Network (SAINT) is a member-based group of investors who have an interest in investing in early stage and growth-focused Saskatchewan companies. These investments cover a broad range of industries, including technology, where there is potential to build sustainable and successful businesses.

> Contact:
> Phone: 306-244-3889
> E-mail: info@saint.sk.ca
> Web site: www.saint.sk.ca

Toronto Angel Group
Markham, Ontario

The Toronto Angel Group has over 40 members that have extensive investment and/or operational business experience. The Toronto Angel Group helps entrepreneurs raise sufficient capital to launch their offering or expand their market. As the company achieves its milestones, the Toronto Angel Group may provide introductions to later stage VC funds, corporate investors, and strategic partners to raise the next round of capital or attract an acquisition offer.

> *Contact:*
> Catarina von Maydell, Manager
> Angel Programs
> Toronto Angel Group
> Phone: 416-673-8481
> Web site: www.tvg.org

Toronto Life Science Angels
Toronto, Ontario

The Toronto Life Science Angels provides investment capital for the commercialization of innovations in life science. Our goal is to support Ontario-based technology investment opportunities by facilitating risk sharing on early opportunities with high upside potential.

> *Contact:*
> Office Location:
> 257 Adelaide Street West, Suite 600, Toronto, Ontario M5H 1X9
> Mailing Address:
> 157 Adelaide Street West, PO Box 133, Toronto, ON M5H 4E7
> Phone: 416-938-0676
> Fax: 416-368-5122
> E-mail: Network@TorontoAngels.ca
> Web site: www.TorontoAngels.ca

Toronto Network of Angels
Toronto, Ontario

The Toronto Network of Angels has developed an association of sector-focused angel investment groups to provide Ontario with a new source of professional capital. The goal is to link emerging technology growth companies with the right management talent, superior mentorship and key strategic connections.

> *Contact:*
> Office Location:
> 257 Adelaide Street West, Suite 600, Toronto, Ontario M5H 1X9
> Mailing Address:
> 157 Adelaide Street West, PO Box 133, Toronto, ON M5H 4E7
> Phone: 416-938-0676

Fax: 416-368-5122
E-mail: Network@TorontoAngels.ca
Web site: www.TorontoAngels.ca

Vancouver Angel Network (VANTEC)
Vancouver, British Columbia

To introduce early stage investors and mentors to promising technology (i.e. all advanced technology fields) ventures mainly in British Columbia.

Contact:
Mike Volker
E-mail: mike@volker.org
or
For Biotech/Life Sciences companies:
Thealzel Lee
Phone: 604-839-5388
E-mail: tlee@rocketbuilders.com
Web site: www.vef.org/angels/index.html

Winnipeg Angel Organization
Winnipeg, Manitoba

WAO is a non-profit organization set up to improve access to risk capital for small business start-ups in the Winnipeg centered area.

Contact:
E-mail: info@wao.ca
Web site: www.wao.ca
Blog: www.waokc.blogspot.com

Angel Organizations in Europe

List of EBAN Members
From EBAN Info No. 6 March 2006

COUNTRY	ORGANIZATION	WEB SITE	MEMBER STATUS
AUSTRIA	Austria Wirtschaftsservice	www.awsg.at	Network (No English translation)
BELGIUM	BAMS	www.bams.be	Network (No English translation)
BELGIUM	BAN Vlaanderen	www.banvlaanderen.be	Network
CZECH REPUBLIC	ANGEL INVESTOR ASSOCIATION	www.aia.cz	Network
CZECH REPUBLIC	BANET	www.bids.cz	Network
CZECH REPUBLIC	Hidalgo Partners	www.investori.cz	Associated (No English translation)
FINLAND	SITRA	www.sitra.fi	Federation
FRANCE	Femmes Business Angels	www.femmesbusinessangels.org	Network (No English translation)
FRANCE	FranceAngels	www.franceangels.org	Federation (No English translation)
GERMANY	BANSON	www.banson.net	Network (No English translation)
GERMANY	BUSINESS ANGEL AGENTUR RUHR	www.baar-ev.de	Network (English summary available for download)

COUNTRY	ORGANIZATION	WEB SITE	MEMBER STATUS
GERMANY	BUSINESS ANGELS NETZWERK DEUTSCHLAND E.V. (BAND)	www.business-angels.de	Federation (No English translation)
GERMANY	Peter Jungen Holding	www.bic-leipzig.de/ip/peterjungen/main.html—	Associated (No English translation)
GERMANY	Venture Forum Neckar E.V.	www.venture-forum-neckar.de	Network (No English translation)
GREECE	Mentoring Business Development Services SA	www.mentoring.com.gr	Network
GERMANY	netzwerk1nordbayern	www.netzwerk-nordbayern.de	Network
ITALY	IBAN	www.iban.it	Federation
Luxembourg	INBIS	www.inbis.com	Associated
MALTA	Malta BAN	www.maltaban.com	Network (Note: link to contact e-mail address)
NORWAY	ArticBAN	www.vinn.no	Network
NORWAY	Roban Business Builders	www.roban.org	Network (No English translation)
POLAND	Lewiatan Business Angels	www.lba.pl	Network
POLAND	PolBAN	www.poiban.pl	Network

COUNTRY	ORGANIZATION	WEB SITE	MEMBER STATUS
PORTUGAL	Gesventure	www.gesventure.pt	Network
PORTUGAL	IAPMEI	www.iapmei.pt	Associated (No English translation)
SPAIN	BANC	www.bancat.com	Network (No English translation)
SPAIN	BAN Madrid	www.madrimasd.org/emprendedores	Network
SPAIN	CIDEM	www.cidem.com/catalonia	Network
SPAIN	ESBAN	www.esban.com	Federation (No English translation)
SPAIN	UNIBAN	www.uniban.org	Network
SWEDEN	NUTEK	www.nutek.se	Federation
SWEDEN	SVCA	www.svca.se	Federation
SWITZERLAND	ASBAN	www.asban.ch	Federation
THE NETHERLANDS	NEBIB	www.nebib.nl	Network (No English translation)
THE NETHERLANDS	Technopartner	www.technopartner.nl	Associated
TURKEY	BANATOLIA	www.banatolia.org	Network
UK	Advantage Business Angels	www.advantagebusinessangels.com	Network
UK	BBAA	www.bbaa.co.uk	Federation
UK	Business Link Devon and Cornwall Business Angels Programme	www.blinkdandc.com	Network

COUNTRY	ORGANIZATION	WEB SITE	MEMBER STATUS
UK	Equity Link	www.exemplas.com	Network
UK	Finance South East Limited	www.financesoutheast.co.uk	Associated
UK	Halo	www.investmentbelfast.com	Network
UK	LINC SCOTLAND	www.lincscot.co.uk	Federation
UK	London Business Angels	www.gle.co.uk	Network
UK	Northwest Regional Development Agency	www.nwda.co.uk	Network
UK	Xenos: Wales Business Angel Network	www.xenos.co.uk	Network
United States	Worldtech Inc.	www.worldtech-inc.com	Associated

Totals:

47 members

20 countries represented

Due Diligence Checklist

*N*ote: Few companies will have as complete a business as this document request contemplates. This list is extensive. Some investors will not request information this detailed and others will make requests in stages. Nonetheless, more and more angels are realizing the importance of thorough, extensive due diligence checklists as a form of insurance. Requesting documents in various areas that are probably not applicable, such as real estate and litigation, assures the investors that in fact you do not have such issues or assets. So don't think you have to have an answer other than "none" or "not applicable" for these inapplicable categories.

Documents Requested

General corporate materials (the company, all subsidiaries, partnerships, and joint ventures).

Business Plan including executive summary, market analysis and plan, operational plan, and complete financials.

Minutes:

Minutes of stockholders' meetings, including those of any predecessor corporations.

Minutes of board meetings, including those of any predecessor corporations.

Minutes of permanent committees of the board, including those of any predecessor corporations.

Authorizing resolutions relating to this offering and related transactions.

Charter documents:

Articles or Certificate of Incorporation, as amended to date, including current drafts of pending charter amendments and recapitalization documents.

Drafts of documents related to proposed reincorporation.

Bylaws, as amended to date.

Good standing (and franchise tax board) certificates.

List of jurisdictions in which the company or any of its subsidiaries or affiliates is qualified to do business, owns or leases real property, or is otherwise operating.

Corporate organization:

List of officers and directors.

Management structure organization chart.

Stockholders' lists (including list of option and warrant holders), including number of shares and dates of issuance, and consideration paid.

Information regarding subsidiaries: ownership, date of acquisition of stock or assets, all closing binders relating to acquisitions.

Information regarding joint ventures or partnerships: partners, date of formation, all closing binders relating to joint ventures or partnerships.

Agreements relating to mergers, acquisitions, or dispositions by the company of its subsidiaries or affiliates of companies, significant assets or operations involving the company or any of its subsidiaries or affiliates since inception, including those of any predecessor or subsidiary corporations.

Capital stock:

Stock records, stock ledgers, and other evidence of securities authorized and issued.

Agreements relating to the purchase, repurchase, sale, or issuance of securities, including oral commitments to sell or issue securities.

Agreements relating to voting of securities and restrictive share transfers.

Agreements relating to preemptive or other preferential rights to acquire securities and any waivers thereof.

Agreements relating to registration rights.

Evidence of qualification or exemption under applicable federal and state blue sky laws for issuance of the company's securities.

Documents relating to any conversion, recapitalization, reorganization, or significant restructuring of the company.

Litigation:

Any litigation, claims, and proceedings settled or concluded, including those of any predecessor corporations and subsidiaries.

Any litigation, claims, and proceedings threatened or pending. Please include potential litigation, for example, employees who may be in breach of non-compete agreements with prior employers.

Any litigation involving an executive officer or director, including executive officers or directors of predecessor corporations and subsidiaries, concerning bankruptcy, crimes, securities law, or business practices.

Any consent decrees, injunctions, judgments, other decrees or orders, settlement agreements or similar matters.

All attorneys' letters to auditors, including those of any predecessor corporation and subsidiaries.

Compliance with laws:

Any citations and notices received from government agencies, including those addressed to any predecessor or subsidiary corporations, or with continuing effect from an earlier date.

Any pending or threatened investigations and governmental proceedings.

All material governmental permits, licenses, and the like of the company presently in force, together with information regarding any such permits, licenses, and so forth that have been canceled or terminated, required to carry out the business or operations of the company or its subsidiaries or affiliates, including such permits, licenses, and so forth required by foreign, federal, provincial, state, or local authorities, and any evidence of exemption from any such permit or license requirement.

All documents filed with the SEC or any state or foreign securities regulatory agency, if any.

Any material reports to and correspondence with any government entity, municipality, or government agency, including the EPA and OSHA, including those of any predecessor corporations or subsidiaries.

Employee matters (including items regarding any predecessor or subsidiary or affiliated corporations and all items presently in force and drafts of any pending amendments or new items):

Employee agreements.

Consulting contracts.

Employee benefit and profit-sharing plans, including stock option, stock purchase, deferred compensation, and bonus plans or arrangements.

All other employee compensation, bonus, incentive, retirement, benefits (for example, life or health insurance, medical reimbursement plans, and the like), or similar plans.

Employee confidentiality and proprietary rights agreement.

Officers and directors questionnaires.

Contracts with unions and other labor agreements.

Loans to and guarantees for the benefit of directors, officers, or employees.

"Key person" insurance policies.

Listing of employees by office and department.

Real property:

Deeds.

Leases of real property.

Other interests in real property.

Any documents showing any certification of compliance with, or any deficiency with respect to, regulatory standards of the company's or any of its subsidiaries' or affiliates' facilities.

Financing leases and sale and lease-back agreements.

Conditional sale agreements.

Equipment leases.

Intellectual property matters:

> List of all foreign and domestic patents, patent applications, copyrights, patent licenses, and copyright licenses held by the company.
>
> List of any trademarks, trademark applications, trade names, or service marks.
>
> Claims of infringement or misappropriation of others' patents, copyrights, trade secrets, or other proprietary rights.
>
> Copies of all agreements in-licensing or acquiring any technology, including without limitation software licenses, patent licenses, or other technology licenses, or any development or joint development agreements.
>
> Copies of all agreements out-licensing or selling any technology, including without limitation any software licenses, patent licenses, or other technology licenses, or any distribution, OEM, VAR, or sales representative agreements.

Debt financing:

> All debt instruments, credit agreements, and guarantees entered into by the company, including lease financing, that are currently in effect.
>
> All material correspondence with lenders, including all compliance reports submitted by the company or its accountants.
>
> Any loans and guarantees of third-party obligations.
>
> Any agreements restricting the payment of cash dividends.

Other agreements:

> Marketing agreements.
>
> Management and service agreements.
>
> Forms of secrecy, confidentiality, and non-disclosure agreements.
>
> Contracts outside the ordinary course of business.
>
> Indemnification contracts and similar arrangements for officers and directors.
>
> Agreements with officers, directors, and affiliated parties.
>
> Any agreements with competitors.
>
> Any agreements with government agencies or institutions.
>
> Any agreements restricting the company's right to compete or other agreements material to the business.

Any material insurance arrangements (including property damage, and third-party liability).

Agreements requiring consents or approvals or resulting in changes in rights in connection with change of control transactions.

Financial information:

Audited or unaudited financial statements, including those of any predecessor corporations.

Interim financial statements.

Budget plan, including revisions to date with respect to the budget plan for the current fiscal year for the company and its subsidiaries and affiliates.

The company's long-range strategic plan, any other documents concerning its long-range plans, and any information concerning the company's compliance therewith.

Disclosure documents used in private placements of the company's or any of its subsidiaries' or affiliates' securities or institutional or bank loan applications since inception.

Any other material agreements with creditors.

Significant correspondence with independent public accountants, including management letters.

Any reports, studies, and projections prepared by management on the company's or its subsidiaries' or affiliates' business, financial condition, or planned operations, including business plan.

Any reports and studies prepared by outside consultants on the company's or its subsidiaries' or affiliates' business or financial condition.

Reports and materials prepared for the company's board of directors or a committee thereof.

Contracts with investment bankers and brokers.

Tax matters:

Federal, state, and local tax returns, including those of any predecessor corporations.

Audit adjustments proposed by the IRS.

Acquisitions and divestitures:

Acquisitions or divestitures (including related documentation).

Current plans or negotiations relating to potential acquisitions or divestitures.

Public relations:

> Annual reports and other reports and communications with stock-holders, employees, suppliers, and customers.

> Advertising, marketing, and other selling materials.

> Press releases and clippings.

> Analyst reports.

Miscellaneous:

> Copies of all market research or marketing studies concerning the company's business.

> Significant agreements currently in draft stage.

Due Diligence Interview Questions

Corporate Structure and Governance

What is the company's corporate structure? C corporation, S corporation, limited liability company, or limited partnership? Does this structure allow for a liquidity event and return on investment?

Is there an exit strategy?

Is the corporate structure overly complicated? If so, why, and might it be simplified?

How many shareholders does the company have? Are shareholders too numerous, and, if so, why?

Does the corporate structure fit with the business model?

Does the corporate structure allow for growth?

What is the founders' share allocation? Does the founder have a large enough stake to have the incentive to succeed, but not so large as to be able to ignore board and other advisers? Is the founders' stock vested over time?

Who is on the board of directors? Do they have the right background for the company? Is the number of outside directors sufficient? How are board members compensated?

Does the company have a board of advisers and, if so, who is on the board? Do the advisers actively participate in the company's development? How are advisers compensated?

Has the company been involved in any litigation or been threatened with litigation?

Does the company have all required permits and licenses?

Financial Assumptions and Revenue Sources

Has the company completed one-, three-, and five-year financial projections?

Have the financial documents been properly developed according to applicable accounting rules?

Has the company used an outside, independent accounting firm to compile, review, or audit financials?

How good are the assumptions? (Rate of growth, acceptance rate, pricing, multiple revenue streams, costs.)

Are revenues realistic?

When does the company reach cash flow positive and what cash requirements will it take to get there?

Has the company already received funding, and, if so, how much; what are pre-money valuation and terms?

What are the follow-on funding requirements and sources? Has the company properly anticipated future needs and is it already working on those?

Have all tax returns been properly filed?

What debt is the company carrying? What are the ratios?

Is the company's current valuation aligned with its current stage of development and market potential?

Market Assessment

Does the company's product or service address a new or existing market?

Is the product or service platform-based, with the opportunity for additional products or services? Or is this potentially a one-trick pony?

Does the company have a well-thought-out sales and marketing plan?

Does the company have key relationships in place? If not, is it working on the same, with marketing or sales partners, or both?

Does the company have or need key joint venture relationships?

Is the company focused on the appropriate market development, or is it trying to do too much at one time?

Have the founders chosen the right first market?

Does their product or service represent a market push or pull?

What is the potential market size?

Have they conducted thorough market research to support their financial assumptions, revenue model, and valuation?

What is their stage of development? Concept, alpha, beta, or shipping?

If the company has already introduced its product or service into the market, what is the number of current and potential customers?

What is the length of its sales cycle?

What are the channels of distribution?

Does the company's product or service have a seasonal aspect?

Is this a stable market and are production costs stable?

Competitive Arena

Who are the company's competitors?

Has the company realistically assessed its competitors?

What is the company's market differentiator? Is this enough to make it superior to competition from the customer's perspective?

Is this a market or product consolidation?

How entrenched are the competitors?

What is the financial stability of competitors?

What does the market share look like?

How will this company win?

Has the company done a detailed feature-by-feature analysis?

Management Team

What is the caliber and pedigree of the team?

What is the team's overall track record?

Do the team members collectively have the requisite skills and experience?

Do they recognize limitations in management and are they seeking candidates?

Is the management team open to discussion and suggestions on improvement to their business model?

Has the management team been previously funded?

How are management and all other employees being compensated?

Does the company have an option plan, and have options been granted to all employees? What percentage do the founders have as compared to other key management personnel?

Technology Assessment

Do they have market requirements and functional specifications?

At what stage is development? Concept, alpha, beta, shipping?

Does the company have any usability studies?

Does the company have adequate intellectual property protection? Does it need it?

Is the company relying on being first to market, rather than on its intellectual property, for competitive advantage, and is this realistic?

What is product quality assurance like?

Is it proprietary architecture or open-source code?

Do they have adequate systems in place to identify and protect intellectual property?

Who in the company is focused on these issues?

Has the company properly set up relationships and documentation to ensure ownership of all intellectual property?

Does the company own all necessary intellectual property through internal development or licenses?

Do any other companies have potential claims to the intellectual property resulting from previous employment relationships, or for any other reason?

Operations

Does the company have an operating plan (or an outline of the same if early-stage)?

Has the company considered all aspects of operation to successfully launch a product or service?

Does the operating plan anticipate growth? Is anticipated growth realistic?

Has the company received any citations or notices of violation?

For more mature companies, does each division of the company have an operating plan and are these plans compatible?

Does management meet regularly to ensure compliance with the plan or make needed adjustments?

Has the company been able to stay on plan?

Does the plan take into consideration all cash needs and anticipated cash flow?

Does the company have an alternative plan if assumptions do not hold, such as for product rollout, cash needs, and market response?

Convertible Promissory Note

*N*ote: This agreement can contain many other terms and conditions, such as the possibility of a security interest, depending on your needs and your lender's demands. All agreements should be reviewed and approved by your legal counsel for compliance with state law and alignment with your needs.

NEITHER THIS NOTE NOR THE SECURITIES INTO WHICH IT IS CONVERTIBLE HAVE BEEN REGISTERED OR QUALIFIED UNDER THE SECURITIES ACT OF 1933, AS AMENDED OR ANY STATE SECURITIES LAWS (COLLECTIVELY, THE "SECURITIES LAWS"), AND HAS BEEN ACQUIRED FOR INVESTMENT PURPOSES ONLY AND NOT WITH A VIEW TO, OR IN CONNECTION WITH, THE SALE OR DISTRIBUTION THEREOF. THEY MAY NOT BE SOLD, OFFERED FOR SALE, OR OTHERWISE TRANSFERRED UNLESS THE SECURITIES (I) ARE REGISTERED UNDER THE SECURITIES LAWS OR (II) ARE EXEMPT FROM REGISTRATION UNDER THE SECURITIES LAWS, AND COMPANY IS PROVIDED AN OPINION OF COUNSEL SATISFACTORY TO COMPANY THAT SUCH REGISTRATION IS NOT REQUIRED.

GREAT STARTS, INC.
[SECURED] CONVERTIBLE PROMISSORY NOTE

$_____   [DATE]

[City, State]

1. Promise to Pay. FOR VALUE RECEIVED, [Borrower], a _____ corporation ("Company"), hereby promises to pay to the order of [Lender], [a _____ company or individual] ("Lender"), in lawful money of the United States of America and in immediately available funds, the principal sum of _____ Dollars ($_____) (the "Loan") together with accrued and unpaid interest thereon, each due and payable on the dates and in the manner set forth below.

[IF THE NOTE IS SECURED, INCLUDE THE FOLLOWING PARA-GRAPH.]

[This Secured Convertible Promissory Note is the Note referred to in and is executed and delivered in connection with that certain Security Agreement dated as of [even date herewith] and executed by Company in favor of [Lender] (the "Security Agreement"). Additional rights of Lender are set forth in the Security Agreement. All capitalized terms used in this Note but not otherwise defined in this Note shall have the respective meanings given to them in the Security Agreement.]

2. Interest. Company further promises to pay interest on the outstanding principal amount of this Note from the date hereof until payment in full, which interest, shall accrue and be payable at the rate of ___ percent (____%) per annum [compounded annually commencing on the date hereof OR calculated on the basis of a 365-day year for the actual number of days elapsed.] Interest shall be due and payable [on demand OR in a single installment at maturity as set forth below OR in monthly/quarterly/annual payments, in arrears not later than thirty (30) days after the end of each calendar month/quarter/year for the preceding month/quarter/year].

[INTEREST CAN BE PAID IN CASH OR IN STOCK OF EQUIVALENT VALUE, TYPICALLY COMMON STOCK.]

3. Due Date. If not sooner converted as provided in Section 4 below, the entire unpaid balance of principal and all accrued and unpaid interest shall be due and payable on [Date] (the "Maturity Date"). Payment of principal and interest hereunder shall be made by check, drawn on a U.S. bank account, delivered to Lender at the address furnished to Company for that purpose.

4. Conversion.

4.1 Upon the consummation of a Qualifying Equity Financing (as defined below) on or before the Maturity Date, the entire outstanding principal balance of, and all accrued and unpaid interest on this Note shall be automatically converted into the number of shares of the capital stock issued by

Company in such Qualifying Equity Financing as is obtained by dividing (a) the outstanding principal balance of, and all accrued and unpaid interest on, this Note as of the date of conversion by (b) the price per share of the [PRE-FERRED] capital stock issued in the Qualified Equity Financing. A "Qualified Equity Financing" shall mean an equity financing in which Company sells [PREFERRED STOCK] equity securities and obtains net proceeds (including conversion of this Note) in an amount not less than _____ dollars ($_____).

[TYPICALLY, THE QUALIFIED EQUITY FINANCING IS A VENTURE CAPITAL ROUND, THUS THE REFERENCE TO PREFERRED STOCK SINCE THE VAST MAJORITY OF VENTURE CAPITAL ROUNDS ARE PREFERRED STOCK OFFERINGS. THIS ALLOWS THE INVESTOR TO OBTAIN THE FAVORABLE TERMS NEGOTIATED BY THE VENTURE CAPITALISTS. CONVERSION CAN ALSO BE UPON THE REALIZATION OF A MILESTONE SUCH AS DEFINED REVENUE AMOUNT, RECEIVING A PATENT ON KEY TECHNOLOGY, CERTAIN NUMBER OF CUSTOMERS SECURED, OR THE LIKE. IN THE ALTERNATIVE CONVERSION CIRCUMSTANCES OTHER THAN A FINANCING, A CONVERSION VALUE (PRICE PER SHARE) SHOULD BE NEGOTIATED UP FRONT ALONG WITH THE RIGHTS, PREFERENCES, AND PRIVILEGES THAT WILL BE ASSOCIATED WITH THE THEN-ISSUED SHARES. IF THE NOTE CONVERTS INTO COMMON STOCK, RIGHTS, PREFERENCES, AND PRIVILEGES ARE NOT RELEVANT.]

4.2 If this Note is automatically converted, written notice shall be delivered to Lender of this Note at the address last shown on the records of Company for Lender or given by Lender to Company for the purpose of notice or, if no such address appears or is given, at the place where the principal executive office of Company is located, notifying Lender of the conversion, specifying the principal amount of the Note converted, the amount of accrued and unpaid interest converted, the date of such conversion and calling upon such Lender to surrender this Note to Company in exchange for equity securities of Company as provided herein, in the manner and at the place designated by Company.

4.3 In connection with the conversion of this Note, Lender shall enter into the subscription or stock purchase agreement relating to the Qualified Equity Financing, together with any other documents that investors in such Qualified Equity Financing enter into generally ("Equity Transaction Documents"). As promptly as practicable after the conversion of this Note and delivery of Equity Transaction Documents signed by Lender, Company at its expense will issue and deliver to Lender of this Note, upon surrender of the Note, a certificate or certificates for the number of full shares of capital stock issuable upon such conversion.

4.4 As additional consideration to Lender for the loan evidenced hereby, upon automatic conversion of this Note in connection with a Qualifying Equity Financing, Company shall issue to Lender additional shares of the capital stock issued in the Qualified Equity Financing, such number of additional shares to be determined by dividing (a) 5 percent (5%) of the original principal amount of this Note by (b) the price per share of the capital stock issued in the Qualified Equity Financing. Concurrent with the delivery of stock certificates to Lender pursuant to Section 4.3, Company at its expense will issue and deliver to Lender a certificate or certificates for the number of additional shares of capital stock issuable pursuant to this Section 4.4.

[THE ADDITIONAL CONSIDERATION CAN BE A FLAT AMOUNT OR CAN BE IN TIERS, INCREASING THE LEVEL OF CONSIDERATION OVER TIME ON THE THEORY THAT THE LONGER IT TAKES FOR COMPANY TO GET TO THE QUALIFYING EVENT, THE GREATER RISK THE INVESTOR IS TAKING. FOR EXAMPLE, CONSIDER A CONVERT-IBLE PROMISSORY NOTE WITH A MATURITY DATE OF DECEMBER 31, 2010, ISSUED ON JANUARY 1, 2007. IF COMPANY IS ABLE TO MEET THE QUALIFYING EVENT, WHICH SHALL BE A QUALIFIED EQUITY FINANCING OF $2,000,000, BY SEPTEMBER 30, 2007, THEN LENDER RECEIVES 5% AS NOTED IN THE ABOVE EXAMPLE PARAGRAPH. HOWEVER, IF COMPANY IS NOT ABLE TO SUCCESSFULLY COM-PLETE A QUALIFIED EQUITY FINANCING UNTIL SEPTEMBER 31, 2008, THEN LENDER RECEIVES 10% INSTEAD OF 5%, AND SO ON IF NECESSARY.]

5. Form and Application of Payment. All payments of interest and prin-cipal shall be in lawful money of the United States of America. All payments shall be applied first to costs of collection, if any, then to accrued and unpaid interest, and thereafter to principal.

6. Prepayment. Company reserves the right to repay this Note in whole or in part at any time or from time to time upon five (5) days' prior written notice to Lender (as provided above), without penalty or additional fees.

7. Waiver of Presentment. Company hereby waives demand, notice, pre-sentment, protest, and notice of dishonor.

8. Attorneys' Fees. Company agrees to pay Lender's reasonable costs in collecting and enforcing this Note, including reasonable attorneys' fees.

9. No Shareholder Rights. Nothing contained in this Note shall be con-strued as conferring upon Lender or any other person the right to vote or to

consent or to receive notice as a shareholder in respect of meetings of shareholder for the election of the directors of Company or any other matters or any rights whatsoever as a shareholder of Company. [IF THE NOTE IS SECURED, INCLUDE THE FOLLOWING PARAGRAPH.]

[Secured Note. The full amount of this Note is secured by the Collateral identified and described as security in the Security Agreement executed by and delivered by Company. Company shall not, directly or indirectly, create, permit, or suffer to exist, and shall defend the Collateral against and take such other action as is necessary to remove, any Lien on or in the Collateral, or in any portion thereof, except as permitted pursuant to the Security Agreement.]

10. Governing Law; Venue. The terms of this Note shall be construed in accordance with the laws of the State of _____ as such laws apply to contracts made and to be performed entirely within the State of _____. The parties consent to the jurisdiction of and venue in any appropriate court in _____ County, _____.

11. Amendment; Waiver. Any of the terms of this Note (including, without limitation, the Maturity Date, the rate of interest, and the conversion features) may be waived or modified only in writing, signed by Company and Lender.

12. General Provisions. No party may voluntarily or involuntarily assign that party's interest in this Note without the prior written consent of the other party. Subject to the above, this Note shall be binding upon and inure to the benefit of the parties and their respective permitted successors and assigns. If any portion of this Note is held to be invalid by a court having jurisdiction, the remaining terms of this Note shall remain in full force and effect to the extent possible.

GREAT STARTS, INC.

By: _____

Angel-Entrepreneur Internet Matching Sites

504 Bank—Fair Oaks, California & Dallas, Texas
www.504bank.com/vc.asp

"504 Bank ('The Bank') connects investors with investment opportunities. The service is performance based so companies seeking financing pay 504 Bank a small transaction fee each time an investor downloads and reads their business plan or profile. The benefit of this approach is that a company seeking financing can significantly increase the quantity of targeted high quality investors who assess their business opportunity (only paying for results), while the investor has a more organized and comprehensive resource."

Cost:
Entrepreneur

- 75 cents per Business Plan downloaded
- 45 cents per Executive Summary read
- 15 cents per Bio clicked on
- 12 cents per Offering Bio clicked on
- 25 cents per Executive Summary downloaded
- 75 cents per Prospectus (Offering Document) downloaded

**NOTE: There is a $50 security deposit required for Private Placements. You may provide credit card info and set up a spending limit.
Angel:
No statement of cost found.

Active Capital—Irvine, California
http://activecapital.org/index.html

"Active Capital is the premier Website for entrepreneurs seeking private investment and private investors seeking deals in a secure and protected environment consistent with all investment laws.

"Active Capital's legal status derives from a no action letter issued by the Securities and Exchange Commission (SEC) and Model Accredited Investor Exemption (MAIE) of 48 states as overseen by the North American Securities Administrators Association (NASAA). They allow Active Capital to post entrepreneurial offerings safely across state lines for accredited investors to view in a highly secure environment for both, without some of the stringent limitations incurred by broker-dealers, so long as Active Capital keeps the offerings within a format acceptable to them.

"Active Capital's action orientation is reflected in the national and regional character of its Website. Active Capital recognizes the local quality of deals. It utilizes local operators to help entrepreneurs translate their business plans into a legally acceptable format and to support entrepreneurs with counseling and mentoring as appropriate.

"Active Capital's cost effectiveness rests on the fact that entrepreneurial companies seeking equity capital to grow and gain legal access to a nationwide network of investors by answering a single basic set of questions derived from their business plan. Once accepted, they have achieved exempt status according to state and federal regulators. By using Active Capital's pre-screened database, investors in angel groups, Small Business Investment Companies (SBICs), and individual accredited investors and intermediaries can deal directly with entrepreneurs instead of having to find investment opportunities through brokers or finders."

Cost:
Entrepreneur:
    Active Capital (ACE-Net) is a fee-based listing service. Through June 2005, the cost of using the online software to generate your U-7 SCOR Offering is $199, payable to a not-for-profit Network Node Operator. Once it is completed, you will be provided an Adobe PDF version (static, to comply with ASAA and SEC regulations). Active Capital will then make your data available to Accredited Investors to search and will automatically notify

Accredited Investors in the database whose saved "search criteria" match your offering. Your offering will continue to remain searchable for the remainder of the sixty-day period. Time extensions are available in ninety-day increments for $100.

Angel:

   ACE-Net is a fee-based listing service. While the maximum amount that any ACE-Net regional Network Operator can charge is $450, some Network Operators are funded by states that compensate the fee for their in-state investors.

Angel Deals
www.angeldeals.com

"AngelDeals.com is a virtual global network for the business community of Entrepreneurs seeking funding and growth, Investors seeking deal flow, Business Professionals seeking visibility and Job Seekers / Employers.

   "This unique virtual network serves as a learning environment, a connection engine and a meeting place wherein our members can post free Listings to find the right 'door openers.'

   Highlights of AngelDeals's robust site are:

- Several mechanisms to connect Entrepreneurs with Investors
- A growing, searchable, global Venture Capital Database
- The ability to post free Listings in several categories
- Access to advice from the Angel and Legal Tips of the week
- The ability to create an investment-grade Executive Summary online
- A toolbox of essential entrepreneurial resources
- A 'Help Section' where members can ask for advice
- Sections to search for entrepreneurial opportunities and strategic alliances
- A consulting service for Business Plan Analysis & Review by an investor
- A comprehensive essential Links section."

Cost:

Entrepreneur:

Annual membership is $19.95.

Angel:
Annual membership is $50.

Angel Legacy—Roseville, California
www.angellegacy.com

"Angel Legacy provides entrepreneurs efficient access to private capital often unavailable through traditional funding channels. We match accredited investors with entrepreneurs from all industries and geographies."

Cost:
Entrepreneur:

   After our public launch date, members will be assessed a membership fee of $100 per year. In addition, a $50 matching fee will be assessed for each angel match that the entrepreneur indicates he or she wishes to pursue. Those participating in the beta period will receive their first year membership free. All matching prior to the public launch will also be free.

   Warrants: —"After the public launch date, Angel Legacy is to receive a warrant from the entrepreneur equal in value to 5% of the amount funded for all funding that occurs from angels that were introduced to the entrepreneur due to an Angel Legacy matching event."
Angel:

   No cost.

Business Plan Posting—Lafayette, Indiana
www.businessplanposting.com/index.php?tid=AVCE

"Business Plan Posting is part of the American Venture Network (AVN), a media and service provider for entrepreneurs and investors of innovative and early stage technology based companies. AVN has over a decade of experience within the venture capital industry and through Business Plan Posting, AVN aims to build successful relationships between aspiring entrepreneurs and investors.

   "Business Plan Posting is the first website to give entrepreneurs the unique opportunity to create an online presentation that allows investors to see the personality behind the business plan. Our innovative approach to capital sourcing allows our members to combine their business plan and video elevator pitch in a digital format to maximize their business plans' impact. We have utilized the latest digital technologies to allow this presentation to be viewed and downloaded by our investor community to PC or personal video player.

"Business Plan Posting also hosts a Venture Resources channel which gives entrepreneurs free access to informative advice and business plan help from professionals in the industry. We have collaborated with industry leaders to develop an effective business planning model to guide you through the planning process. With over fifty sample business plans available and expert advice to help entrepreneurs secure investor funding—Venture Resources is an essential guide for entrepreneurs at all stages of the business planning process.

"To aid in the exhausting task of finding funding, we have compiled a database of nearly 3500 Venture Capital Firms, Angel Associations, Venture Clubs, Law firms, Investment Banks, Incubators and other related service providers. Our free Venture Capital Directory is constantly being reviewed and updated to help us provide our members with the most accurate venture capital information available."

Cost:

Entrepreneur:

- No initial set up or monthly fees.
- Executive Summary: Introduction and overview of your business plan -(Maximum 3000 characters)—FREE.
- Full Business Plan Document: Upload file in Word, PDF, or Power-Point, $79.95.
- Upload Video Elevator Pitch: Upload a maximum 2 minute or 35Mb filmed pitch—One Month free upload, after this period you will be given the option to retain this feature for only $120.

Angel:
No charge

California Investment Network—Los Angeles, California & Toronto, Ontario
www.californiainvestmentnetwork.com

"California web based portal and matching service of angel investors seeking investments, with entrepreneurs seeking capital. The website is owned by California Investment Network Inc. which has created the site in response to the growing demand of California angel investors to invest in things that are more tangible, predictable and closer to home."

Cost:
Entrepreneur:
One-time fee of $199 after you respond to the first angel investor.

Angel:
   No fee.
Regional Focus: State of California

Canadian Angel Investment Network—Canada
www.angelinvestmentnetwork.ca

"Canadian web based portal and matching service of angel investors seeking investments, with entrepreneurs seeking capital. The site is owned by the Canadian Angel Investment Network Inc. which has created the site in response to the growing demand of Canadian angel investors to invest in things that are more tangible, predictable and closer to home."

Cost:
Entrepreneur:
   One-time fee of $199 after you respond to the first angel investor.
Angel:
   $29.99 bi-annual membership fee.
Regional Focus: Canada

Capital Acquisition Strategies & Hedge (CASH)—Columbus, Ohio
www.theentrepreneur.net/C.A.S.H.htm

"Capital Acquisition Strategies & Hedge (CASH) can assist your company in raising $100,000 to $20,000,000 or more in capital. CASH specializes in working closely with start-up and early-stage companies, mentoring the process of raising capital in the same manner Wall Street does—through a series of securities offerings with "Marketable" deal structures."
Cost:
   Send e-mail to request list of product services and schedule of fees.

Capital Connexion—Canada
www.capital-connexion.com/carrefour_capital.asp

"Capital Connexion™ is a local databases network containing business projects and venture capital sources configured according to a common model. Registration of business projects and private venture capital investors is entirely free of charge, but must be validated by a local economic development organization that has been accredited."

Cost:
Entrepreneur:
   No cost.

Angel:
   No cost.

Capital Match—Dallas, Texas
www.capmatch.com/index.cfm?fuseaction=entrepreneurs

"We serve Entrepreneurs from all industries, at all stages of development. We welcome talented women, resourceful minorities, and those without cozy VC connections. We target "potential" Angels who have the means and sophistication, but who haven't yet found their wings. Capital Match has two distinct levels of service. In the *Open Market,* Entrepreneurs post 250-word pitches for secure browsing by qualified Angels. In *Venture Direct,* selected Entrepreneurs prepare a five-page venture summary that is delivered directly to Angels for review. At their sole discretion, Angels may contact Entrepreneurs for more information. Capital Match is not involved in any discussions, due diligence, or negotiations. These are the sole responsibility of those matched and their advisors."

Cost:
Entrepreneur:
   $30 registration fee.
Angel:
   No cost.

Cloud Start—Salt Lake City, Utah
www.cloudstart.com

"CloudStart.com is a national angel club made up of a select group of active angel investors. In addition, we partner with local angel clubs, venture capital firms, and other accredited investors to insure a solid base of active investors. To succeed, you must ultimately get face to face with an interested investor. This is your meeting place. By nature, the world of venture capital is an inefficient marketplace. Our goal is to bring everyone together from the entrepreneur to the VC to the angel.

"CloudStart.com is committed to bringing together entrepreneurs and active angel investors. Our mission and dedication is two fold. For entrepreneurs, we provide access to active investors outside of their personal networks in ways that foster investor action. For investors, we provide screened deal flow and opportunities to network, share due diligence, and spread risk by investing in groups. We also focus on large institutions such as venture capital firms, private equity concerns and other CPA firms which are looking to bring their clients opportunities from the VC world."

Cost:
Entrepreneur:
   One-time application fee of $100.
Angel:
   Free for accredited investors.

DEALFLOW—Lake Forest, Illinois
www.dealflow.com

"DEALFLOW is designed to decrease the time and effort it takes an Entrepreneur to find and attract angel investors. Private Angel Investors can download detailed Venture listings immediately while online, to capture product opportunity windows which close quickly. DEALFLOW's goal is to take a lot of friction out of the Venture funding process, thereby speeding good products and ideas to market."

Cost:
Entrepreneur:
   No cost.
Angel:
   No cost.

Deal Generator—Edmonton, Alberta
www.dealgenerator.com

"We work to facilitate investment in high-growth Alberta technology companies.

"Alberta Deal Generator (ADG) has established the largest network of accredited investors in Canada who are actively pursuing opportunities in Alberta's early and growth-stage companies.

"Through a screening process ADG identifies technology companies that are 'investment ready' and then connects these firms with our network of angel investors, Venture Capital firms and other investor groups in special presentation forums.

"If you are an investor serious about partnering with a high-growth, advanced-technology enterprise, join the Alberta Deal Generator network.

"If you are an entrepreneur requiring early stage financing to grow your Alberta based technology company to the next level of operations, register with ADG."

Cost:
Entrepreneur:

The registration and the initial screening process is at no cost. Should the company pass the screening process, there is a $1500 fee to proceed to the investor forum.

Angel:

No statement of cost found.

Regional Focus: Alberta

Florida Angel Investors—Miami/Boca Raton, Florida
www.floridaangel.com

"Florida Angel Investors aims to create networks and funds to assist early stage venture capital formation in the State of Florida."

Cost:

Entrepreneur:

No statement of cost found.

Angel:

No statement of cost found.

Regional Focus: State of Florida

Florida Investment Network—Tampa, Florida, and Toronto, Ontario
www.floridainvestmentnetwork.com

"Florida web based portal and matching service of angel investors seeking investments, with entrepreneurs seeking capital. This website has been created in response to the growing demand of Florida angel investors to invest in things that are more tangible, predictable and closer to home."

Cost:

Entrepreneur:

One-time fee of $199 after you respond to the first angel investor.

Angel:

No fee.

Regional Focus: State of Florida

Funding Post—Stratford, Connecticut
www.fundingpost.com

"Showcase entrepreneurs to interested investors, while increasing exposure and shortening time to capital."

Cost:

Entrepreneur:

$100 for initial three-month listing, $30/month thereafter. In-person pitch (fifteen minutes) directly to investors—$2000.

Angel:

No cost

Funding Universe—Orem, Utah
www.fundinguniverse.com

"The FundingUniverse.com network of sites is a free service, connecting entrepreneurs with angel investors. FundingUniverse.com provides individual websites for all 50 states in the U.S. because more than 90% of angel investors invest within a six-hour drive of their homes. After registering for FundingUniverse.com, entrepreneurs create a business profile and have the opportunity to upload their business plan, executive summary, etc. Investors login and view business plans."

Cost:
Entrepreneur:

No cost.
Angel:

No cost.

GO BIG Network—Columbus, Ohio
www.gobignetwork.com

"The Go BIG Network allows professionals to connect with small businesses, entrepreneurs, investors, customers, vendors, employees and advisors. The Web site is like a "virtual rolodex" that people like yourself can use at any time to connect with people that can help your business.

"The fastest way for an Entrepreneur or Startup Company to find Angel Investors, Small Business Funding and Early Stage Venture Capital.

"The Go BIG Network is an on-line community for start-up companies. We facilitate the interaction between startups, investors, advisors, job-seekers and service providers. Members of Go BIG post a request for what they are looking for—investment capital, job opportunities, partners, etc.—and we route that request to other members who have expressed interest in that type of opportunity. Members can also post their requests publicly so that everyone can see who needs what."

Cost:
Entrepreneur:

Free to create profile but charges a "small premium" to post a public request.
Angel:

No statement of cost found.

Gould Financial Network—Nashua, New Hampshire
www.gouldreport.com

"The Gould Financial Network has a seasoned team of advisors with decades of experience assisting entrepreneurs, inventors and business owners in marketing their companies, products and ideas to the financial community. Since 1985, the Gould Financial Network has built a proprietary database of Private, Corporate and Venture Finance Sources throughout the USA. These include, but are not limited to:

- Investment Groups
- Merchant Bankers
- Pension Fund Managers
- Corporate Players
- Venture Capital Firms
- Family Trust Advisors & Managers
- High Net Worth Individuals (Angels)

"Our innovative Public Relations and Marketing Services are designed to enhance the efforts of an entrepreneur or business owner to obtain financing for the purpose of starting or growing a business enterprise."

Cost:
Entrepreneur:
Yes, but no specific details provided.
Angel:
No statement of cost found.

Indiana Venture Center—AngelNet—Indianapolis, Indiana
www.indianaventurecenter.org/angelnet.asp

"AngelNet is a private network that provides connections, knowledge, and resources for Angel investors and Indiana high growth businesses. This network is a key link between potentially high growth entrepreneurial companies and Angel investors across the state of Indiana. By showcasing emerging companies at Angel-only receptions held at the Indiana Venture Center and via a webinar process utilizing the internet and telephone, Angels meet peer Angels and collaborate on business opportunities that are not often made widely available.

"AngelNet brings investors, businesses, and civic leaders together for the purpose of:

- Providing Angel investors with a more rational method for seeing a wider selection of investment opportunities and enhancing their deal choices while protecting the Angels from unwanted intrusions into their privacy

- Presenting Indiana businesses with a way of reaching a statewide audience of Angel investors who might have an interest in providing funding and business expertise

- Streamlining the process for presenting deals so Angel investors are not inconvenienced

- Providing Angel investors with intelligence on deal terms and trends

- AngelNet is the meeting place for investors wanting to easily find opportunities and Indiana businesses seeking funding. Membership into AngelNet—for both investors and businesses—is selective."

Cost:
Entrepreneur:
   No statement of cost found.
Angel:
   No statement of cost found.
Regional Focus: State of Indiana

Investors' Circle—San Francisco, California, and Brookline, Massachusetts
www.investorscircle.net/index.php?tg=articles&topics=16

"Investors' Circle is a national network of early-stage private equity investors who seek financial, social and environmental returns on their investments. Investors' Circle reviews company applications to our website on a monthly basis. Investors' Circle will only approve companies that meet its criteria. Each application is reviewed by an IC staff member who may request additional information or suggest you edit your profile.

   "Businesses that are reviewed by Investors' Circle members must fall into one or more of five specific interest areas:

- Energy & Environment
- Food & Organics
- Community & International development
- Education & Media
- Health & Wellness

We also strongly encourage minority- and woman-led businesses to apply, as long as the underlying business is consistent with the mission of Investors' Circle."

Cost:

Entrepreneur:

$350 posting fee; there is an additional fee to present in person at a "venture fair," ranging from $350 to $850 depending on the scale of the event (good for eight months).

Angel:

$2495/one-year membership; $3790/two-year membership.

Kentucky Enterprise Fund—Lexington, Kentucky
www.kyicc.com

"Kentucky Science and Technology Corporation (KSTC) is a private non-profit organization managing the Kentucky Enterprise Fund. The Fund encourages the enhancement of technology-based economic development by leveraging resources throughout the Commonwealth to create jobs and wealth for the citizens of Kentucky and enhance the state's image as an attractive and successful location in which to live, learn, and grow. We work with early stage business and technology development activities including business plan creation, early seed capital funding, team creation, technology planning, and proof of concept development. We work with all private and public entities to create new companies and big ideas in the Commonwealth of Kentucky."

Cost:

Entrepreneur:

No statement of cost found.

Angel:

No statement of cost found.

Launch Funding Network—Atlanta, Georgia
www.launchfn.com/index.html

"Launch Funding Network, Inc. (LAUNCHfn) bridges the gap for companies that know they need capital, but don't know what they need to do to attract it. We facilitate private equity capital formation by maximizing the entrepreneur's affinity group and our own private network of investors and lenders during the Capital Campaign stage. We deliver on the services necessary for entrepreneurs and management teams, investors and board members to execute their strategic business plans so that they can maximize the return on investment and build thriving, scalable businesses. Our Capital

Campaign services are appropriate for early stage companies as well as established businesses that are seeking to grow to a new level to ready their company for optimum value for acquisition."

Cost:

Entrepreneur:

Showcase your business enterprise to serious investors for $349. (includes three months of online hosting. Hosting can be renewed for $39/month.)

Angel:

No cost.

LocalFund—All over the United States
www.localfund.com

"LocalFund provides an Internet-based platform for local entrepreneur-investor networks.

"LocalFund's vision is to build an international network of local entrepreneur-investor networks.

"LocalFund's mission is to provide private and public organizations with innovative solutions for matching local entrepreneurs with private 'angel' investors."

Cost:

Entrepreneur:

$150.00 for a lifetime membership.

Angel:

No cost.

Minnesota Investment Network—St. Paul, Minnesota
www.mincorp.org

"Our investments span from early stage to expansions, turnarounds, and ownership transitions. Our investment strategy targets growth companies in the manufacturing and technology sectors located in Minnesota with a focus outside the metropolitan area of Minneapolis and St. Paul.

"Minnesota Investment Network invests in growth companies capable of yielding financial returns appropriate for the risk to investors and creating quality jobs.

"Our long-term goal is to optimize the value of Minnesota Investment Network's portfolio companies that benefit all stakeholders—the business owner(s), employees, our Equity Fund and other investors."

Cost:
Entrepreneur:
   A fee of 2 percent of capital provided is payable at transaction closing.
Angel:
   No statement of cost found.
Regional Focus: State of Minnesota

National Association of Seed and Venture Funds—Chicago, Illinois
www.nasvf.org

"The National Association of Seed and Venture Funds is an organization of private, public and nonprofit organizations committed to building their local economies by investing and facilitating investment in local entrepreneurs."

Cost:
"Membership dues are $650 annually; Membership in NASVF is by invitation only."

Network of Business Angel and Investors—Atlanta, Georgia
www.nbai.net

"We are committed to bringing more qualified investors into the market to provide small growing companies with capital and resources. Our economy depends on free enterprise and the growth of small companies into large companies. Angel Investors are critical to bridge the gap as companies move from start-up to 'bankable.' We will accomplish this by bringing value to the investor community through events, offerings, and association. We plan to grow the NBA&I brand so that it will be known in communities around the United States as the organization that connects Capital, Ventures and Resource."

   Cost:
Entrepreneur:
   Initial phone consultation is $20, cost is unknown if you decide to hire them.
Angel:
   Guardian Angel Membership: $350 annually.
   Active Angel Investor Membership: $1000 annually.

New Product Development Consortium (NPDC)—New York, New York
www.npdcinc.com

"Bring together in a selective membership environment high net worth individuals with an interest in early stage business situations. This network seeks to build and nurture successful businesses whose value can sharply appreciate in a few years. All investments are independently made by members based on the due diligence provided by Spencer Clarke; NPDC never invests its members' funds and does not operate a blind pool. Ideas may be submitted to the NPDC website by non-members. In fact, most ideas are submitted by non-members."

Cost:

Entrepreneur:

   Yes, but no details given.

Angel:

   Yes, but no details given.

New York Investment Network—Melville, New York
www.newyorkinvestmentnetwork.com

"New York web based portal and matching service of angel investors seeking investments, with entrepreneurs seeking capital. The website has been created in response to the growing demand of New York angel investors to invest in things that are more tangible, predictable and closer to home."

Cost:

Entrepreneur:

   One-time fee of $199 after you respond to the first angel investor.

Angel:

   No fee.

Regional Focus: State of New York

NVST—Seattle, Washington
www.nvst.com

"NVST is an Internet hub (or portal) for the worldwide private equity and finance community. The NVST.com website provides online access to Venture Capital or Merger & Acquisition investment opportunities, professional journals, research databases and educational resources for professional training. NVST.com is the only company providing this broad range of private equity investment resources.

"Here, entrepreneurs and professionals in the private equity industry can find new deals, meet one another, access online business tools and learn more about their marketplace.

"Private equity is generally utilized to fund entrepreneurial businesses through venture capital and mergers and acquisitions. NVST.com gives the entire industry instant access to deals, financing resources, online business tools and education."

Cost:
Entrepreneur:
   No statement of cost found.
Angel:
   No statement of cost found.

Texas Investment Network—Dallas, Texas, and Toronto, Ontario
www.texasinvestmentnetwork.com

"Texas web based portal and matching service of angel investors seeking investments, with entrepreneurs seeking capital. This website has been created in response to the growing demand of Texas angel investors to invest in things that are more tangible, predictable and closer to home."

Cost:
Entrepreneur:
   One-time fee of $199 after you respond to the first angel investor.
Angel:
   No Fee.
Regional Focus: State of Texas

The Angel Network—Escondido, California
www.angelnetwork.com/index.php

"In business, there are no guarantees. There is simply no way to eliminate all the risks associated with starting a small business—but you can improve your chances of success with good planning, preparation, and insight. And that is exactly what you will empower yourself to do with an Entrepreneur Membership at Angel Network.

"You will gain instant access to the Angel Investor database, Business Plan Services to help you chart your course, and access to our Venture Capital database that you can use to find capital to jump start your project!

"Select from a monthly membership or an annual payment plan. It is, in our opinion, the best investment in the success of your ventures that you can possibly make."

Cost:
Entrepreneur:
   Annual membership—$197.
   Monthly membership—$27.

Angel:
   Annual membership—$447.
   Monthly membership—$47.

The Angel People—Boise, Idaho
www.TheAngelPeople.com

"Our aim is to list qualified investors and quality opportunities within our database.

   "Northwest Angel Network, Inc. founded theAngelPeople.com to build strong associations with companies and accredited investors. TheAngelPeople.com supports a significantly detailed financing database for new start-up companies seeking capital investment or companies that need next round financing to improve their product or service. This data base is a list of individual investors who provide financing in return for an equity stake in the business with new opportunities."

Cost:
Entrepreneur:
   Placement fee of 2 percent of all monies invested by the Angel Investors.
   Nonrefundable $500 deposit upon signing and listing in the database.
Angel:
   No statement of cost found.

The Entrée Network—Raleigh, North Carolina
www.entreeventurenetwork.com

"Entrée provides a unique networking service to companies and organizations that require sales and/or angel investor access and penetration of certain industries, strategic partners, angel investors and clients.

   "We work with clients, on valuation enhancement and strategic partnering options, sales revenue ramp-up, angel investors, angel funding and market penetration plans."

Cost:
Entrepreneur:
   No statement of cost found.
Angel:
   No statement of cost found.

The Swap—Washington, D.C.
www.investorswap.com

"Exchanging investment opportunities is the core of The SWAP. Investors can exchange opportunities by referring to The SWAP any start-up that they believe has potential, but are not interested in financing. By exchanging, investors provide each other with more investment opportunities. Exchange is mutually beneficial!"

Cost:
Entrepreneur:
   No charge (must be referred).
Angel:
   No charge.

Tribe of Angels
www.tribeofangels.com

"Tribe of Angels is an international community of Jewish entrepreneurs, executives, investors, and researchers. Tribe of Angels is a private membership organization consisting of influential industry executives, entrepreneurs, investors, and researchers. Members join Tribe of Angels to collaborate, share ideas, and discover new opportunities. Membership is highly selective, and special consideration is given to applicants with prior relationships with Tribe of Angels members. Those denied membership may reapply the following year. Members receive access to TribeWire, a Web-based collaboration service that connects Tribe members worldwide. In addition, members may occasionally be invited to attend discrete, private dinner parties hosted by other Tribe members."

Cost:
Entrepreneur:
   No statement of cost found.
Angel:
   No statement of cost found.

USVisionaries—Newport Beach, California
www.usvisionaries.com

"USVisionaries.com is providing a free stage for Growing Businesses and Established Businesses as well as Individuals with innovative ideas to assist them to develop and network their enterprises."

Cost:
Entrepreneur:
   No cost.
Angel:
   No cost.

VentureChoice Inc.—Santa Clara, California
www.venturechoice.com

"VentureChoice is a global deal sourcing, screening, and syndication service provider for an exclusive network of PE and VC Investors who are looking for higher quality deals to (co-)invest in. VentureChoice service is enabled by innovative collaboration technology to be more efficient, effective, and secure than traditional deal flow services providing investment choices otherwise unreachable."

Cost:
Entrepreneur:
   No statement of cost found.
Angel:
   No statement of cost found.

Venturescape
www.venturescape.com

"Venturescape.com is the world's premiere online venture capital portal and will be an invaluable strategic resource for all members of the global Silicon Valley community. Membership is extremely affordable and provides many tangible benefits.

   "As a Venturescape™ member, you can:

- Search our Global VC Plaza database to learn about & target specific VC firms

- Uncover detailed information on 3000+ VC firms worldwide

- Find details on 3700+ office locations

- Search 11,000+ VC contacts by educational background and experience (i.e., search for VCs in Paris that have a Harvard MBA; search for VCs in New York that have worked at Goldman Sachs; search for VCs in Hong Kong that have studied Philosophy at Stanford, etc.)

- Includes over 1000+ face photographs and 1900+ website links

- Updated constantly in real-time

- Have your business plan selectively routed to the most appropriate venture capital firms and private investors worldwide using our intelligent GateKeeper Routing Engine™

- Evaluate pre-screened and post high-potential opportunities in our online GateKeeper Arena™

- Earn significant cash commissions with our generous Affiliates Program

- Utilize our global Rolodex database to professionally network & develop new business

- Acquire valuable industry intelligence through our online Info Plaza

- Keep up with the latest industry news headlines through our global News Plaza"

Cost:
Entrepreneur:
   No statement of cost found.
Angel:
   No statement of cost found.

vFinance—Boca Raton, Florida
www.vfinance.com

"vFinance Investments, Inc. (the 'Company'), a subsidiary of vFinance, Inc. (www.vfinance.com), is a financial services company which specializes in emerging opportunities, providing investment banking, trading, trend forecasting, and consulting services to micro, small and mid-cap high-growth companies, and to institutional and high net-worth investors seeking above-market returns."

Cost:
Entrepreneur:
   No statement of cost found.
Angel:
   No statement of cost found.

Wisconsin Angel Network—Madison, Wisconsin
www.wisconsinangelnetwork.com

"The mission of the Wisconsin Angel Network (WAN) is to build early-stage capital capacity throughout Wisconsin, increasing the number and amount of equity investments in Wisconsin's entrepreneurs. WAN was founded in January 2005 as an umbrella organization providing services and resources to the early-stage investing community. WAN does not operate a fund or make recommendations on potential investments. WAN is a public-private initiative rooted in Governor Jim Doyle's Grow Wisconsin plan and the Legislature's Act 255 initiative; it is operated by the Wisconsin Technology Council."

Cost:
Entrepreneur:
   No statement of cost found.
Angel:
   No statement of cost found.
Regional Focus: State of Wisconsin.

Experts' Profiles

LAURENCE BRIGGS

Laurence Briggs is an English national, becoming a permanent U.S. resident in 1992 and making his home in Dallas, Texas. Currently, he is president and founder of The InvestIN Forum of Angel Investors in the Dallas/Fort Worth, Texas area. The forum now has more than fifty members and has invested in more than a dozen deals.

In addition, Briggs is co-founder of the InvestIN Group (Member NASD, SIPC) and has been CEO since 1995. His industry knowledge includes financial services, robotics, anti-terrorist devices, metal transformation, medical devices, oil and gas, and staffing services. He has negotiated twenty-eight acquisitions and raised capital for numerous companies, and has founded several companies in Egypt, France, and the United States.

Briggs is an avid supporter and member of the Dallas chapter of The Association for Corporate Growth, the Dallas chapter of TexChange, The Greater Dallas Chambers' Tech Business Council, and its Capital Connections Committee. He is also a regular speaker on angel investing, specifically explaining how entrepreneurs and angels help "fuel the entrepreneurial ecosystem." He has been a regular speaker on French and British radio and television and particularly a regular guest of the European version of CNBC *Power Lunch*. Companies he has advised include Mobil Oil, Colgate-Palmolive Co., and a subsidiary of United Technologies Corp. on overseas transactions. He qualified as a professional accountant at the London School of Accountancy (London University), and was a Fellow of the Sloan Fellowship program—London Business School (London University). He holds the NASD series 7, 63, and 24 securities licenses.

BOB GERAS

Bob Geras is president of LaSalle Investments, Inc. He has been an active participant in the venture capital and angel community in Chicago for more than forty years. Termed "a virtual Renaissance Man of Entrepreneurship" in a David Lundy *Chicago Sun-Times* interview, "one of the Big Three 'old-timer' angels in Chicago" in *Crain's Chicago Business,* and featured in a July 2005 cover story in *INC.* magazine titled "Angels in America," Geras is the one many venture capitalists, accountants, attorneys, and other consultants call when they have a client who needs experienced advice and a good dose of mentoring as well as seed or early-stage money for their young company. He has been a frequent featured panelist, lecturer, mentor, or business plan judge for the Illinois Coalition and has taught entrepreneurship courses at the University of Illinois, University of Chicago, Kellogg, Roosevelt, and De Paul Universities, as well as seminars sponsored by Chicago Software Association, Garage Technology Ventures, Midwest Entrepreneurship Forum, Association for Corporate Growth, MIT forum, Technology, and many more. In 1970, he co-founded the budget motel chain Sixpence Inns, which was acquired by Motel 6 for more than $200 million in 1989. He has done turnarounds with highly profitable results. In addition, he is an investor or adviser to Kettle Venture Partners, Chicago Ventures, Dunrath Venture Partners, K-B Partners, Crestview Capital, Artesian Capital, and Ceres Venture Fund, and is a founding member and director of the Illinois Venture Capital Association.

BOB GOFF

Bob Goff is founder and chairman of the Sierra Angels, along with myriad other accomplishments. Bob's career was primarily in semiconductors in Silicon Valley, where he had the opportunity to manage three successive high-growth businesses from early stage through IPO and subsequent strategic mergers with Fortune 500 companies. These "gazelle" companies were primarily a result of commercializing and marketing the innovative advances from the companies' R&D laboratories. Concurrently, he became active in specialized venture capital investments and subsequently became a principal in an investment banking firm specializing in strategic mergers.

Upon retiring to Lake Tahoe in 1997 he led the founding of the Sierra Angels to provide coaching, venture capital, and connectivity to early-stage technology companies in the region. He also made a commitment to devote time and energy to his post-career passion: the confluence of education, entrepreneurship, and technology. He applies his strong advocacy for collaboration among complementary organizations to help accelerate the commercialization of innovations throughout the state and region. The Sierra Angels has been featured nationally in articles in *Business Week Small Business, Worth* (Robb Report), and also in numerous regional publications. In 2002 Goff was inducted by TBAN into Nevada's High Tech Hall of Fame, and in 2005 he was honored by the Kauffman Foundation–funded Angel Capital Association as the first recipient of the Hans Severiens Award.

In addition to his active role as chair of Sierra Angels, Goff serves on a number of nonprofit and for-profit boards in support of his collaborative and converging interests. These include chair emeritus of Golden Capital Network (a Nevada and California collaboration), initial chairman of Nevada's Center for Entrepreneurship & Technology, member of the UC Davis External Research Advisory Board, founding board member of Research Ventures, Inc., a joint venture between University of Nevada, Reno (UNR) and Desert Research Institute (DRI) to promote commercialization of their technology, a trustee of DRI Foundation, former trustee of Sierra Nevada College, former chair of UNR Engineering Advisory Board, former member of Santa Clara College Business Advisory Board, and president emeritus of Nevada Technology Council. Following his undergraduate studies in electrical engineering at the University of Missouri and business at San Jose State, he received his MBA from Santa Clara University and completed postgrad executive programs with Stanford University. He and his wife live at North Lake Tahoe, Nevada, where they enjoy the great variety of activities that the High Sierra offers throughout the year.

MITCHELL D. GOLDSMITH

Mitchell Goldsmith is a director and shareholder with Shefsky & Froelich in Chicago, Illinois. He concentrates his practice in the areas of federal and state regulation of securities, corporate finance, general corporate representation, and real estate development and syndication. He is a graduate of the University of Chicago Law School and a summa cum laude, Phi Beta Kappa graduate of the University of Pennsylvania (BS in economics).

His securities practice has led to the successful structuring and placement of numerous debt and equity offerings in both public and private markets for clients in a diverse array of industries:

- Health care and medical products and services
- Computer software
- Internet
- Telecommunications
- Electronics
- Biotechnology
- Automotive
- Banking and finance
- Manufacturing and food service
- Multi-family, commercial, industrial, and nursing home properties

Goldsmith gives particular emphasis to value-added efforts in introducing clients to sources of finance and business opportunities. His closely related activities are financing start-up and emerging growth businesses, and transactions including venture capital, public offerings, and reverse mergers into public shells, coupled with PIPE financings. He provides all aspects of general corporate counseling for these and more established operating entities. He has also represented a variety of banking institutions in their organizational and lending efforts.

DAVID GRAHAME

David Grahame graduated MA Honours from the University of St. Andrews in 1976 and managed and then owned businesses in the hospitality industry for several years before developing the LINC Scotland business angel initiative, becoming its first chief executive in 1994. Since then LINC has facilitated more than 470 investment deals for fast-growing Scottish companies, making it one of the most successful and effective angel organizations in Europe. LINC has also pioneered initiatives in investment readiness, syndicate building, public-private co-investment, and sustainable intervention. Other positions Grahame has held include

- Founding board of EBAN (the European Business Angels Network)
- Bank of England Small Firms Consultation Group
- The Scottish Hospital Endowments Research Trust
- Advisory Board of CONNECT Scotland
- Advisory Board of Technology Ventures Scotland
- Expert Panel (Business Angels) for Enterprise Directorate General of the European Commission
- Business Rating Valuation Appeals Panel

In 2003 he was awarded an OBE by the Queen for his services to entrepreneurship.

NELSON GRAY

Nelson Gray is a Chartered Accountant with an entrepreneurial background, who, following the sale of his own business (debt recovery), became a hands-on business angel investor, mentor, non-executive director, and fund manager. Gray has been involved in a wide range of companies as diverse as biotech manufacturing, diagnostic platforms, intelligence software systems, medical devices, call centers, and construction. He acted as the fund manager for Scotland's leading angel investment syndicate. Later, he managed two early-stage investment funds that invested in more than fifty Scottish companies.

He has provided advice on funding to Scottish enterprise, the Scottish executive, and the Enterprise Committee of the Scottish Parliament. Between 1999 and 2004 he managed gap fund managers on behalf of Noble, the independent investment bank (www.noblegp.com), and remained a consultant with Noble Fund Managers (NFM) until March 2006. NFM manages six investment funds ranging in size between £10 million and £100 million. Since 1996 Gray has made sixteen personal angel investments in new and developing companies. These include

- Tissue Science Laboratories PLC, (medical devices, floated on AIM in 2002)
- Optos PLC (medical devices, main market flotation February 2006)
- Excel Biotech Ltd. (manufacture of monoclonal antibodies and other material for clinical trials, sold to QBiogene of Canada in 2002)
- Eleksen Group PLC (smart fabric for control of electrical devices— AIM float May 2006)

Gray is a board member of the Entrepreneurial Exchange (www .entrepreneurial-exchange.co.uk) and a former board member of Connect (www.connectonthenet.com), and he was a founding board member of the Scottish Institute for Enterprise (www.sie.ac.uk). In 2001 he received the Entrepreneurial Exchange's Entrepreneurial Supporter of the Year Award. He is a frequent speaker in Scotland on the topics of angel investing and "Investor Ready" and has been asked to present on these topics in Chile, Holland, Sweden, Estonia, and Latvia. He holds a diploma in company direction from the Institute of Directors, and is a Financial Services Authority–registered investment manager and adviser.

BRANNON LAMBERT

Brannon Lambert is co-founder, president, and COO of VHT. Lambert began his career working for U.S. Frontier as a financial analyst, coordinating lenders and professional service firms that were developing a golf course residential community. Several years later, he formed Excelsior Group, Inc. (EGI), to develop, own, and manage affordable housing for older adults. Over a six-year period, EGI was the developing partner for more than three hundred affordable residential units in the Chicago metropolitan area. The developments were financed using various sources of funding, including Low Income Housing Tax Credits, Tax Increment Financing Funds, Community Development Block Grant Funds, and conventional bank loans. Lambert worked with local and state public officials, lending experts, and professional service firms to provide quality housing and services for seniors for less than half the market rate in the respective communities.

Lambert graduated from the University of Wisconsin–Madison in 1990 with degrees in marketing and real estate finance. He has held his real estate broker's license in Illinois since 1992. He serves on the Board of Directors for Neumann Association, a fifty-five-year-old nonprofit group helping physically and mentally disabled individuals enrich their quality of life with choice and independence. Neumann has an annual budget of $9.5 million for 152 housing units providing services for over five hundred individuals.

KNOX MASSEY

Knox Massey has served as executive director of the Atlanta Technology Angels since 2002. He is also a member of the Atlanta Technology Angels and an active angel investor in the group. In his role of executive director at ATA, Massey has participated in the initial funding of Invistics, Qcept Technologies, Fortel DTV, Oversight Systems, OpenSpan Software, Jacket Micro Devices, Asankya, Zeewise, Beacon Software, and Invirtus. He has also participated in the execution of more than twenty-five additional financing rounds associated with ATA portfolio companies, two M&A events, and one shutdown.

Massey is currently an investor in ATA portfolio companies' Marketworks, Market Velocity, and Beacon Software. Prior to 2002, he held senior sales positions at America Online, served in a management position at the West-Wayne Advertising Agency, and worked within regional sales offices of the *New York Times* Regional Newspaper Group. He sits on the Board of Directors of ATA and is chairman of the board of Beacon Software, as well as a general partner of Keith-Massey Partnership, LLP. He has an MBA from the GEM Program at Georgia State University and holds Series 7 and Series 63 securities licenses.

LON MCGOWAN

Lon McGowan founded iClick, a promotional electronics company that supplies product to the niche market of advertising specialties. He started the company in 2001 with no outside financing other than fourteen credit cards. In the first four years it managed to survive off cash flow and profits and has only recently raised its first round of outside private capital. iClick employs ten people in its Seattle office and has launched more than thirty-five products since its inception. Before iClick, McGowan attended the University of Colorado at Boulder and graduated with a degree in business and marketing from the Leeds School of Business.

STEPHEN G. ROBINSON

Stephen Robinson is active in both business and nonprofit sectors in the Pittsburgh area. He is managing general partner of Robinson Properties, LP, and 105 Delta Drive, LP, family real estate investment and development partnerships; and vice president and director of Gateway Travel Management, the largest independent travel management and meeting planning company in Western Pennsylvania. He is also a director of or investor in numerous early-stage venture capital-backed technology-oriented companies in Western Pennsylvania, including TimeSys, True Commerce, Quantapoint, Precision Therapeutics, and Webmedx among others.

His current and past nonprofit board positions have included the I Have A Dream Foundation of Pittsburgh (past president), Pittsburgh Venture Capital

Association (past president), Advisory Committee of the Donald Jones Center for Entrepreneurship at GSIA—Carnegie Mellon University, the Pittsburgh Social Venture Partners Foundation (founding partner, treasurer), Western Pennsylvania Conservancy, Winchester Thurston School, and the Family Tyes fly-fishing school. Robinson graduated magna cum laude from the University of Pittsburgh in 1975 with a BA in political science.

LAWRENCE D. SCHWARTZ

Lawrence Schwartz is the founder of Stampede Brewing Co., maker of the first-ever government-approved vitamin beer. Prior to founding Stampede, he was the founder and CEO of Attenza, a leading-edge software company. He also spent several years in marketing at Anheuser-Busch, where he was involved with the marketing of O'Doul's, Michelob Dry, and Bud Dry. He received his BA from the University of Oklahoma at Norman. He is a member of Young Entrepreneurs' Organization and a former member of the American Management Association, the North Dallas Chamber of Commerce, and Who's Who in Technology Executives. He was nominated for the prestigious Ernst & Young Entrepreneur of the Year award in 1999, and was the winner of the North Dallas Chamber of Commerce Small Business of the Year Award in 2000 and the Texas eComm "Tens" award in 2001. In the June 10, 2005, issue of the *Dallas Business Journal,* Schwartz was recognized as one of the "Top 40 Entrepreneurs Under 40." He has been interviewed on the radio on topics of entrepreneurship, customer service, venture capital, and health and fitness, and has authored two books: *The Professional's Guide to Fitness* (Taylor, 1999) and *Fat Daddy/Fit Daddy* (Rowman & Littlefield, 2003).

COLLEEN STONE

Colleen Stone, founder and CEO of InSpa, started the corporation in 1999 in the belief that there was enormous pent-up demand from mass market consumers for services and products that were at that time only available in the high-end day spa industry. InSpa, with its tag line "Feel Great Now," was created especially for everyday people and their everyday lives. Each 2,000-square-foot InSpa store is designed with a clean, beach-themed look, a welcoming environment, and well-priced, unintimidating operations (including ordering from menu boards and a firm "No Tipping" policy). InSpa now has six successful stores open in the greater Seattle area, with additional stores scheduled to open in Washington and California by the end of 2006. InSpa intends to expand its branded stores throughout the United States in all major markets in coming years. Stone was formerly executive vice president of Merle Norman Cosmetics Company in Los Angeles, California. Previously, she had been an investment banker with Salomon Brothers in New York City for five years, including three years when she was chief of staff for the Domestic Corporate Finance division. She holds both a BA in economics (1977) and an MBA (1989) from Stanford University.

HENRY VEHOVEC

Henry Vehovec is an entrepreneur and investor providing funding and consulting services through Mindfirst, Inc., a private company he founded in 1998. He is a current board member for several nonprofit organizations including the National Angel Organization and the CHIN UP Fund, which supports nerve research at Toronto's Hospital for Sick Children. He is a member of the nine-person Investment Committee of Sustainable Development Technology Canada, which is deploying $350 million over five years, and recently joined the Advisory Board of the Museum of Canadian Contemporary Art. He has served on several public and private boards of small and medium-sized companies.

Vehovec started his business career with IBM Canada in 1980, before leaving to help launch and take public a medical imaging start-up, ISG Technologies (Cedara). He subsequently founded, grew, and sold ADAM Peripherals, after eight years of operation. In 2005 he achieved ICD.D certification by completing the Directors Education Program of the Institute of Corporate Directors Corporate Governance College. He completed the Owner/President Management Program at the Harvard Business School (1996), an MBA from the Richard Ivey School of Business (1984), and an engineering degree from the University of Toronto (1979). He works primarily from his home office, is married to Ann Louise, is father to Eric (age fifteen) and Graham (twelve), shovels his own walk, and sometimes mows his own lawn.

~~~ References

Web Sites

Angel Capital Education Foundation: www.angelcapitalfoundation.org. Information on angel organizations in the United States and Canada.

European Business Angel Network (EBAN): www.eban.org. Listing of current EBAN members.

Global Entrepreneurship Monitor: www.gemconsortium.org. Various statistics on venture capital and informal investing.

National Venture Capital Association: www.nvca.org. Various reports and statistics on venture capital financing.

PricewaterhouseCoopers MoneyTree: www.pwcmoneytree.com. Various reports and statistics on venture capital financings.

TechCoast Angels: www.techcoastangels.com. Presentation guidelines.

Published Sources

Goff, Robert. (2005, Nov. 16). "Making a Good First Impression." Kauffman Foundation. Available online: www.eventuring.org (search on author and title). Access date: September 8, 2006.

Keeley, Robert H., Cooper, Jeffrey M., & Bloomer, Gary D. (1998). "Business Angels: A Guide to Private Investing." Colorado Springs, CO: Colorado Capital Alliance.

Sandler, Daniel. (2004). "Venture Capital and Tax Incentives: A Comparative Study of Canada and the United States." Toronto, ON: Canadian Tax Foundation.

Wiltbank, Robert. (2006). "At the Individual Level: Outlining Angel Investing in the United States." White paper, Willamette University, Salem, Oregon.

Wiltbank, Robert. (2006). "Investment Practices and Outcomes of Informal Venture Investors." White paper, Willamette University, Salem, Oregon.

⟶ Acknowledgments

It takes a village to raise a child and a team to build a successful company, because we know any young company is first an infant, then a toddler, and only—after the struggling teen years—an adult full of lessons and love of its parents. So is the development of a book. Many people who care about me, and I them, provided invaluable intelligence and countless hours to help me out of friendship and love. I am forever in their debt and I look forward to the day when I can give of my time and mind to Bradley Knox, a cherished friend with a heart as big as the world and an incredible mind that I so admire; to Joseph Rubin, my taskmaster, reality check, and entire project coordinator, with a gentle way and wonderful soul; to Heather Aldrich, willing to help in any way with a very sharp mind, and who will some day set the world on fire; to Mary Baker Anderson, financial strategist extraordinaire, with the biggest heart one could imagine; to Jeanne Bliss, for introducing me to my editor Neal Maillet and for being an inspiration; to all my friends and all the interviewees who so willingly gave of their time to add substance to my book, and, most important, to my family for putting up with my preoccupation, maniac focus, and absences from home to allow me to fulfill a dream. Thank you so much. I am truly blessed.

⎯⎯ The Author

Ms. Preston is an Entrepreneur-in-Residence with Ewing Marion Kauffman Foundation, specifically focusing on initiatives related to the capital community, particularly in the areas of angel investing and angel organizations. In addition, she is Director of Attorney Training and Professional Development for Davis Wright Tremaine, a 450-lawyer national/international law firm. Ms. Preston has held several board positions with public and privately held corporations, as well as serving on non-profit boards. Ms. Preston is Chairman of the Board for The Hope Heart Institute, a leading cardiovascular research institute with national and international recognition. She is the chair of the Entrepreneurship Center at Seattle University and is a member of the Board of Visitors for Washington State University. In addition, Ms. Preston was on the board of advisors for Nokia/Innovent. Additionally, Ms. Preston is the author of *Angel Investment Groups, Networks and Funds: A Guidebook to Developing the Right Angel Organization for Your Community,* a comprehensive guidebook on the establishment and operation of angel investment groups. She was also a contributing author to *State of the Art: An Executive Briefing on the Cutting-Edge Practices in American Angel Investing.*

Ms. Preston has been and continues to be a national and international speaker on economic development and angel and venture financing, for such programs as Goldman Sachs, Northern Trust, NYU Business School, OECD, Industry Canada, Alberta California Venture Channel, Angel Capital Association, National Angel Organization, NASVF, SSTI, NBIA, MASVF, Jamaican Government, Governor's Conference on Economic Development, Washington State legislation, Pittsburgh Venture Capital Association, and many others. Ms. Preston has been profiled in *Inc. Magazine* and in other local and national publications, and has contributed to numerous nationally published articles on women entrepreneurship or angel investing. Ms. Preston is a founder and immediate past-president of Seraph Capital Forum, an all-women's accredited investor angel investment organization. She testified at a United States Congressional hearing in support for the $4 Billion Small Business Investment Company (SBIC) program as the national expert on angel financing, and most recently regarding H.R. 5198 (and S. 3950), a Federal income tax credit for private equity investments. Ms. Preston is the architect of H.R. 5198 and S. 3950, with the bill concept originating from Ms. Preston's discussions and interactions with the House Small Business Committee on solutions to the loss of the SBIC participating equity program. Ms. Preston continues to actively participate in the promotion and furtherance of the bill on Capital Hill and elsewhere.

Ms. Preston has significant experience in senior management of companies including CEO of Reality Based Learning Company, a privately held company that designed, developed, and produced web-delivered educational curriculum and assessment products for the pre-K through 6th grade market. Until taking the CEO position, Ms. Preston was a partner with Cooley Godward and was a founding partner in the firm's Pacific Northwest office, and prior to that COO and General Counsel for Source Scientific, Inc., a publicly traded medical device company, and VP, General Counsel for MicroProbe Corporation, a public biotech research and development company. Ms. Preston received her JD, cum laude, from Seattle University School of Law and her BS, magna cum laude, Phi Beta Kappa, in Microbiology and Public Health from Washington State University.

~~~ Subject Index

⟞⟝ Business, Angel Organization, and Web Site Index